POWER BEYOND REASON

THE

MENTAL COLLAPSE

OF

LYNDON JOHNSON

POWER BEYOND REASON

THE

MENTAL COLLAPSE

OF

LYNDON JOHNSON

D. JABLOW HERSHMAN
WITH A PREFACE BY
GERALD TOLCHIN, PH.D.

BARRICADE
BOOKS

Fort Lee • New Jersey

Published by Barricade Books Inc.
185 Bridge Plaza North
Suite 308-A
Fort Lee, NJ 07024
www.barricadebooks.com

Library of Congress Cataloging-in-Publication Data
Hershman, D. Jablow.
   Power beyond reason : the mental collapse of Lyndon Johnson / D. Jablow
   Hershman and Gerald Tolchin.
      p. cm.
   Includes bibliographical references (p.) and index.
   ISBN 1-56980-243-2 (casebound)
      1. Johnson, Lyndon B. (Lyndon Baines), 1908-1973--Psychology. 2.
   United States--Politics and government--1963-1969--Psychological
   aspects. I. Tolchin, Gerald. II. Title.

E847.2 .H47 2002
973.923'092--dc21   2002026061

First Printing
Manufactured in the United States of America

This book is dedicated to my family, in gratitude for their encouragement and support.

CONTENTS

★ ★ ★ ★ ★ ★

Preface		1
PART I	**LAYING THE GROUNDWORK**	8
1.	Manic Depression Makes History	9
2.	A Born Manic-Depressive	21
3.	Lyndon Prepares for Politics	34
4.	The Lion in Congress	51
5.	Escape From Congress	66
6.	Tyranny in the Senate	79
7.	The Heartbreak Hotel	93
8.	Hell in Second Place	110
PART II	**LBJ BECOMES THE MOST POWERFUL MAN IN THE WORLD**	124
9.	The Accidental President	125
10.	Sex, Lies, and LBJ	141
11.	The Peace Candidate	150
12.	"The Only President You Have"	165
13.	Fear and Loathing in the Oval Office	184
14.	The Year Without a Tunnel	195

15.	"Downright Frightening"	207
16.	Burning the Olive Branch	220
17.	"I Don't Need the Job"	228
18.	Back at the Ranch	241

POSTSCRIPT 250

	Why Vietnam?	251
	Was This War Necessary?	252
	A War That Could Have Been Avoided	268
	War and Madness	282
	Delusion's Web	291

APPENDIX   An Introduction to Manic Depression   307

Bibliography   327

End Notes   333

PREFACE

"There are more instances of the abridgement of freedom by grad-
ual and silent encroachments of those in power than by violent and
sudden usurpations."

—James Madison

Determining whether Lyndon Baines Johnson had bipolar disorder and answering the more significant question of how his bipolar disorder affected his life and his career in politics are the tasks that this book seeks to accomplish.

It is dangerous to engage in retrospective psychiatric diagnosis and, it is all too easy to be cavalier in assigning diagnostic labels. One danger stems from the false sense of security that arises when we feel that we have explained a person's behavior merely by giv- ing him a diagnosis. For example, that we could somehow grasp the evil of a Jeffrey Dahmer (who kept skulls and body parts of his victims in his refrigerator), by assigning him to a psychiatric cate- gory. Perhaps it is because we feel we can reduce even the most inexplicable behavior to a more human scale and thereby gain a sense of understanding. He did it because he was crazy, not because of some unfathomable evil. But in truth, making a diag- nosis rarely provides us with much additional understanding. A diagnosis provides little more than a description of a problem, in medical terms. It has only limited value.

Given any two individuals with the same diagnosis, we might expect to find certain similarities in their behavior. Actually the differences between them can be astonishing. Understanding how and why a disorder plays out in a particular individual is a far more difficult problem than assigning that person a diagnosis.

A diagnosis has only limited utility but this doesn't mean that an investigation into the relationship between a mental disorder and the trajectory that it imparts to a person's life should be ignored. To do so would be folly, for it could shed light on important historical questions, and to ignore this information could prove disastrous. To paraphrase Santayana's famous dictum (1905): If we are unwilling to examine the mistakes of our past we are likely to repeat them. Examining the life of Lyndon Baines Johnson from a psychological (or psychiatric) perspective could prove valuable for the future. It is a task that needs doing but one that must be approached with caution.

Mental disorder is something which most of us have had at least a casual (if not intimate) relationship. Who among us can say that they have never experienced a problem with impulse control, or depression, or anxiety? Who could say that their own lives have not been impacted by the mental suffering of others? The fact is that our very familiarity with such life problems gives us the sense that we have an intuitive understanding of mental disorder.

It is difficult to be objective when we become the subject of our own inquiry. Mental disorders exist on a spectrum that in their mildest forms shade easily into common acceptance. At the extremes however, are those disorders that can wreak devastation on a person. Bipolar or manic depressive disorder falls into this category.

It is unclear whether Lyndon Johnson was ever formally diagnosed. Certainly, if he were to have been diagnosed with manic depressive disorder and this were to have been made public, it could have had a crippling impact on his political career. It took far less than this to scuttle Senator Eagelton's vice presidential aspirations in 1972.

A diagnosis of mental disorder has always been a double-edged sword. On the one hand, it could open the possibility for treatment but it also carries with it a powerful stigma. This book does not pretend to be a medical text, nor does it attempt to provide a complete biography of the life of Lyndon Johnson. Its value comes from its ability to study and clarify the complex interplay of the personality, mental disorder, behavior and judgment of one of the strongest political figures in 20th Century politics.

The office of president of the United States of America carries with it enormous powers and responsibilities. In 1973 Congress passed the War Powers Resolution, allowing the president, without a declaration of war, to act on his own to use the full might of the armed forces without having to notify Congress until forty-eight hours after the fact. In essence, a mentally disordered president could unilaterally launch an attack that would end the world as we know it, but not bother to tell anyone until it was a fait accompli.

Was President Johnson merely misguided in his handling of the war in Vietnam or was his behavior shaped by and a product of mental disorder? And if the latter is true, did he lack the competency to serve as Commander in Chief? Is the presence of a mental disorder sufficient reason to disqualify a president from continuing in office? Does it follow that a president with a mental disorder would of necessity lack the competence to make wise or sound choices?

In both psychology and law an important distinction is drawn between mental disorder and mental competency. A mentally disordered person is generally assumed competent unless it could be proven otherwise.

To be sure, this was not always the case. In the not so distant past, mentally ill persons were assumed to lack capacity to make decisions in most areas of their lives. But a growing body of psychological research, bolstered by a number of legal decisions, have redrawn the boundary between mental competency and mental disorder. There is no reason to assume that a mentally disordered person would be an incompetent decision maker. Conversely, it does not follow that a mentally disordered person, or in this case a mentally disordered president, would necessarily be a good decision maker.

Many completely sane presidents were awful decision makers. Still it would be folly to conclude that a person's mental disorder could not adversely affect their decision making ability. Manics sometimes show poor judgment in their personal and professional lives, often inflicting damage to themselves and to those closest to them. They rarely have insight into the distortions caused by their grandiose thinking and exaggerated sense of purpose.

A manic can act impulsively and precipitously with little regard for consequences. Attempts by others to curtail their activity are usually met with bursts of anger and rejection. Needless to say, when it is the President of the United States who is in a manic state there is legitimate cause for concern. (The appendix to this volume provides an accurate portrait of bipolar disorder from a medical point of view and should prove a useful resource while reading the text.)

What qualifications exist in guiding the selection of the person who is to become the President of the United States? The framers tell us in the Constitution that the president must be a natural-born citizen of the United States, 35 years of age or older, and "fourteen years a resident within the United States." Nothing more. No education or experience is required. Nor is a prior felony conviction a disqualifier for election to public office so long as the sentence has been served.

The Constitution provides no further guidance regarding the fitness of a person to occupy the office of president and little concerning what to do when the president becomes disabled in office. The 25th Amendment to the Constitution passed in 1967, in Section 3 states: "Whenever the President transmits to the President pro tempore of the Senate and the Speaker of the House of Representatives his written declaration that he is unable to discharge the powers and duties of his office, and until he transmits to them a written declaration to the contrary, such powers and duties shall be discharged by the Vice President as Acting President."

The amendment becomes operative only after the president acknowledges that he has become disabled and notifies the

Congress of his inability to carry out the duties of office. The amendment appears to apply primarily to physical disabilities. Lack of insight by a president with a mental disability would usually preclude his taking any action.

It is widely known that Woodrow Wilson suffered a series of strokes in the waning months of his presidency. He was bedridden and may have been mentally incapacitated. It is widely suspected that his wife, Edith Bolling Wilson, acting for her husband, assumed many of the functions of the ailing president.

By 1984, it was becoming clear that Ronald Reagan was having serious problems discharging his duties as president. He was confused and had real difficulties with his memory. Contrary to reports coming from the White House at the time, it appears likely that he had become disabled while in office, showing signs of what later was to be diagnosed as Alzheimer's disease.

Do we need a better process to screen candidates for public office (as we do with police officers, teachers, military personnel and many other civil servants)? Once elected should a mentally ill or disabled president be permitted to remain in office? If not, what would be an appropriate process to remove or furlough such a person?

In principle at least there is nothing standing in the way of committing a sitting president to a mental hospital in a civil law proceeding as long as it could be demonstrated clearly and convincingly, that his mental illness is dangerous. But would we even consider such an action against a sitting president? Would we find ourselves having to illuminate all a president's decisions under the scrutiny of psychiatric evaluation? Should a president be asked to undergo regular fitness for duty examinations by a White House psychiatrist?

Should a president be held to the same standards as we do everyone else? Lord Acton in a letter to Bishop Creighton commented: "I cannot accept your canon that we judge Pope and King unlike other men, with a favorable presumption that they did no wrong. If there is any presumption it is the other way against holders of power, increasing as the power increases. Historic responsibility has to make up for the want of legal responsibility."

There have been numerous biographies and countless biographical sketches of Lyndon Baines Johnson, 36th President of The United States, though none has approached their subject in quite the manner of D. J. Hershman. *Power Beyond Reason* is a chilling psychological portrait, unblinking and meticulous in its search for truth. It tells a story that is spellbinding. Having read it it is difficult to view Lyndon Johnson other than through the remarkable lens that Hershman provides.

Lyndon Johnson remains a puzzling and controversial figure. He presided over perhaps the most ambitious civil rights legislation since the Emancipation Proclamation. And, he plunged the nation ever more deeply into a futile and desperate war in Vietnam; a war from which the nation is yet to recover.

Johnson may well have been the most psychologically unstable person ever to assume the presidency. He was at once an astute and skillful politician who could be ruthless and cunning in his pursuit of power; flamboyant, impulsive and mindless as a decision maker as well as in his personal life; generous and deeply empathic; self-centered, cruel, suspicious and unforgiving; tireless, robust and driven by his enthusiasm, optimism, euphoria and sense of urgency; grandiose, narcissistic, impatient, but then alternately, catastrophic, exhausted, confused, melancholic, self-critical, deeply pessimistic, and from time to time, nearly immobilized and sickly with recurrent thoughts of death.

He was a tragic figure pursued by demons, real and imagined.

To those who dealt with him, Johnson's moodiness was obvious and difficult to ignore but few, if any recognized the extent to which it dominated his life. To the casual observer, he was a big man of big appetites and ambitions. He could be charming and ruthless at the same time. His energy and enthusiasm were magnets drawing in those around him but he could also be daunting, frightening, and even downright terrifying.

6

Examining the evidence that Hershman presents, it seems clear that the extremes of Johnson's mood swings went far beyond what could be accounted for by the events that were unfolding in his life. His moods appeared to have a mind of their own, taking Johnson along and often those around him, (not always willingly), on their quixotic journeys. It appears likely that Lyndon Johnson suffered from bipolar (manic-depressive) disorder throughout his life, a condition that grew worse as he grew older, peaking just as he reached the zenith of his influence and power.

We can only wonder how history might have been written had he been diagnosed and treated early in his career.

Dr. Gerald Tolchin
Madison, Connecticut

Part One:
Laying the Groundwork

CHAPTER 1

MANIC DEPRESSION MAKES HISTORY

★　★　★　★　★　★

Texan is president again and this country is fighting a war again. Beyond that, there seem to be few parallels between the Vietnam War and the war against terrorism in which we are currently engaged. But this promises to be another long war and only the passage of years will show us that there are no additional similarities. In the meantime, the Vietnam War itself remains a mine of mysteries. One of the most fundamental of those mysteries is why did it become an American war?

How much sense did the Vietnam War really make? The government of the United States claimed to be preserving democracy in South Vietnam, while the truth was that it was defending a dictatorship lead by a dizzying succession of corrupt leaders. The U.S. was napalming and defoliating Vietnam to save it. Even Robert McNamara, Secretary of Defense to both Kennedy and Johnson, and initially one of the war's staunchest advocates, finally said: "The picture of the world's greatest superpower killing or seriously injuring 1,000 noncombatants a week, while trying to pound a tiny backward nation into submission on an issue whose merits are hotly disputed, is not a pretty one."[1]

It was the first war we Americans fought in which there was no aggression against us. It gained us nothing. Although we lost the war, and Vietnam became Communist South as well as North, no dominos fell and Chinese troops did not land in San Francisco, as Lyndon Baines Johnson predicted they would. This of course, is hindsight, but why fight Communism in Southeast Asia when we had Cuba on our doorstep? Where was the greater threat? If ever we fought an irrational war, this one was it.

Another mystery of the Vietnam War is that it dragged on after much of the public and Congress wanted it to end and even Lyndon Johnson despaired of victory. By 1967, it was considered a miserable war by most Americans. The economy was headed towards inflation, riots were igniting the cities, and the President had seen his approval ratings fall from 70 % to 39%. He complained in August of that year: "I don't know how in hell to get out."[2]

To what extent was President Lyndon Johnson responsible for sinking America in the quicksand of Vietnam? He'd won a huge majority partly because voters feared that Republican Barry Goldwater would do exactly what Johnson later actually did himself: Escalate in Vietnam.

The President cleverly kept the war on hold when he campaigned as a peace candidate. There was no mandate from "the People" to get over there and fight, although for a while the general public was persuaded that fighting was necessary.

Who was the real LBJ? Beneath the mask of the peace candidate was the face of a war lover that LBJ showed only to the generals. A month after Kennedy's assassination Johnson told the Joint Chiefs of Staff: "Just let me get elected, and then you can have your war."[3]

The military establishment was delighted with the new occupant of the White House. The Constitution designates the President of the United States as Commander in Chief of the Armed Forces. The relationship between the President and the nation's military leaders was intended to be one of cooperation and mutual respect. With a Cold Warrior for Commander in Chief, the generals expected the relationship to be especially congenial.

The Joint Chiefs of Staff offered their own war plan to the President in November of 1965, says Marine Lieutenant General Charles S. Cooper, "He responded with an explosion of invective that stunned them. He screamed obscenities, he cursed them personally, he ridiculed them for coming to his office with their 'military advice.'

"…He then accused them of trying to pass the buck for starting World War III to him. It was unnerving. It was degrading. He told them he was disgusted with their naïve approach to him, that he was not going to let some military idiots talk him into World War III. It ended when he told them to 'get the hell out of my office!'"[4] The generals were lucky to escape without bruises. The face of the war lover was merely another mask.

For now, we can accept LBJ's claim for responsibility. "If it belongs to anybody, it's my war," he declared in 1966.[5] His war is the longest, most expensive one this nation has ever fought. North Vietnam suffered the heaviest bombing in the history of warfare. And the cost of this to the American side included—more than nine hundred aircraft shot down in three years.[6] More than two million Americans were sent to Vietnam from 1965 to 1975.[7] The Americans lost 58,000 dead in fighting that losing war. Out of a population of 27 million people, the Vietnamese lost 3.8 million. We killed two civilians for every enemy soldier.[8]

In the United States no single person can launch a war. Johnson did not do that: he inherited Vietnam. However, he steadfastly kept the United States in the war. Every year that he was in office there were opportunities to negotiate a pull out. But he flatly refused to consider that course of action.

Along with the mystery of why Vietnam became an American battleground is the mystery of why LBJ ignored John Kennedy's plan to end American involvement in the conflict after the election. Instead, while proclaiming that he was continuing Kennedy's policies, Johnson gave the generals an army of more than half a million with which to pursue victory. On one occasion, Johnson became exasperated with the reporters who kept asking why the United States was fighting in Vietnam. The President unzipped his pants, extracted his penis, and announced: "This is why!"[9]

Apparently, it never occurred to LBJ that anyone was unwilling to die for that part of his anatomy, or the manhood that he thought it symbolized. Lyndon Johnson declared many times that he refused to be the first American President to accept defeat. He had repeated nightmares about being called a coward. His monumental ego and his devotion to what he considered macho qualities were sufficient to prevent him from entering into serious negotiations with North Vietnam even if his paranoia and megalomania had not kept him on his disastrous course.

During his presidency, Johnson's sanity became a popular topic for discussion among psychiatrists and psychologists who viewed him from afar. Those who saw him close had gone beyond wondering about the mental stability of the President. His one time friend and right-hand man, Bobby Baker commented: "...Johnson may have been the classic manic-depressive, with all the wide swings of the emotional pendulum typical of the breed...."[10] Harry McPherson, LBJ's special counsel, was in agreement with that and speechwriter Richard Goodwin said the President had, by 1965, "taken a huge leap into unreason." Senator William Fulbright considered Johnson incapable of discussing Vietnam rationally and worried that LBJ might bomb China.[11]

Just before the Democratic National Convention in August, 1964, Johnson expressed his own doubts about his fitness for office: "...I do not believe I can physically and mentally carry the responsibilities of the bomb, and the world, and the Nigras and the South, and so on...." He added, "I don't see any reason I ought to seek the right to endure the anguish of being here. ... They think I want great power. What I want is great solace and a little love, that's all I want."[12]

That mood passed. While he wanted love, he kept a tight grip on power.

For psychiatrists the label "psychosis" is reserved for the extremes of mental illness. Two indicators of that condition are delusions and hallucinations. LBJ showed signs of having both while he was president. Grandiosity is the condition of having delusions about the magnitude of one's greatness or importance. This is not an easy thing to identify in a President of the United States. But here is a sample from Johnson. On one occasion, a Secret Service agent felt his leg becoming wet and warm. When he realized what was happening, he informed the President that he was "pissing on the agent's leg." Johnson smiled. "I know I am," he said. "It's my prerogative."[13]

Paranoia is a word that is casually applied to a lot of relatively normal people who merely have isolated suspicions, well-founded or otherwise. However, when the suspicions become all-consuming, and one sees oneself surrounded by enemies and plotters, we are looking at the kind of paranoia that is seen in psychosis. Three people that knew Johnson well: Richard Goodwin, Johnson's press secretary, Bill Moyers, and Doris Kearns, his biographer, all thought that the President was, to some degree paranoid.[14]

Richard Goodwin believed that the President saw himself struggling in the coils of a gigantic Communist conspiracy that had coopted or duped LBJ's political adversaries into joining in his persecution. The President's' paranoia was out in the open for all to see when he informed his staff that most of the communications media were under Communist control.[15] Few of his staff recognized what they saw, however: people are reluctant to admit the possibility that their President is a psychotic.

Paranoids find enemies wherever they look. Johnson's favorite enemy was Robert Kennedy, whom LBJ feared and hated since his days as Vice President. In December of 1966, when Johnson still had two more years in office, he told his old friend, Supreme Court Justice Abe Fortas, "I believe that Bobby is having his governors jump on me, and he's having his mayors, and he's having his nigras, and he's having his Catholics."[16] The same year Johnson told a *Time-*

Life journalist that reporter David Halberstam made the Americans assassinate the leader of South Vietnam, Ngo Dinh Diem.[17]

Johnson's paranoia was already noticeable during his Senate years, but there is no hint of his having hallucinations until he was president. By 1966, there were rumors afloat that he claimed to be entertaining the Holy Ghost in the White House after midnight. He mentioned this to the Austrian Ambassador, Dr. Ernst Lemberger. According to the Ambassador, the President told him: "He comes and speaks to me about two o'clock in the morning—when I have to give the word to the boys, and I get the word from God whether to bomb or not."

How does one respond to a statement like that?

What Dr. Lemberger replied is not recorded, but he began to worry that the Soviets would hear about this madness. If they wondered when God would tell LBJ to destroy Moscow, the Russian leadership might decide to do something preemptive, like bomb Washington.[18] While the Ambassador's story is not conclusive evidence that Johnson was having hallucinations, it certainly was not the only strange thing Johnson said while he was president.

After a White House dinner with aide Ronnie Dugger, LBJ declared that the decisions to bomb and to send more troops were his, and his alone. Then, Dugger related, "…he shouted at me with terrible intensity, jamming his thumb down on an imaginary spot in the air beside him, 'I'm the one who has to mash the button!'"[19]

Future generations may well wonder at the fact that although some of the people around the President suspected that he was mentally ill, nothing was done to remove his finger from the nuclear button. Indeed, it would have been difficult for them to do this, and no one to whom they could report their suspicions. There are professionals and procedures in place to deal with a president's physical illness, but no machinery to deal with mental illness. No psychiatrist is assigned to monitor a president's mental health, diagnose whatever disorders might arise, or treat them. Unfortunately, ignoring the possibility of a mental collapse does not prevent its occurrence.

The mental illness that afflicted Lyndon Johnson was, as Bobby Baker said, manic depression. LBJ showed signs of this disorder from childhood on, as well as during a stormy adolescence, a remarkable college career, and throughout his adult years. Johnson's illness molded his personality and character.

Manic depression was in large part responsible for his rise in politics and his self-destruction as president. It contributed to his sexual excesses and his alcoholism. It gave him the acquisitiveness, drive and semi-criminality that would make him the richest president in American history. It turned him into a terror in the office and a Napoleon in the Senate. His ugly treatment of his Vice President, Hubert Humphrey, and his record-breaking production of domestic legislation both have their source in his manic depression. Finally, his illness also left its fingerprints on the Vietnam War which, absent his egotism and paranoia, could have started winding down, as Kennedy had planned, before it became an American war.

Benjamin Franklin had some perceptive things to say about the type of person who enters politics: "It will not be the wise and moderate, the lovers of peace and good order, the men fittest for trust. It will be the bold and the violent, the men of strong passions and indefatigable activity in their selfish pursuits. These will thrust themselves into your Government and be your rulers." He made this comment on June 2, 1787, during the sixth working session of the Constitutional Convention.[20] This certainly sounds like the voice of experience. And it sounds like he was talking about hypomanics, or manics, for that matter. The difference is largely one of degree, and the latter term will be used henceforth to include all degrees of mania. The "strong passions," "indefatigable activity," "selfish pursuits," and "thrusting ambition," fit Johnson perfectly.

It is not necessarily a bad thing for a nation to have a manic depressive leader. Three of the better known who still command respect are Abraham Lincoln, Theodore Roosevelt, and Winston

Churchill. Some voters would rather have a president of their own party who takes medication for manic depression than a president of the opposing party who doesn't need it.

Be that as it may, having a president under the sway of paranoia is an unacceptable risk, like riding on a bus on a busy highway during a blizzard with a nearsighted bus driver who left his glasses home. Today, there is a multitude of medications that can correct the distortions through which paranoids view the world. When Johnson was in the White House, such medications were few and not widely available.

LBJ was paranoid before he became president, and in an ideal world, he would have been diagnosed as such and either treated or disqualified. Unfortunately, the psychiatric evaluation of political candidates and office holders is not considered necessary. Tests are required to obtain drivers' licenses, to practice numerous professions, to enter government service and the military. No tests of any kind are required to become President of the United States.

This neglect of the mental health of politicians has severe personal consequences as well as lamentable historical results. The career of an untreated manic-depressive can take on the dark colors of a Greek tragedy. It is not just a question of hubris. The illness which sets him on a high trajectory may also lead to his downfall, as LBJ demonstrated.

A detailed discussion of manic depression appears in this book's appendix. As an aid to understanding Lyndon Johnson, here is a brief introduction to a complex and paradoxical illness:

Manic depression is a family illness, sometimes traceable back several generations, as it was among Johnson's forebears. However, a family history of the illness does not guarantee that all or any of one's children will have it, or have it to the same degree.[21] Both inheritance and upbringing play a part. Manic depressives even in the same family vary tremendously in the severity of their illness, the particular symptoms they have, and the course the illness may take.

The families of these people never know what to expect. The person who enjoyed the euphoria and sociability of mania one day can the next day wake up in an irritable, hostile, and even paranoid state.[22] Some manic depressives start the evening at a party and finish it at a hospital, drunk or high, and out of control.

More than half of the people who suffer from a depressive or manic depressive illness will also experience a period of alcoholism or drug dependency or both.[23] Abuse of alcohol and/or drugs can occur in mania as well as in depression. The manic wants to enjoy himself, the depressive to dull his pain. The irritable, paranoid manic is more likely than the euphoric manic to get drunk or high.[24] Irritable and paranoid is the kind of manic depressive Lyndon Johnson was, and alcohol was his drug of choice.

The fortunate few will experience mania or severe depression only once, but for the rest, emotional instability is a condition of existence, like having a life sentence to ride a Ferris wheel. It is impossible to predict the length of a manic or depressive episode: some are as brief as a few hours, while others last for days, months, or years. When the illness hits, an attack may bring nothing more than minor discomfort, or it may confine a person to his bed, as did some of Johnson's depressions. However terrible it may be, though, the mania or depression will eventually pass by itself, if it is not terminated by suicide.[25]

People with the mildest form of this illness may be noted for their moods, but are rarely considered sick. At the extreme end of the spectrum, people leave reality behind and enter the zone of frightful suffering. The manic is sleepless but constantly on the move, ready to jump out of his skin, eager for a fight, and incapable of thinking clearly. The depressive is suffering unbearable mental agony. He may be considering ways to kill himself, or he may become increasingly immobile, sinking into catatonia. These are the invisible victims, hiding at home or haunting the halls of psychiatric wards. Hallucinations can occur in both mania and depression.[26]

The general public rarely sees severely ill manic depressives outside of mental hospitals or prisons. The manic depressive that is most familiar to the general public is the hypomanic. This person is manic a lot of the time. But the mania is mild, and many hypomanics seem able to maintain a steady state of high energy and good humor, with very little time given to depression. The hypomanic is familiar, though unrecognized as such, because he or she is the model of the successful American. These people are leading artists, scientists, doctors, CEOs, military officers—they are the cream that rises to the top.[27]

Hypomanics and even manics also succeed in politics. Manic depression could almost be called the "political disease." The historical record shows that many prominent politicians were affected by this illness to some degree. That is because politics is a character filter. Most of those who pass through it are ambitious, energetic, gregarious, talkative, optimistic (or they would never be candidates), confident and dominating. Anyone who has these symptoms of hypomania or mania is more likely to succeed in politics than people who lack them, as the career of LBJ demonstrates.

It is the busy, bossy hypomanic who is most likely to achieve wealth, fame and power. That is because his symptoms are so useful. Who can compete with someone who can work longer and harder than any normal person, and does it on four hours' sleep? Moreover, he (or she, of course) is bubbling with ideas, and daring enough to carry them out. The hypomanic can be very inspiring and carry people away with his optimism and self-confidence.[28] When there is a party, he is the life of it and often the host too. He loves to make friends. His cheerfulness, humor, charm and sexual magnetism make him irresistible.[29] He is exciting to be with and loves to make friends.[30] These characteristics are always useful in politics, as is the hypomanic's talkativeness and ambition, his altruism, public spirit and generosity. He is a tireless and ardent campaigner. All of this was true of Johnson.

There are, however, significant drawbacks to hypomania. The

roving eye, the impatience, and the impulsive, thoughtless behavior so often seen in these people make hypomanics difficult to live with despite their charm. They are prone to exaggerate and lie. They can become dangers to the businesses they run, spending too much money, taking too many risks, ignoring any rule but their own will and their own greed. Hypomanics meddle in everything. They can be excessively critical of even the best performance, and innocent employees may become targets of the boss's screaming anger.[31] The work of hypomanics is frequently scattered and disorganized, and they often fail to carry things through.[32] Most of this was reflected in LBJ.

As conversationalists, their favorite topic is themselves. They can drive people away with their boasting and pornographic humor. Although they are oblivious to the hurts they inflict, they have tender skins and cannot themselves abide criticism. Rather than obey orders, they to try to control others.[33] The greatest liability, however is that the popular, successful hypomanic is always at risk for a major manic or depressive breakdown.[34] All of this also applied to Johnson.

Hypomanics do not necessarily have all of the assets or liabilities mentioned above. The successful hypomanics may have too few liabilities to scuttle a career, or at least they may be able to hide their flaws.

Any manic depressive whose symptoms occur often or for long periods may develop personalities and idea systems shaped by those symptoms.[35] These people may continue to have the negative outlook of a depression even when not depressed, for example. Or they may develop a desire to dominate people even when they are not manic. Johnson, who alternated between hypomania and mania, developed an irritable, tyrannical version of the manic personality.

Because many symptoms of manic depression are experienced at one time or another by normal people and because the malady varies tremendously both among individuals and within individuals' lifetimes, the conclusion that someone is a manic depressive should not be made on the basis of a few behaviors or traits. That label is justified only by the appearance of a constellation of symptoms displayed consistently over time. This is particularly true for historical personages, who are not available for observation, interview, or testing. Furthermore, in the light of the secrecy that surrounds mental health issues among politicians, one might conclude that the truth about the people who thrust themselves into our government, to paraphrase Benjamin Franklin, can never be determined with any certainty. This is not the case with Lyndon Johnson. He dealt with multitudes of people, many of them wrote about him, and though they were unaware of it, they were recording evidence of his illness.

Many recognized that Johnson was a phenomenal man, although they had no idea that mania was so closely tied to his abilities. James Reston of the *New York Times* observed: "President Johnson's strength is that he can outwork, outtalk, and outwit almost any other member of the human race....He overwhelms the opponent with power. You know exactly where he's going, but he rolls over you anyway."

LBJ often displayed the prodigious energy, pressure of speech, quick thinking and persuasiveness that mania can provide. Johnson's monumental ego was noted by journalists Haynes Johnson and Richard Harwood who wrote that the President's self-absorbtion prevented him from understanding the issues of the day.[36] Joseph Califano, a senior aide, said that Johnson's insistence on complete control of his universe gave new meaning to the word "Machiavellian.[37]

LBJ had the need to dominate seen in many manic personalities. But he could not master his own desires, anxieties or rage. The expansion of the war in Vietnam became inevitable when this afflicted individual became the most powerful man on earth.

CHAPTER 2

A BORN MANIC-DEPRESSIVE

★ ★ ★ ★ ★ ★

L BJ declared in his later years: "Listen, goddammit, my ances-
tors were teachers and lawyers and college presidents and
governors when the Kennedys of this country were still
tending bar."[1] This was typical Johnson talk: bragging while, at the
same time, expressing jealousy of the Kennedy family. What he
does not tell us is that the maternal line was, one might say, genet-
ically cursed. Lyndon's maternal great-grandfather suffered depressions after his service as a physician in the Civil War. A culminating
"nervous breakdown" is blamed for his death at 41. Lyndon's
grandfather lost all his money on a business deal that went bad. He
had to sell his house, and fell into a two-year depression at the end
of which he, too, died.[2] While risking and losing everything at once
is the kind of investment that people make during mania, it is hardly conclusive evidence of manic depression. However, it is clear
that Rebekah, Lyndon's mother, had an inheritance of two generations of severe, incapacitating depression.

Rebekah was a tough, domineering woman. She graduated
from college, edited a local weekly paper, and became an elocution
teacher in a place and at a time when careers required unusual initiative for a woman.[3] However, after the birth of her fifth child in

1916, she fell into a series of completely disabling depressions, staying in bed for several days at a time and sometimes for weeks. During these periods, unless someone stepped in to do her housework, the dishes for meal after meal collected in the sink, and clothes were piled in heaps waiting for an ironing that never came. She could not even rally sufficient will to break up her children's fights.

Unable to control her children, she asked neighbors to spank them for her. She stopped going to school meetings and church, and rarely left the house. When her husband was away on business, Lyndon, her oldest child, witnessed her crying spells and she shared her fears and anxieties with him.[4]

He recalled: "I knew how much she needed me, that she needed me to take care of her. I liked that."[5]

There is not much to suggest that Rebekah Johnson was manic except for her show of initiative in her early years and her domineering behavior. Not so with Sam, Lyndon's father. He had a typical manic's career: many changes of occupation, and the taking of risks that eventually reduced him to poverty. He was also a politician, elected to the Texas legislature six times.[6] Sam Houston, Lyndon's brother recalled that their father spent many a night talking politics 'till the morning. [7] Here we have a hint of those standard symptoms, pressure of speech and diminished need for sleep.

Before examining other indicators of Sam Johnson's illness, it is important to note that he introduced Lyndon to politics, taking the boy along with him on his campaigns and into the chamber of the legislature. The father would attract attention by wearing a gun and dressing like a cowboy. His son would later also seek to be the center of attention in Congress, but by using subtler means.

It was Sam Johnson who invented the "Johnson treatment," which consisted of grabbing a man by his arm or lapels, or reaching around the man's shoulder, going nose to nose, and then arguing. This, too Lyndon adopted. Like the son, the father was loud and given to bragging. They shared a lively sense of humor. They

were also both fond of teasing, the kind of intrusive, subtly bullying behavior that manics can develop.

The unique style in which Lyndon's manic depression mani-
fested itself was probably learned from his father. He clearly adopted his father's populist politics.[8] When Lyndon was a new congressman, his father said to him: "Son, measure each vote you cast
by this standard: Is this vote for the benefit of the people? What
does this do for human beings? How have I helped the lame and the
halt and the ignorant and the diseased?" He added: "Now you get
up there, support FDR all the way…and give 'em hell."[9] One can
hear the voice of Sam Johnson in his son's speeches about the Great
Society.

However, in one crucial respect the son did not walk in the
father's footsteps. Sam Johnson was a man of principle, one of the
few in Texas who did not work for and accept money from special
interests.[10] His political career was marked throughout by the
manic's altruism: he was a stalwart champion of the poor and disadvantaged, and he tried to imbue his son with his own concern for
the downtrodden.

Having seen his father end up as a state bus inspector, the son
would do whatever it took to be elected and reelected, which eventually meant serving those rich enough to pay for his extravagant
campaigns. Here we have a clear example of two manic depressives
who had similar symptoms and personalities yet who differed in an
important way, one being a man of integrity and the other being a
law unto himself.

Sam was notably friendly, a humorous man who could walk
into a bank and get everyone within earshot laughing. He loved to
talk. He was a warm, caring, generous man. As a legislator he
helped veterans and soldiers' widows get pensions. He had the
manic's energy and fertile, quick mind. Like his son Lyndon, he
was persuasive and a lot of the people who knew him were quite
fond of him.

However, he also had some of the less attractive attributes of his illness. He could be not just self-confident, but arrogant, over-bearing and verbally abusive. As a boy, he wanted to be first in every competition, whether it was racing horses or picking cotton. He needed to dominate. He refused to give way to anyone.[11] In these characteristics his son was a carbon copy.

He liked to buy the most expensive clothes, cars, and gifts, and his son was the same kind of shopper. But fatally, Sam was blind to risk and refused to save money, the combination that sends people into debt and poverty. Lyndon recalled: "We had great ups and downs in our family.... One year things would go just right. We'd all be riding high.... But then two years later we'd lose it all."[12]

A lot of Sam's money was spent in the capital's whorehouses, suggesting that he had not only the manic's extravagance but the intense sex drive as well.

There is no evidence in the father of the paranoia that was to plague Lyndon's later years, but grandiosity was somethiing of a family tradition. This instance of Sam's grandiosity became part of the family legend. When Lyndon was born, Sam announced to a neighbor that the baby would one day be governor of Texas.[13] What made the remark grandiose was that the father could not have had a clue how high his son would rise. When Lyndon was an adolescent and Sam was better acquainted with him, he told his wife: "That boy of yours isn't worth a damn, Rebekah. ...He'll never amount to a Goddamned thing!"[14]

The father, like the son, was impatient and unwilling to give people time to answer his questions. Sam's illness was also manifest in his sudden, explosive temper. Unlike his son's explosions, Sam's rages were quickly over and he could acknowledge his wrong, then make amends.[15] Sometimes, though, the rages resulted in violence. He frequently went after Lyndon, who recalled: "My father, he'd take a razor strap and just whip the hell out of us."[16] Sam used a gun barrel on a couple of men who crossed him and a rail from a fence on another.[17] This was bad temper even for Texas.[18]

Lyndon noted: "When he had too much to drink, he'd lose control of himself. He'd use bad language." Lyndon did the same, but perhaps he was a bit more discrete in his drinking than his father. Sam Johnson once made an unforgettable entrance into a meeting at the school auditorium. Too drunk to stand up, he crawled in on his hands and knees. When Sam's business ventures went belly up, the drinking increased.[19]

Before that happened, from age 5 to age 12, Lyndon lived the life of a rich boy, as a member of the best dressed family in town, riding around in the fanciest car. In those years, his father did very well selling real estate and cattle, well enough to afford a maid, well enough to be ranked among the three most successful men in the area.[20] But Sam Johnson, like many others, came to grief betting on cotton futures. When the cotton market crashed, Sam lost everything.

LBJ said that they lost "…one of the largest and best farms in this section of Texas."[21] Sam moved his family to Johnson City and retreated to his bed, with "nervous exhaustion" from September of 1922 through much of 1923.[22] His legislative career ended the following year. He was unable to work and the money was gone. At times, neighbors brought food to the family. Sam remained, for the balance of his life, penniless, and ill tempered. And he kept drinking, even though he had to borrow the money to drive to the bars in Austin, where he'd sometimes be found the next morning lying in a wagon yard.[23]

The marriage was difficult. At times, Sam and Rebekah didn't speak and used separate doors to the house. It didn't help that, as Lyndon remarked, "We had dropped to the bottom of the heap."[24] Having a large family only raised the stress level in the house. Lyndon's birth had been followed by those of three girls and a boy.[25]

Sam Houston, who was Lyndon's junior by six years, would eventually become a frequent participant in his life in Washington. When they were both adults, Lyndon relied on his brother for encouragement, particularly during periods of depression.

Sam never quite achieved a life of his own. He was cheerful and gregarious, but could not hold a job in the business world and relied on his brother for government jobs and salaries. His two marriages failed. His reputation in Texas was "No-good, a periodic drunk, a gambler, a chaser after loose women" (So far, this could also describe the father.) "A man who all his life had been doing his brother's dirty work in politics. ...His greatest pleasure was to set up intricately devious schemes for bringing about the discomfiture of any Texas or Washington politician who dared to oppose his brother."[26] This is the opinion of Johnson's assistant and speechwriter, Booth Mooney.

The Lyndon Johnsons had many homes over the years, where Sam was often found in the morning by an annoyed Lady Bird. He was sleeping off a drunk in the living room of whatever place they were in.[27] When LBJ was president, the Secret Service had to keep an eye on Sam, who would disappear on binges for days at a time.[28]

Lyndon's sister Josefa had her own problems with stability. She developed a reputation for sexual promiscuity, a behavior that often occurs when women become manic. She also shared the family alcohol abuse problem. Her marriage ended in divorce and her attempts at employment were not successful. Lyndon's sisters Rebekah and Lucia also appear to have been emotionally fragile, but they escaped the heaviest burdens of the Johnson's genetic load.[29]

What sets the stage for the entrance for over 80% of manic-depressive children is inheriting a mood disorder from both parents, combined with parental alcoholism or some other chemical dependency.[30] Lyndon's mother's and father's disabling depressions and his father's alcoholism suggested severe genetic risk even if the father had not been a manic depressive. In addition, Lyndon was a paradigmatic manic depressive child.

The picture of this illness in children is not a pretty one. The single spot of brightness in it is that these afflicted children are often gifted; they may show early artistic talent or, as did Lyndon, precocious verbal ability.[31] But they are difficult to raise, especially for parents who have their own symptoms to deal with. This was the case in Lyndon's family.

The fact that Lyndon was a manic depressive from childhood

26

on is important because this is a disorder from which there is no recovery in any absolute sense. The child is indeed a preview of the man. At best, with psychotherapy and appropriate medications, one can learn to minimize the effects of the illness, and lead a relatively normal life. But to be successful, this management of the illness must be a daily affair and requires a constant vigilance for the appearance of symptoms. Lyndon Johnson never had either therapy, adequate medication, or even a diagnosis for his condition.

Lyndon, the oldest of the Johnson children, was born on August 27, 1908, a year and a week after his parents were married. During the first two years of his life, he had his mother to himself and she had time to teach him the alphabet. His two sisters, brother and a final sister arrived at two-year intervals thereafter. Nevertheless, Rebekah took the time to teach Lyndon poems by Longfellow and Tennyson when her son was three. The following year she taught him to read, and sent him to school in a one-room schoolhouse nearby.[32] His mother being unavailable there, he literally clung to the teacher and was not happy at school although the teacher allowed him to sit on her lap while he was reading.[33]

By the time he was five, he was in constant motion and when the Johnson family went visiting, someone had to be assigned to keep an eye on Lyndon. His hyperactivity in school encouraged his teachers to give him extra work, but the same restlessness that made him a troublemaker prevented him from completing his lessons.[34]

At the age of five, in addition to his manic energy, poor concentration and mischievousness, he had developed the trait of defiance so often seen in children with his illness. His mother had to give him an order several times before he would obey it. And, adds a family friend, "He was also a boy who could be very arrogant."[35]

At that early age, Lyndon was already known for his compulsion to talk and to argue.[36] He would thrust himself in the faces of his playmates and harangue them until they agreed with him just to get away.[37] Here we have three traits that are notable in manic children: pressure of speech, arguing, and invasion of another's boundaries, in this case, physical space. [38]

The abnormal self-centeredness of the manic also emerged early in Lyndon. He gave his mother ceaseless demands, and she usually gave him what he wanted. He exacted attention from everyone, and according to his classmates, Lyndon wanted his superiority to be acknowledged.[39] By the time he was eleven, people were complaining about Lyndon's tremendous ego.[40]

He later recalled that his mother's need of him during her depressions "...made me feel big and important...made me believe I could do anything in the whole world."[41] Another child in his shoes might have felt overwhelmed and abandoned, but Lyndon not only had the manic's feeling of omnipotence, he made grandiose assertions as a boy, insisting that he would be a congressman. By the time he was twelve, he announced to a bunch of incredulous children: "Some day, I'm going to be President of the United States."[42] This may become a fixed idea that encourages a few of these afflicted children, later in life, to pursue fame and power and achieve it. If they live long enough, that is. They get into serious accidents because they are so reckless, and in depression, they may commit suicide.

Lyndon was a precocious tyrant. His sister Rebekah recalled that the boy bossed everyone as though he were the head of the family.[43] His brother Sam said that Lyndon, from boyhood on, was "Always checking on his three sisters and only brother to make damn sure none of them get out of line."[44] According to Sam, Lyndon designated himself the family foreman, seeing to it that his brother and sisters did their and his work around the farm, bringing the wood in for the stove, feeding the pigs, and collecting the eggs. Sam thought that Lyndon gave orders and their mother followed them, rather than the other way around.[45] A friend noted that Lyndon turned his mother into his personal servant. He would demand "Where's my shirt, where's my britches?" She would scurry to supply them.[46]

A cousin recalled that Lyndon insisted on being the leader in whatever games were going on.[47] He preferred to play with boys who were older, but this did nothing to curb his will to dominate. He was the classic boy who took the baseball home if he wasn't chosen as pitcher.[48] When bossiness failed, Lyndon fell back on manipulation. He would get his friends to do his job of stacking the firewood on the porch by challenging them to see who could make the biggest pile in the least time.[49]

The flip side of the manic's need to dominate is the refusal to let another dominate him. Lyndon's brother Sam said: "No one could boss him or even persuade him to do anything he didn't want to do."[50] Most mothers can get their children at least to wear shoes. Lyndon refused to do so until he decided it was time, and that was when he was fifteen. When teachers tried to deprive him of the privilege of recess because his homework had not been done for some time, he spit at them and walked out.[51]

This child seemed to thrive on the discomfiture of others. The woman who tutored him in his early grades called him "a real hellion."[52] At home, he would hide under beds and grab at the legs of everyone who passed. He was a demon in dancing class, unrelentingly teasing the girls. He teased his mother and sisters so regularly that his father got into the habit of asking, when he came home from work, "Well, what has Lyndon done today?" The answer often resulted in a spanking, but nothing deterred Lyndon from tormenting his family the next day.[53] Family fishing trips did nothing to moderate his behavior. He liked to use the fishing poles to toss people's hats into the water. His poor, frantic mother went around asking people what she could do to make her son behave.[54] Parents of other chemically unbalanced children often ask the same question.

It is not easy to discipline a child who runs away from home. The parents' fear of what might happen to him often gives the child the upper hand. Lyndon started this youthful form of extortion when he was four, and warnings about falling into the river or being bitten by rattlesnakes never made him hesitate when he wanted to go. Twisting the knife in the wound, he would hide in the woods for hours while his father called for him to come home and his mother cried.[55] When he was ten, his risk-taking took the form of jumping off the barn roof. Even the resulting broken leg did not curtail his recklessness.[56]

The boy had a strong resistance to getting up in the morning. He was frequently late to school. Despite his evident intelligence, when he was in the higher grades, his schoolwork followed his already poor behavior downhill. By the time he was twelve, he missed 50 school days out of 180.[57] He stole peaches from his grandfather. He was also becoming a fighter, throwing rocks to drive black children out of a swimming hole, getting into battles with them.[58] All of this was symptomatic for his illness.[59]

Lyndon thought that he had a hard childhood because his home lacked electricity and indoor plumbing during his family's descent into poverty.[60] What may well have been the cause of greater suffering in the Johnson home was the fact that a depressive and an alcoholic manic depressive were raising a manic depressive child. That is never easy.

Despite his oppositional and at times unbearable behavior, Lyndon, like many manic depressive children, showed a lot of potential. If politicians received the same kind of recognition as composers, Lyndon would have been recognized as the Mozart of his profession. He was unusually gregarious and, like a miniature politician, would get into conversations with everybody he encountered.[61]

When Lyndon was ten, his father began the boy's political training. Father and son would go to the legislature. Amazingly, Lyndon summoned the patience to sit hour after hour in the gallery, watching the legislators going about their business on the floor below. Sam turned his son into an unofficial page to run errands for his father and his father's friends.[62]

Sam also took Lyndon with him on campaigns in his district. These trips were among the boy's happiest memories. He and his dad would have impromptu picnics by the side of the road, sharing bread and jam. Or, during hot weather, farm families would invite them inside for talk and homemade ice cream. Lyndon recalled that "....Christ, sometimes I wished it could go on forever."[63] These were possibly the most harmonious moments the two ever had together. Lyndon, at least before his father's downfall, was quite proud of him. The boy told a playmate: "I want to wind up just like my Daddy, getting pensions for old people." As an adult, he recalled: "I wanted to copy my father always, emulate him, do the things he did."[64]

Lyndon went on to have the career of a political prodigy. While still in college, he ran an election campaign for three weeks for Texas State Senate candidate Willy Hopkins. He set up twelve small rallies and two big ones, placing newspaper ads, producing and distributing campaign literature, raising money for all this, and even organizing a portable claque.

Hopkins won.

As a newly minted congressional aide, at the age of 23 Lyndon took over the Little Congress, an organization of congressional aides. Three years later he was the youngest state director of the National Youth Administration. At 28, he was elected to Congress. Five years later he raised and controlled the funds for the Democratic congressional campaigns.

But the real power and glory lay far ahead.

The manic's preference for conspicuous dress emerged when Lyndon was in high school. In an overalls and blue jeans school he alone among the students wore slacks, a white shirt and a tie, which he eventually augmented with a yellow silk shirt and ascot, or on occasion, the only Palm Beach suit and straw boater in town. When he wasn't astonishing his schoolmates with his clothes, his ceaseless activity awed them. His friends considered him possesed of inhuman, inexhaustible energy.[65]

Lyndon treated high school as either a joke or an obstacle course. He avoided doing the work, convincing numerous female classmates to do it for him. If this failed, he would involve the teacher in an argument until the bell rang.[66] He already had "the Johnson Treatment" perfected. A friend recorded: "He'd lean over into your face, talking all the time, and lean right into your face until you were leaning backward."[67]

The manipulation went on at home too. He talked his younger brother into paying for a bike that only Lyndon was tall enough to ride.[68] The adolescent continued to ignore the authority of his father and his mother still jumped to obey his orders.[69] He continued to bully his younger brother and sisters into doing his chores. He got at his parents with a kind of water torture, a continual stream of minor defiances that included using his father's shaving equipment without permission. There were major infractions too. At night he sneaked out with the car, despite the whippings his father continued to administer.[70]

Sam and Rebekah, in desperation, sent their eldest to live with Sam's brother and sister-in-law. They could not control him either. He missed so much schoolwork that he was threatened with having to repeat the year. His parents sent him for eight weeks of summer school to San Marcos. No doubt they were relieved to have him out of the house. But the trouble did not stop. In a display of manic extravagance and generosity, in the first week, their son spent all of the money that was to have lasted eight weeks. He spent it buying candy and ice cream for his schoolmates. Then he had the audacity to hitch the thirty miles home to demand more money. All he got for his trouble was a ride back to school with his father.[71]

Lyndon regularly stayed out 'till early morning partying with his friends. They got drunk on prohibition liquor, drove around town, and according to a friend, fearless Lyndon was constantly getting into fights over anything at all.[72] By the time he was fifteen, Lyndon had attracted the attention of the local law. Once he and a friend stole two horses and ran them down a main street until the town Marshall went after them. Another time, they burned down a barn. Lyndon's grandmother declared: "That boy is going to end up in the penitentiary."[73]

Lyndon managed to stay in school long enough to graduate from the eleventh grade, which was the highest grade there. He enrolled in summer school to take the additional courses he would need for college eligibility. He later claimed that the school expelled him. Then, despite his parents' vigorous protests in July he ran off to California with some friends. Lyndon stayed for a while, with a lawyer who was supposed to impart his legal knowledge. The man was an alcoholic, and Lyndon, returned to Texas the following year. Sam got him a job for two to three dollars a day working on a road gang. On that salary, Lyndon had no choice but to live at home.

His oppositional behavior was evident at work, where he refused to take direction from anyone.[74] Despite his obdurateness, he was considered to be "full of fun." A certain amount of grandiosity stayed with Lyndon at this time. Here he was, in a dead end job, with not much education and no plans to get more, and he was bragging about what a big man he would one day be.[75]

He also continued with his flashy clothes, going to dances and looking for fights. Finally he had one that left him sufficiently bloody and beaten to end his enthusiasm for the way he was living. The next day he told his parents he would go to college. Without that decision, none of Lyndon's grandiose ambitions could ever have been realized.

CHAPTER 3

LYNDON PREPARES FOR POLITICS

★　★　★　★　★　★

San Marcos was a quiet, small town teachers' college that was unprepared for Lyndon. He ran around the campus, a perpetual motion machine that seemed to sweep everything before it. Even when he was pinned to a desk for a class, his fingers drummed on the wood, and when he had to stand still to talk to someone, his arms kept sweeping the air with grand gestures.[1] He joined every club or activity he could, from the literary society to the business administration club. He also became president of the Press Club and worked on the yearbook.

Political activity was not neglected as he served on the Student Council and, in his senior year, as class "senior legislator."[2] To earn money he sold silk socks and worked for the president of the college. To top it off, he completed four years' of college in less than three.[3] A dean of the college observed of Lyndon: "He had too many irons in the fire."[4]

Johnson delivered a torrent of talk, invading his friends' nocturnal poker games to subject the young cardplayers to long monologues about people in politics.[5] Pressure of speech colored his interactions at his boarding house too. A fellow boarder complained that Lyndon pushed his way into conversations like a bulldozer, and from that moment on, no one else was given a chance to say much.[6] Anyone who has spent time with a person who is even moderately manic knows what it is to be a captive audience.

Not only was Lyndon's fast, nonstop style of talking symptomatic, so was the content of his outpouring. People who spent time with him were likely to be treated to his repertoire of dirty stories. And he was still a braggart. A teacher recalled that Lyndon was vain, constantly demanding recognition for whatever he did.[7] His boasting about his family's social and political position and his own accomplishments at San Marcos, including his sexual ones, didn't always go down well with other students.[8]

Lyndon earned the nickname "bull," but not because of his strength or sexual prowess. A fellow student explained that it was "Because of this constant braggadocio. Because he was so full of bullshit, manure, that people just didn't believe him. Because he was a man who just could not tell the truth." Lyndon earned a reputation as the college's most outrageous liar.[9] According to a teacher, neither his arrogance nor his lies made him popular with the other students.[10]

Lyndon may have been a manic spender earlier, but his extravagance was especially noted in college, particularly by those who lent him money.[11] Although his family had no money to spare, he wore the most expensive clothes on campus, made a big splash on dates, took expensive trips to Houston, Austin and San Antonio and even bought a car with no way to keep up the payments. When he earned a small bonanza selling socks he drove to Nuevo Laredo with a friend and spent it all in one day.

The future LBJ may not have been liked by everyone, but he established "instant friendships" with strangers he met when he was travelling with the university debating team.[12] He was a person who was universally friendly, greeting everybody, taking an interest in everyone's affairs. Some fellow students found this irresistible.[13] But, as many friendly manics do, Lyndon took liberties. To the dismay of faculty members who were watching, he greeted the college president with a slap on the back, as though he were a colleague.[14]

The people who saw only the sunnier side of Lyndon's illness liked him a lot. It was the darker side that made enemies. He was already a master of the art of manipulation. He would begin with persuasion, for which he had more of that manic gift than most people. A teacher at the college said that neither he nor anyone else could refrain from buying socks from Lyndon, who was a master salesman.

Lyndon wanted more than to sell socks. He mounted a campaign of flattery against his target, and it was usually a teacher. He saturated the faculty with his admiration. A classmate describes him in action, sitting at a teacher's feet, giving worshipfull attention to every word from the teacher's mouth. This happened even when chairs were available. Lyndon expressed agreement with absolutely everything said by the objects of his courtship. The college yearbook marveled: "Believe it or not—Bull Johnson has never taken a course in suction."[15]

Lyndon apparently looked on those who peopled his world as raw clay to be shaped into tools, or broken if they were refractory. And his lifelong practice of cloaking his acts in secrecy was already established. One student who understood what was afoot said: "Lyndon was always the string-puller behind the scenes. He found those he could use, and used them, and those he couldn't, he worked behind the scenes to put down."[16]

The man on campus who could help Lyndon Johnson the most was President Cecil Evans. One day while Lyndon's cousin Ava was visiting him on campus, he told her his modus operandus: "The first thing you want to do is to know people...and don't play sandlot ball; play in the big leagues...get to know the first team."

Ava demurred that she would never have the nerve to go to the office of the president. Lyndon insisted, "That's where you want to start."[17]

President Evans was besieged with flattery as though he were a castle with a treasure inside. Lyndon not only ran the president's errands, he invented additional ones to run. It paid off with jobs that Lyndon also created for himself, such as painting a garage that didn't need painting. He became Evan's office boy. He was paid for this but the money, was secondary to his having a protector so well placed that the protégé could afford to make enemies.[18] Which he did.

He became known as a ruthless opportunist. A college friend said that everything Lyndon did was designed to bring him some advantage, and that he omitted nothing that would advance his ambitions.[19] Lyndon respected no limits to his will. A fellow student noted: "He was likeable. He was smart. But he would do anything to get his way. ...He'd cut your throat to get what he wanted."[20]

When Lyndon was unable to get into the fraternity of his choice, he secretly organized one of his own and in a campus election took all the power from the fraternity which had blackballed him.[21] He managed this reversal of fortune by stealing his first election. A friend stated that the election smelled to high heaven and that it was widely known who was responsible for the stink.[22] Lyndon, in fond reminiscence said: "It was a pretty vicious operation....They lost everything I could have them lose. My first real Hitler-type operation....I broke their back.... It's been broke for a good long time."[23]

Although it did not happen often, depression came to Lyndon during his college years. One of the students describes him in terms of contrasts: outgoing, cheerful, noisy, and then occasionally, quiet and sad.[24] Only when Lyndon was depressed did the normally gregarious young man complain of feeling lonely. And one such time was the spring of 1927, when he was 18. He was discouraged enough to consider quitting college and running off to a friend in California.[25]

One benefit of President Evan's patronage was a teaching job that Lyndon needed to pay for the remainder of his college education. In 1928, he went to the small, predominantly poor, Chicano town of Cotulla where for one school year he held the position of principal of the Welhausen Ward Elementary School.[26] It was a town where many of the citizens lived in adobe hovels. Most of the students lacked everything, including hope, but Lyndon was finally boss of something and he blew in on a wind of mania.

Someone who knew him there noted that Lyndon was constantly rushing around.[27] People were amazed at his energy.[28] He got a lot done. He took over the school's office work. He organized regular school assemblies and competitions with other schools in baseball, track, spelling, and public speaking, as well as organizing the car pools to get students to these events. He organized a volleyball team. He created a debating team, became its coach, and founded a literary society.[29] He started a parent-teachers association.

Having his personal little kingdom brought out the generous, altruistic manic in Lyndon. Despite his own pinched budget, he bought musical instruments and songbooks for the school. He even took on the job of landscaping the school, personally planting the flowers and shrubs.[30] As though he were not fully occupied at his own school, he became coach of the high school's basketball team, took correspondence courses for extra credit, and courted a neighborhood girl.[31]

He was struck by the poverty of the children. They came to school without breakfast. Often they were driven away in trucks to spend days working in the fields, though school was in session. He had his mother send him packages of toothpaste to give to the children. He bought them a volleyball with his first paycheck so that they would have something to do during recesses besides fight with each other.

Perhaps his greatest gift was the gift of hope. Here was manic optimism at its best: he taught them that they need not have to remain trapped in poverty, that with education, they could become anything, even President of the United States.[32] It was true in theory, although a Chicano president has yet to be elected.

Before long, Lyndon knew and was known by just about everyone in town. He loved to talk politics, and insisted that he would follow in his father's footsteps.

Lyndon's grandiosity was emerging. He became incensed when

he believed some students had made fun of him. He loftily informed them that he would one day be their President.[33] He also did what many dictators do when they establish their cults of personality: he wrote or commissioned a little worshipful song for the students. He required them to stand when he entered the classroom and sing it to him: "Is there anything that we can do for you? We will do it if we can, we'll stand by you to a man."[34] This is precisely the attitude he demanded from everyone who worked for him in later years.

One teacher, while acknowledging his energy and creativity, noted that he had a hair trigger temper.[35] Lyndon expressed his rages the same way his father had done: "I disciplined 'em, I gave 'em hell." "I'd drive 'em, whip 'em."[36]

Lyndon's final year at San Marcos was another manic marathon. He resumed working for President Evans, was student-teaching, and took extra courses. But even this schedule didn't burn up all his energy. He was dating every night. This left him only three or four hours for sleep.[37]

Lyndon spent the following year, teaching at Sam Houston High School in Houston. He made a tremendous impression on his students. Lyndon had an overpowering personality and nagged without mercy, but he made the students feel that what they did mattered tremendously to him. Moreover, he set standards for himself that made him work harder than the students. Sometimes he would stay up all night correcting papers just so that he could hand them back the next day.[38]

In Houston, where he was a young teacher on the bottom rung of the ladder, the manic benevolence seen in Cotulla was replaced by cruelty. As coach of the debating team, he set a pattern he would follow faithfully and which would make him a nightmare boss. "If they'd take one side of a question, I'd take the other," he remembered. "I'd just try to run 'em under the ground, just almost stomp 'em, but always would make it clear that I loved 'em, where they'd never completely run off. I would humiliate and embarrass

'em and make fun of 'em and everything" (here comes his ratio-
nalization) "until they got to where they could take care of themselves, which they did."[39]

According to his mother, depression was his frequent compan-
ion in Houston. She recalled: "Lyndon was very lonely in Houston.
Quite downhearted and blue."[40] But the wheel of his life was about
to turn again.

While a senior in San Marcos, Lyndon had managed a successful
campaign for a Texas legislator. The legislator remembered the political prodigy when Congressman Richard Kleberg was seeking a legislative secretary. Lyndon was beginning his second year of teaching
when he received a call from Kleberg offering the job. He took it and
was off to Washington as soon as the school let him go.[41]

The magnetic manic hit the Hill with "charm to burn." And, his
coworker adds, optimism: to Lyndon Johnson, there was no such
thing as a problem without a solution. (This attitude would prove
immensely costly when applied to Vietnam.) Lyndon had an
unsinkable optimism that was often quite contagious.[42] The term
"manic contagion," the ability of the manic to influence and
swamp others with his excitement, applies to situations like this.
Strong emotions are often contagious, especially among people
who are working together for the same goals.

In Kleberg's office, the staff was obligated to try to make the
government deliver what it owed to their constituents. When their
efforts succeeded, everyone was pleased, but Lyndon would cheer
and all but leap into the air. As a worker noted, "He would get
ecstatic."[43] Who wouldn't be carried away with him? Of course, his
magnified emotions were not limited to the cheery ones. A friend
noted with understatement that Lyndon's were rather emotional.
An ordinary letter from his mother could bring the young man to
tears.[44]

During his first night at his new Washington lodgings in the
Dodge Hotel's sub- sub-basement, instead of sleeping, he spent
hours getting to know everybody, joking, arms around their shoul-

ders, becoming instant buddies as though he were giving a text-book demonstration of sociability.[45] He soon was acknowledged to know more of the people who actually made the government function than anyone else in town.[46]

During this part of his life, he was too excited to stay seated in a movie theater for more than a couple of minutes. He'd get up and leave. He treated the cafeteria as a place where food was going out of fashion, racing to the head of the line, racing to his table, gulping down his meal, and then barraging his fellow congressional secretaries with political questions as they ate at a normal speed.[47]

According to one secretary, Lyndon was like a tornado in the office.[48] He arrived before anyone arrived, left after everyone left, and often returned after dinner to work another 3 or 4 hours. Seven-day weeks of twelve-hour days were normal to him. Besides feeling the goad of ambition, he was propelled by the incredible energy of mania. According to a fellow office worker: "...he was moving, going all the time. He would never rest."

Speech speed is an unmistakable indicator of mania. According to his future wife, Lady Bird, who met him when he worked for Kleberg, "he talked incessantly."[49] Much of his speech was given to arguing. One of his fellow aides affirmed that Lyndon was a heavyweight champion of disputation. He used arguments as a way to gather information from others. He sought to discover who wielded power in Washington.[50] In the opinion of another aide, Lyndon, during the brief interval of only a few months, had acquired a mastery of Washington equal to that of many a 20-year veteran.[51] Here we have another early display of his political talent. His only failure so far was the failure to get a rich wife. But that was about to be remedied.

Lyndon was so open in his pursuit of girls with wealthy fathers that it was mentioned as a joke in his college yearbook. From high school on, he set his sights on the daughters of the richest men in town. Usually, the fathers sent him on his way.[52]

One who did not was the father of Claudia Alta Taylor, a quiet girl four years younger than LBJ. Whirlwind courtship hardly describes what happened. He told her: "I see something I *know* I *want* and I *immediately exert efforts* to get it…." With typical impetuosity, he proposed to her within 24 hours of meeting her.[53] She recalled: "I just thought it was sheer lunacy."[54] She also told people: "I knew I had met something remarkable, but I didn't know what." She found him "a little bit scary— so dynamic and so insistent."[55]

He courted her with love letters such as the following: "This morning I'm ambitious, proud, energetic and very madly in love with you. I want to see people. I want to walk through the throngs, want to do things with a drive. If I had a box, I would almost make a speech this minute. Plans, ideas, hopes, I'm bubbling over with them.…when I feel as I do this morning, I think how cruel it was to even let you know how despondent I felt last week."[56] Claudia Taylor held him off for seven weeks. Then he insisted that they had to get married immediately if they were ever going to do it. They married the following week, on November 17, 1934.[57] They had a brief honeymoon in Mexico, during which the man an aide called a "sexual gorilla" bragged to his bride about the (other) women he'd known intimately.[58]

In one regard, Lady Bird had made a good marriage: her husband enriched both her and her father, Thomas Taylor. Mr. Taylor had a construction company that, thanks to LBJ's influence, eventually received government contracts for rural electrification systems that were worth several hundred thousand dollars, a large sum in those days. In 1941 LBJ saw to it that Taylor got the highest going price for 7,804 acres that the government bought from him.[59] Some twenty years later, Lady Bird's business holdings were worth $9,000,000.00.[60]

Working for Congressman Kleberg, Lyndon continued honing the manipulative skills that he'd developed in college. Having found out who was important in Washington, he wooed these people with flattering letters. When someone he thought would be useful to him entered Kleberg's office, Lyndon took up a worshipful position seated on the floor at the man's feet.[61]

One of the men Lyndon cultivated was Texas Congressman Wright Patman, whom he visited nearly every day. Lyndon induced Patman to play the role of professor of advanced political mechanics, treating politics as though it were an immensely complex machine. If you move this gear or that lever, what will happen? Lyndon's questions were not always that abstract, however. He particularly wanted to know who was doing what to whom and why. Patman adds: "He … also liked to ask questions about the dirty political fighting that was part of Texas electioneering."

Lyndon turned Washington into his personal university. Whatever political event was occurring in town, he tried to be there, like an avid music student going to the degree recitals of the advanced students. In Washington, these performances consisted of committee hearings and speeches by important people. Lyndon also repeated what he had done as a boy and became a temporary congressional page carrying messages. In the course of that activity he met many more congressmen and learned how Congress worked. He was obsessed with power and determined to get it. A friend said that remaining a nobody was absolutely intolerable to Lyndon.[62]

The manic's tendency is to move into a position of dominance, and before long, Lyndon claimed that location in his employer's office. Richard Kleberg was an easy mark, a spoiled prince of Texas, heir to the kingdom-sized King Ranch. Lyndon worked his usual twelve-hour, seven-day week, while Kleberg's main concern was to continue his playboy lifestyle, which included poker games, the attending of horse races, and making trips to Mexico.

When Kleberg was absent, Lyndon took over his functions as congressman, not only seeing to constituents' needs, and running the office, but also deciding how the Congressman should vote on the bills that came up.

Lyndon pretended to be Kleberg on the phone and wrote all of the Congressman's letters, including personal ones. In time Lyndon controlled all access to Kleberg. The secretary's domination of the

Congressman reached the point where Lyndon threatened to leave if Kleberg did not vote as instructed, and the Congressman caved in.[63]

Eventually, Lyndon took over Kleberg's personal life too, paying bills and signing checks for him. The young man got embroiled, as a confidant to both sides, in the conflict between the adulterous Congressman and his wife. Finally, Lyndon held a party for Congressman Patman aboard Kleberg's yacht while the owner was nowhere to be seen.[64] This process of creeping usurpation reached the point where Lyndon began taking personal credit for Kleberg's political actions. Not only did his name replace Kleberg's in press releases that Lyndon dictated, the aide made sure that people appointed by Kleberg knew who really was responsible for selecting them. He was now using Kleberg's assets to make friends for himself.[65]

Despite his heavy schedule, Lyndon found time to steal another election, this one to the presidency of the Little Congress. The members were congressional aides who gathered regularly to discuss political issues. Not satisfied with stuffing the ballot box, Lyndon also cheated on the count of votes.[66] It's as though he were practicing for running in Texas.

Speaking of Texas politics, Lyndon had a chance to buy votes there, which he did, at five dollars per vote on behalf of Congressman Maury Maverick.[67]

Again, no account of Lyndon's behavior is complete without mentioning depression. A fellow staff member observed: "Now Lyndon had a side to him. He could get very low. When he got real quiet it was bad." And sometimes "very bad." She would ask Congressman Kleberg to talk to Lyndon to cheer him up—which often worked, but the depression would quickly return.[68]

Kleberg's office was a training school and stepping-stone. Lyndon planned to move on even before he got there.[69] What he wanted was a chance to build his own constituency in Texas.

Opportunity appeared when President Franklin D. Roosevelt created the National Youth Administration. The NYA was charged with the responsibility of finding work for as many young victims of the Depression as time and money allowed. Hours after the Executive Order was signed, Lyndon was calling every influential man he knew in Texas. This instant leap at opportunity, so characteristic of the manic, paid off. A month later he had the job and took leave of absence from Kleberg's office.[70]

The NYA was tailored to Lyndon's requirements. He could buzz around Texas getting to know people, doing good things for people, and building an unofficial political organization for himself. He was only 27 years old and he had just become the Good Fairy of Texas. He wasted no time setting up an office in Austin and working until 10 P. M., when the electricity went off for the night. Then he'd stop just long enough to light gas lamps and go on for another 5 hours.[71] At any sign of progress, and, says a staff member, "He was beside himself with happiness."[72]

Lyndon did not stay inside the office for long. He wanted to find out what was needed in the state, and this he did not only by phone but by visiting schools, libraries, hospitals, recreational facilities, conservation bureaus and transportation departments. In no time he had 350 sponsors to provide housing for the oncoming young people and materials for the projects.[73] Playgrounds, parks, new buildings and repairs for old ones began to grow in number, and within 18 months 190,000 young people were being paid to make all that happen, while another 428,000 were being assisted with their training or studies.[74]

The NYA directorship was good practice for a political career. Half of the job was persuading people to do something, while the other half was persuading people to pay for what was to be done. This wasn't Cotulla, where the bushes were planted by Lyndon himself.

He was already a gold medalist in the sport of persuasion. A staffer states: "...he had what they now call charisma. He was dynamic, and he had this piercing look, and he knew exactly where he was going, and what he was going to do next, and he had you sold down the river on whatever he was telling you. And you had no doubts that he was going to do what he said—no doubts at all."[75] Manics often rise to the top of whatever organization they are in, be it academia, corporations, the military, or whatever.

The effect of his energy, charisma and persuasiveness on people who worked with him was clear to the Southern Regional Director of the NYA who said that Lyndon had created an organization that, inspired as it was with loyalty and dedication to duty, was a model for all.[76] The director would have realized how truly remarkable that loyalty was if he had seen what Lyndon did to his staff when no one was looking.

Despite the strict segregation prevalent in Texas at that time, he would stay overnight in black colleges when he was checking on their progress. He got a reputation among blacks as the rare NYA person who was taking care of them.[77] It was not deserved, though. The proportion of funds going from the NYA to the young blacks of Texas was below the national average, as was the number of them working in NYA projects. This was true too for Chicanos. Despite the requirements of the national administration, Johnson refused to give staff jobs to members of either group.[78]

In 1936, LBJ was Director of the NYA for Texas and was being interviewed. If he did not give away the shirt on his back, he did the next best thing. The interviewer, Charles Green, reports that, after he had admired Lyndon's Mexican sandals, they were thrust upon him.[79] This was politically astute behavior on LBJ's part, but it was also evidence of pure generosity.

Even before he could afford to spend much on gifts, he arranged to have gifts given. In July, 1933, while he was only a congressional secretary, his assistant, Gene Latimer, got married. LBJ talked their employer, Congressman Richard Kleberg, into giving the newlyweds a gift of $100 and the use of a car for the honeymoon. LBJ also got a higher paying job for Latimer at the Federal Housing Authority.[80]

While mania made Lyndon an inspiring boss, it also made it

hard to work for him. His flights of ideas overburdened his staff with orders. One of them recalled that the boss could, think of hundreds of things to do and the staff was expected to accomplish them at once. And then the questions would begin. If there were satisfactory answers, a new list of jobs to be done was announced.[81]

A depressive probably makes an easy boss. He won't be able to think of orders to give and he won't have the motivation to give the orders anyway. The term "flight of ideas," a prime indicator of mania, means not only that someone has a lot of ideas, but that they come to him at high speed. This was true for Lyndon, who dictated very fast. If one did not have to take the dictation, he must have been entertaining, marching back and forth as he talked, waving his arms, and acting out the contents of a letter. The problem was that not only was he incapable of rest, he was incapable of waiting for anything. "Everything had to be done NOW!" said a staffer. "And he could get very, very angry if something couldn't be done immediately."[82]

At the NYA, Lyndon became the boss from Hell. His demands were ceaseless. Not only did he insist that the staff work on Saturdays, he held staff meetings every Sunday at his home. These sometimes lasted the entire day. Some staff members had to drive two or three hundred miles to reach his home.

LBJ's first office manager was on the job regularly from 7 or 8 A.M. 'till midnight or 1 A.M. and this man could only last for a year. His replacement, Gene Latimer, eventually suffered a breakdown and left.[83]

Whatever his intentions were, LBJ's need seems to have been total control over every minute of his employees' lives.[84] Gene Latimer recalled: "If he caught you reading a letter from your mother, or if you were taking a crap, he'd say, 'Son, can't you please try a little harder to do that on your own time?'"[85] The problem was that he didn't allow them any time of their own. Private lives were not allowed.

Undoubtedly, people put up with this office autocrat for a variety of reasons. One of the reasons was fear of what would happen if they left. When Gene Latimer talked about quitting, his boss warned him that he would be unable to find work in Washington because of the Depression and therefore would not be able to stay in the city and marry his fiancee.[86]

With rare exceptions, the only people who stayed long with LBJ were those willing to live without dignity and pride of any kind. Luther Jones, who worked with LBJ in Kleberg's office, said that LBJ required his workers to surrender completely any shred of personality or individuality to his domination. With few exceptions, LBJ would not keep people who failed to deliver his version of "loyalty" regardless of their competence and hard work.[87]

John Gwyn, a veteran of the office, put it this way: "Johnson didn't demand a great ability. He demanded 'loyalty', and what he meant by loyalty was a kind of total submission. If you worked for Lyndon Johnson, you sold your soul to him. You could see it happening to other people around you. You saw that Jesse Kellem had no soul of his own."[88] Kellem was known as a brute on the San Marcos football team, but in later years, when he worked for LBJ at the Johnsons' radio station, the boss could reduce him to tears.[89]

Having his own kingdom in Texas seems to have fully unleashed Lyndon's temper. People were cursed at the top of his lungs for having neat desks as well as for having sloppy ones. A tidy desk made him believe no work was being done. According to one staffer, "God, he could rip a man up and down."

Lyndon threatened to fire people many times, and this was no joke with unemployment high.[90] Even a perfect performance was no protection from his rage. He would tear into a person without any discernible provocation. And unfortunately, not only could he sense where one's greatest vulnerability was, that was the spot he hit again and again, like a fighter hitting a bleeding eye.[91]

But few at this time knew about the merciless side of Lyndon Johnson. That would change when he returned to Washington.

Almost from the start, LBJ insisted that his wife, now nicknamed Lady Bird, become a team player. He transformed her appearance to meet the standard he set for his other women. One might think he was trying to create a Stepford wife. She noted: "Lyndon was always prodding me to look better, learn more, work harder. He always expects more of you than you think you are really mentally or physically capable of putting out. It is really very stimulating. It's also very tiring."[92]

That was putting his treatment of her in the best possible light. John Connally and his wife saw it as cruelty. LBJ constantly criticized his wife's appearance regardless of who was present. Nellie Connally recalled: "He would say things like.... 'Get out of those funny-looking shoes, Bird. Why can't you wear shoes like Nellie!' Right in front of us all! Now, can you think of anything more cruel?"[93]

One of the first things Lady Bird learned was that her husband was intolerant of opposition. Journalist William S. White observed that Lady Bird never contradicted Lyndon or questioned anything he said.[94]

Another rule she accepted from the beginning of their marriage was to expect surprises. Her husband was impulsive. When he was a director of the NYA, he might not show up for dinner until one in the morning.[95] As a congressman, he frequently brought guests home for dinner with only a last minute call to inform his wife that they were on their way.[96]

During the White House years that followed the only difference, was that Lady Bird no longer did the cooking. McGeorge Bundy recalled: "He would say, 'I'm not coming home.' Then he'd call, 'I'll be home for a hamburger at 7, dear.' At 9 he'd arrive with 12 speechwriters for dinner."[97]

Even early in the marriage, when he was an NYA director, LBJ combined incessant demands with lack of appreciation. He would insist that his wife come along as he dashed back and forth across the state. Then, on reaching their destination he would ignore her.[98] He turned his wife into a servant, and, says journalist Jack

Gwyn, spoke to her as though she were one.[99] A friend, Wingate Lucas, observed that when Lyndon wanted something, he'd yell orders at his wife even if she were on the other side of a room full of people. Lucas thought that all of Texas was full of pity for Lady Bird and was amazed that she continued to endure this treatment.[100]

Her duties included bringing her husband his breakfast and the newspaper in bed, having his clothes ready for the day, the shoes shined, the pockets supplied with pens, handkerchief, cigarette lighter and money. While he shaved, she took dictation like a secretary.[101] She told people: "Lyndon is the leader....Lyndon sets the pattern, I execute what he wants. Lyndon's wishes dominate our household....Lyndon's tastes dominate our household."[102] Perhaps this explains why the Johnsons, in manic style, moved ten times in five years.[103]

In addition to being LBJ's valet, running the household like a restaurant, and frequently packing and moving, Lady Bird also became the family accountant; the LBJ historian, keeping scrapbooks of LBJ's career, recording his life on film; and finally, a Washington tour guide for his constituents.[104] With a husband who came home only to eat and sleep, who spent Sundays entertaining politicians who could be useful to him, Lady Bird bore all the burden of parental responsibility, accommodating her children's needs only after Lyndon's were met.[105]

Her reward for all this was to be treated with contempt. He would, in her presence, tell others what a bad housekeeper she was and he would make fun of her accent.[106] This must have sounded strange, considering his own accent.

Subjugation and humiliation were petty annoyances for Lady Bird, compared to the other stresses that her husband's illness would place on their marriage.

CHAPTER 4

THE LION IN CONGRESS

★　★　★　★　★　★

Congressman James P. Buchanan's death in office on February 22, 1937, left a vacancy for which a special election would be held. Johnson had never run for an elective office. This didn't discourage him. He set off like a rocket. A political veteran said: "I never saw anyone campaign as hard as that.... I never thought it was *possible* for anyone to work that hard"[1]

Johnson was not widely known and there was no television, so he had to mount a person-to-person campaign. He seemed determined to shake every hand in every town in the Tenth Congressional District. Crisscrossing the district, he went up and down streets and into stores, shaking hands and introducing himself, then asking for votes. He gave more than 200 speeches in the month before the voting. Volunteers at his headquarters nicknamed him the "Blanco Blitz."[2]

Energy that intense seems inseparable from an inability to rest and is usually accompanied by near total insomnia. Both of these plagued the candidate. When he tried to relax in the car, while travelling to the next town, a witness relates, "...I would see him close his eyes, but never for more than a minute of two, then he'd just jerk up. He couldn't sleep.... So he'd start talking again." Not even the use of a black eye-mask helped him to take a nap. In the course of the campaign, another symptom of intense mania appeared: Johnson lost weight.[3]

Fortunately, mania supplied LBJ with a love of campaigning. And yet depressions during his campaigns caused him to consider withdrawing from the race. Campaigning was for LBJ like a chain reaction that kept him energized. His brother Sam thought that campaigning was a life-sustaining elixir for Lyndon. The campaign fed the candidate's ego as nothing else in his existence could, and a well-fed ego made him manic. Sam describes the astonishing trans- formation that the return of mania could provide: "I have been with him on the campaign trail when he seemed totally exhaust- ed— slouched in the rear seat of a car, his eyes glazed and his face gray and slack with a weariness that verged on sadness. Then, quite suddenly, as we got near the crowd that was waiting to hear him, he would straighten up and lean forward as the color flowed back to his face and an eager glint came back to his eyes. You would think someone had just given him a massive dose of adrenalin."[4]

This of course did not happen when LBJ thought he was losing. But a flourishing political campaign generates a tremendous excite- ment even for people on its periphery. Imagine what it does to the candidate himself. In later years, George Reedy, his Press Secretary, observed that effect more than once as the roar of the crowd drove Lyndon into a state of ecstasy.

During this first campaign Johnson didn't have his hands in a lot of deep pockets. His initial financing came from a $10,000.00 por- tion of Lady Bird's inheritance from her mother.[5] This did not stop him from running one of the most expensive congressional cam- paigns Texas had ever seen. It would set the precedent for Johnson's future record-breaking senatorial campaigns.[6] Mania makes the spending of money effortless, and how to meet expenses is not a concern.

Appendicitis arrived during the last week of the campaign. The candidate was vomiting between speeches, and clutching his belly in extreme pain. Despite everyone's insistence that he see a doctor, he refused to lose an hour that he could spend shaking hands or giving speeches. He continued in agony for five days, then was rushed to the hospital just two days before the election. He had waited until it was almost too late. As the operation began, the appendix was ready to rupture.[7]

This is one Johnson story that has a happy ending. He was sworn in as a Congressman on May 13, 1937.

Depression was a dead weight for LBJ's political career. It pulled him out of the action even in the midst of a campaign, it turned him into an ineffectual legislator in his final years in the Congress, and it often made him want to withdraw from politics altogether. Mania, by contrast, was the fuel for his rocket. It gave him unmatchable energy and kept him running through 20-hour days.

Mania quickened his mind, and increased his powers of persuasion. Mania endowed him with hospitality, charm, charisma, a genuine enjoyment of people, and, as we saw, a love of campaigning. Mania also gave him the will and unquenchable ambition needed in such a competitive profession. These gifts combined with high intelligence, formidable powers of concentration, and an encyclopedic memory amounted to what could be termed political genius.

Of the two sexes, women are usually credited with being more insightful about and better able to read their fellow human beings. According to journalist June White, LBJ also possessed that very useful form of intelligence: "...he could read people almost on meeting them.... It's almost as though he knew their assets, their plusses and their negative points, so that he could go ... to their plus points and use them...."[8]

This extraordinary sensitivity to what was going on in other people's minds was most in evidence when LBJ first came to Congress, although there were notable lapses. As he had done with the President of his college, so Johnson overstepped the bounds with the President of his country. When he met FDR for the first time, he gossiped with him as though they were buddies from grade school, referring to famous political figures by their first names, whether Johnson knew them or not. He also asked the President personal questions about the other Roosevelts.[9]

A man so generously endowed with political talent should have enjoyed a flawless career. However, the gifs of mania, remarkable though they were, had a downside, especially for those people with whom he was in frequent contact. This damaging side was to become increasingly prominent as the years went by. It made him a dangerous man to be around. It turned him into a tyrant in the office and in his own home, while the hypersexuality that mania can engender made him a sexual predator everywhere.

Johnson came to Congress as a New Dealer, a populist like his father, and a defender of the poor, which were numerous in Texas. Said a friend: "His belief in what he was fighting for just poured out of him." Johnson impressed people as having "passion," "intensity," "vibrancy," and "urgency." He was "eloquent" and "spellbinding."[10]

He was a great storyteller, his jokes and language often unfit for the ears of ladies. Abe Fortas considered the young Congressman to be the life of any party: "If Lyndon Johnson was there, the party would be livelier. The moment he walked in the door, it would take fire."[11] And in those early years, Johnson's impulsivity and sociability combined to produce many an impromptu party. He'd call his guests to invite them as he was leaving the office for the day.[12] The man was high. Visits to the White House would launch him even higher.[13]

Johnson seemed custom-made for Congress, and became adept at working the pork barrel. He secured the record sum of 70 million dollars for his district.[14] He went after and got most of what money and services the New Deal could deliver to his constituents. A staff member recalled that Johnson found no consituent request too trivial, and the voters at home were highly pleased with the service flowing from Washington. Letters were answered on the day they arrived.[15] Those who worked for Johnson had to match his manic pace.

The young Congressman impressed almost everyone who met him. One of these was James Rowe, a friend and Washington insider, who considered him "...a great operator. He stood out." (What follows is a veritable catalogue of manic assets.) " ...besides the drive and the energy and the doing favors, which he did for everybody, there was a great deal of charm in this man.... This was a very bright man and...a very ambitious man. You put them all together, you knew he was going a long way."

In those early years, Johnson was out to make friends, particularly powerful ones.[16] One of the most powerful of these was the Speaker of the House, Sam Rayburn of Texas. On one occasion, Johnson complained of the endless flattery that he felt he had to deliver: "Oh, Rayburn's so goddamned difficult—I've got to go over there...and kiss his ass, and I don't want to do it."[17]

If he omitted that particular ass-kissing session, he certainly went often enough to win Rayburn over. Johnson did not invent the art of acquiring political daddies, but he was a practitioner without peer. He was too impatient to follow the customary, slow, seniority route to power.[18] This was a man for shortcuts, and becoming the right person's protégé was one of the best.

His first political daddy was the influential lawyer and man about Texas politics, Alvin Wirtz, who backed Johnson for Congress and was later to get the federal contract to build the Marshal Ford Dam for the Brown and Root construction company. Wirtz would hug Johnson and call him "m'boy."[19]

Rayburn was the obvious choice for the first Washington "daddy," not only because of his power but because he had known and respected Lyndon's father, Sam, during their days together in the state legislature. While Lyndon was still working in Congressman Kleberg's office, he invited Rayburn to dinner. The invitations multiplied after Johnson came to Congress. Lady Bird was a warm, considerate hostess who adopted the lonely, old bachelor. Before long, Johnson was kissing Rayburn on the top of his head.[20]

Johnson aimed for the top. Thomas Corcoran, who was close to FDR, was a witness to Johnson's wooing of the President: "…the Boss met Lyndon in Galveston and invited him to ride across the state in his train. That was all it took—one train ride.…By the time Lyndon arrived in Washington the word had gone out: 'Be nice to this boy!' The Navy was the President's pet. He asked Carl Vinson to put Johnson on the Naval Affairs Committee and there he became Vinson's pet. Lyndon was an operator. He got more projects and more money for his district than any other man in Congress—but they were worthwhile projects.…"

Corcoran sheds additional light on how valuable FDR's patronage was. He says that it became known around Washington that Johnson had ready access to the President. This conferred not only high prestige on the young Congressman, but power, as other congressmen came begging for favors.[21] FDR would later protect Johnson and his main contributors, Brown and Root, from the consequences of their illegal activities.

Before that happened, Johnson managed to set up Rayburn and FDR as props for a photo opportunity. It happened when the young Congressman proposed that the President give a birthday party for Rayburn. Corcoran again tells the tale. "The President went for it, and Lyndon arranged it, brought Rayburn down to the White House on some pretext, and all the Texas (congressmen) went with him.… I couldn't figure out why he was doing all this. Then the papers came out the next day and there was Lyndon, standing right beside the President of the United States and Rayburn. That was the first time I really knew that an operator was loose."[22] That anecdote has a place in this case history because the scheming, the arranging, the sheer chutzpah of this young nonentity (as a first term congressman) were so typical of a manic personality.

The conception and execution of long-term planning are not characteristic of manic methods, but Lyndon's chosen career did not require it: in fact, politics discourages the making of elaborate plans. You cannot become a chess master when your opponent can dump the board in your lap at the next election. The only thing that is predictable about politics is its defiance of predictions. The ladder of office was there before Lyndon, with the White House gleaming at the top. All he needed was ambition, and a readiness to seize the moment

Johnson also co-opted the people around the President. Again, we have testimony from witness Corcoran that the indefatigable Lyndon courted the young New Dealers on FDR's team, as well as the President's White House staff and any young lawyers in town who might become or already were important contacts. Eventually, Lyndon pressed these people into his own service as messengers and advocates bearing his requests to heads of agencies or to the President himself.[23]

Politics was never the only thing on Lyndon's mind. As his secretaries could affirm, he was a man of affairs, many quick ones, one after the other. Affairs that LBJ had outside of the office often lasted much longer than the several weeks' duration of office romances. One that continued for many years was his entanglement with Alice Glass, who was the mistress and later wife of Charles Marsh.

LBJ met Marsh, a wealthy Texas oilman in 1937. He wooed Marsh, flattering him, treating him like a political sage, asking for advice about speeches. He told Marsh: "I need the inspiration that a couple of hours with you always gives me." He also gave Alice's and Marsh's two children appreciation and praise more appropriate for angels descended direcly from heaven. Marsh helped LBJ on the road to wealth by selling him land far below its current price. As for LBJ's political fortunes, the unwitting cuckold helped there too, by giving him favorable coverage in Marsh's newspapers.[24]

Within two years of their meeting, the tall, striking, sophisticated, strawberry blonde Alice and LBJ were lovers, spending weekends together.[25] Between them, there was even talk of marriage, though it would have threatened LBJ's political career. The affair continued into the war years when Harold Young, an assistant to Vice President Henry Wallace, saw them together: "Lyndon would be sittin' out there flirtin' with her a little, and Lady Bird would be out there very distressed about her husband."[26]

In 1944, another woman of the same type as Alice entered Congress, where she met LBJ. She was Helen Gahagan Douglas a former actress, and as liberal as LBJ. Richard Nixon began his rise to the presidency by running against her for the California Senate seat in 1950. His victory was largely due to his smearing her with the Communist label. According to Horace Busby, an old friend, the Douglas-LBJ affair went on for years. She spent a weekend with LBJ when he was Vice President and the relationship was still ardent.[27]

In 1947, another of LBJ's women was telling people that Lyndon was going to leave politics and Lady Bird to make a fortune on Wall Street and marry her.[28]

Important though sex was for Johnson, it was money and power, power and money, that he went after with a concentrated energy. He augmented his power in Congress by keeping the Texas NYA organization as his private political army and CIA combined.[29]

In 1940, during his second term in Congress, Johnson went after power and money simultaneously, taking a job no one else wanted and showing Washington how it really should be done. Money had to be raised for the Democratic candidates for Congress. He set up an office and was making calls in a matter of hours. Johnson raised large amounts of money, tapping the construction company Brown and Root, and the big oil interests in Texas.[30]

He also contacted each candidate to find out exactly what was wanted most, up to and including a speech by a Cabinet member if need be, or even a personal appearance by FDR. Johnson got it for them more times than not. James Rowe saw him at work: "...he got in with both feet the way he did everything, and he raised a hell of a lot of money. Of course, he was really trying to build a power base as a new congressman." Johnson succeeded. His hard work turned an anticipated loss of seats into a gain for the Democrats. And not incidentally, 30 to 40 Congressmen gave Johnson the credit for their victories. These became allies that he could rely on for votes.[31]

One could say that Johnson wanted it all. Even when he was in Congress, with a $10,000.00 yearly salary, LBJ had a fortune in his closet. The mystery is how he paid for things. He bought only the most expensive, custom-made, Frenchcuffed silk shirts, and by the box-full. Suits, shoes and boots were all custom-made.[32] On one occasion, he ordered nine suits at once.[33] He liked to buy Lady Bird's clothing too and one day brought home five hats for her.[34] LBJ was a manic shopper, which meant that price was of no importance and too much was never enough.

The root of the Johnson wealth was KTBC, a failing radio station in Austin. LBJ bought for $17,500.00 in 1943.[35] The first year's profit was $18. The myth that he spread claimed that Lady Bird ran the radio station. Actually, LBJ, the inveterate meddler, was as thoroughly involved in the radio station as he was in politics. He appointed Walter Jenkins, his chief of staff, (whose salary was paid by the U.S. government) to take care of KTBC affairs[36] LBJ personally hired, monitored, and fired the people who worked at the station. He also watched every penny. While he didn't hesitate to spend his money, he didn't want others spending it without his close supervision. He also payed the lowest salaries he could get away with. He kept the union out of KTBC by having the station guarded with guns.[37]

Although LBJ did not like to "kiss ass" to sell radio time, he was an indefatigable and insistent salesman. He would use his political office to gather advertisers, often calling them from Washington. It was easy to get their accounts when they already had or wanted to receive government contracts.[38]

The brothers Herman and George Brown became as deeply enmeshed in LBJ's career and campaign financing violations as he became in getting them the government contracts that turned their construction company into a behemoth. Brown and Root not only built roads and laid gas pipelines, but earned tens of millions of dollars on other government contracts.

In 1939, George Brown wrote to LBJ: "Remember I am for you, right or wrong and it makes no difference whether I think you are right or wrong. If you want it, I am for it 100%."[39]

LBJ was probably the best investment Brown and Root ever made. He paid off in the contract for the Corpus Christie Naval Air Training Base, which eventually covered 20,000 acres in 3 counties and cost 100 million dollars. The company branched out to make hundreds of destroyer escorts, and went into the production of oil and gas.

LBJ, as a member of the Naval Affairs Committee, made sure that Brown and Root knew whatever federal projects were in the offing. With his help, the company became one of the largest construction companies in the world.[40] He was also tremendously helpful when Brown and Root had dealings with federal agencies such as the Federal Power Commission and the Interstate Commerce Commission.[41]

What LBJ got out of it, besides free office space in the Brown Building in Austin and free rides on the company planes was as much money as he wanted, not only for his campaigns but also for those of political allies that he wanted to assist.[42]

Until now, mania was a tremendous advantage politically for Johnson. But inevitably, there were thorns in the bouquet. When the young Congressman arrived in Washington, he brought with him the King Kong of egos. This gorilla was quickly noticed when Johnson went to parties. The wife of an insider reported, "He demanded attention. He demanded it—and he got it."[43] Johnson would walk into a room and sweep other conversations away like a bulldozer. He would deliver passionate monologues. As soon as others entered the conversational arena, however, he lost interest and often fell asleep.[44]

Self-interest limited Johnson's role in the House of

Representatives. During the eleven years he served in Congress, he introduced only four bills of national interest. He was interested only in bills that paid off in Texas votes. In his entire career in Congress, he made only ten speeches. One would have expected the opposite. However Johnson preferred to be a political chameleon, and speeches woud have revealed his true colors.

Johnson's penchant for secrecy now started to work against him. He preferred to take on the political coloring of his surroundings, a conservative with the conservatives, a liberal with the New Dealers. Other congressmen soon figured out the game he was playing, and it backfired. Congressman Wingate Lucas said: "Johnson was so insincere. He would tell everyone what he thought they wanted to hear. As a result, you couldn't believe anything he said."[45] The manic disregard for truth had begun to damage Johnson's reputation.

Unfortunately, when he was not on the floor of the House, manic indiscretion took over. Johnson talked too much, and about the wrong things. In the Congressional dining room, he would seat himself at a table full of his fellow legislators and subject them to a dose of bragging. This was especially offensive to congressmen who had their own oversized egos to nurture. During these performances, Congressman Albert Thomas would say: "Listen to that sonofabitch talking about himself."[46] Congressman Ray Roberts, a friend from the NYA days, observed that Johnson's aggressive style and habit of wearing his ego on his sleeve was grating to a lot of his colleagues.[47]

Columnists Rowland Evans and Robert Novak noted that Johnson could be "ingratiating, gay, cocksure and, on occasion, hilariously funny," especially with those who could be entertaining or useful. But those who were neither one got a taste of the manic's arrogance. Evans and Novak continue: "to the rest of the world his manner changed with his mood and his mood was frequently overbearing."[48]

As had been the case in college, in Congress Johnson was considered too pushy and nakedly ambitious by his peers. Many disliked him. A fellow congressman from Texas said that Johnson would polish the apples of the powerful and ignore everyone else.

By the autumn of 1937, Johnson's honeymoon in Congress was over and the mania that had launched him so spectacularly had run out, to be replaced by a depression of several month's duration. Twice during that period, he felt bad enough to enter a hospital. The depression may have been prolonged by the death of his father Samuel on October 23. The public was told the standard excuses for Johnson's absence: lung infections or plain "nervous exhaustion."[49]

Lady Bird Johnson said of her husband: "Passion has propelled Lyndon all his life."[50] One could hardly find a more appropriate epitaph for a manic depressive. She learned to protect him whenever she could from whatever might upset his equilibrium. One of her measures was to keep him from attending funerals because his reaction to his father's death had been so agonized.[51]

She could hardly send him away when his children became ill, though she may have wanted to. The infant Lynda developed colic, as do many infants. LBJ wanted to invoke the assistance of J. Edgar Hoover, though it is hard to see what good that would have done. The distraught father shrieked so loudly that a neighbor came over to see what had happened. Later, Lynda developed impetigo, a mild rash. LBJ overreacted again, and panicked that his daughter had something fatal.[52]

Johnson was a person who contributed a lot of stress to the life of his family, and from the beginning of his career, he treated his staff like family. One of his staff said: "He was interested in what I was doing, what I did on weekends, what the children were doing, how they were doing in school, when they had the mumps, as if they had been his own." The Johnsons had staff members come over to their home every Sunday. The staffer adds: "They used to call it the 'Johnson togetherness' because we just seemed to be a little clan all of our own."[53] This must have been very comforting to the staff members who were far from their own friends and family.

With the unstinting help of Lady Bird, LBJ could be a caring and generous father to his employees.

But if poisonous mushrooms did not look edible, they would cause no fatalities. Similarly, the employers who do the greatest psychological damage to those who work for them are the ones who combine charm and other attractive qualities with oppression. There has to be bait for the trap. LBJ was at times an exciting, inspiring man to work for. When his mania was tinged by euphoria rather than darkened by irritability, his good cheer infected everyone around him and turned his offices into great places to work.[54] Unfortunately the good cheer could disappear in an instant.

If you have ever trained young animals, or for that matter, raised children, you know that it confuses and frightens them when reward and punishment have no clear connection to their behavior. That was one of the problems wherever people worked for LBJ. His employees learned to be wary of his moods because these were unpredictable and subject to sudden change.

Sometimes LBJ would single out an employee for persecution. The first of these was Luther Jones. LBJ ridiculed and criticized the man's work. But that was not enough. One way of demonstrating one's dominance is to make someone do what is extremely distasteful to him as well as obviously unnecessary. He insisted that Jones take dictation while his boss was sitting on the toilet.[55]

The office developed an atmosphere of terror. Some days, the office manager, who was LBJ's sister-in-law, would warn everyone that the red flag was up. At once, says staff member John Skuce, "...instant spastic tension occurred....Then, the door would blow open and Johnson—Jesus God, he filled up the whole room the minute he came in, and if he was really in a bad mood, he would be so excruciatingly rude I would gasp."[56]

His staff learned not only to agree with everything LBJ said, but also to withhold anything that might upset him. LBJ's brother Sam attests: "With Lyndon's notoriously short temper a matter of common knowledge, some of his aides felt it was best not to broach any unpleasant subjects for fear of being put on the fire themselves."[57]

Some of the people who worked for him were not only screamed at but were lied to and cheated. A case in point is that of Harfield Weedin who in 1944 had a well-paying job as the general manager of a radio station in Dallas. LBJ offered him the same job at the Johnson's Austin station, which was smaller, and at a lower salary. To provide an incentive, LBJ promised Weedin complete control over the station and in addition to salary, an employment contract guaranteeing 10% of the station's profits. Neither contract, control, nor any of the profits were ever delivered, and LBJ was offended that Weedin finally asked for the money due to him. Weedin said it came to $5,000.00. LBJ refused to give him more than $1,000.00. Weedin had to settle for it.[58]

On occasion, LBJ deliberately tried to make someone a perpetual debtor, like a field hand who could never pay off what he owed at the company store. In 1944, when LBJ wanted to hire John Hicks as general manager of the radio station, he tempted Hicks with the offer of a loan of $10,000. Bryce Harlowe, then an aide for the Naval Affairs Committee observed: "Lyndon would maneuver people into positions of dependency and vulnerability so he could do what he wanted...."[59]

When LBJ ran a subcommittee to investigate Navy procurement practices, he ruled the committee staff as though it were his own. A member recorded that Johnson demanded that the committee staff work nights and weekends. He threatened that complainers would be shipped out to sea.[60]

Johnson was back to his manic form, seeking federal housing funds for Austin. There was only enough money for three cities in the country, so the odds were not good, but the need in Austin was stark. The deputy administrator of the U.S.H.A. saw the young Congressman in action: "There was this first term Congressman who was so on his toes and so active and so overwhelming that he was up and down our corridors all the time....It was his gogetitness that got that first project for Austin."[61]

That was Austin, where there were potential votes, so it is not clear how much altruism had to do with it. However, altruism was clearly at work in 1940, when Johnson helped Jews escape Nazi persecution in Germany. He and others got them false passports and brought them to the NYA training camps, thus breaking a law. Only U.S. citizens could legally be housed and trained there. Here the manic willingness to transgress had a beneficial result. Because his actions had been illegal, however, Johnson could not benefit from them by making them public and the secret was kept for 20 years.[62]

CHAPTER 5

ESCAPE FROM CONGRESS

★ ★ ★ ★ ★ ★

Death seemed to be opening the door to opportunity for Johnson a second time when Texas Senator Morris Sheppard died on April 4, 1941. Johnson decided to run for the Senate. He got off to his usual frenzied start, travelling five to six hundred miles a day. Now he had the entire state to cover and was running against people who were better known statewide. Willard Deason, who had followed Johnson from college to Washington, said that the candidate "...hardly ever slept, never relaxed, never stopped fretting, seldom ate...."[1]

Johnson was not euphoric during this campaign, but he was spending like a manic on a personal plane, billboards, newspaper ads and statewide radio broadcasts all over the state, as well as on an army of campaign workers, and even on cash prizes to be distributed to people who came to his rallies. Much of the nearly half a million dollars that all this cost came from the construction company of Brown and Root. Johnson only admitted to receiving $9,645.00 and spending $11,818.00, which was laughable to anyone who had watched his campaign.[2]

By May tenth, Johnson's anxious mania had been reversed by his trailing position in the polls and depression took over. He was no longer campaigning harder than the other candidates.[3] He said that the polls "...made me feel mighty bad when my mother and wife told me I was the last man in the race. I know that my throat got bad on me and I had to spend a few days in the hospital."[4] He refused to let his principal assistant, John Connally, tell the press about the hospitalization. When Connally asked how he should explain Johnson's absence, Connally reports, "...he just threw a fit, went into a tirade, ordered us out of the house, said he never wanted to talk to us again."[5]

Johnson declared that he was pulling out of the race. During depressions he usually decided to give up whatever he was doing. This time his wife and campaign assistants talked him out of withdrawing. The candidate stayed in the hospital nine days. Then a poll showed that his support had nearly doubled.[6] With this encouragement, Johnson's depression vanished.

A week before Election Day, Johnson's polls proclaimed him the winner by 43% to 22% over his only real rival, Governor O'Daniel. He was euphoric again. On Election Day his lead of 13,000 votes had him shouting with joy.[7] Both candidates were stealing votes. But Johnson's mania had him so confident that he stopped handing in fraudulent votes before his competitor, who was thus able to fake enough additional votes to win, Texas style.[8]

Johnson lost, Lyndon style. He turned on an entirely innocent and unsuspecting low-level campaign worker and blamed the man for everything, screaming, cursing, and flailing his arms.[9] It is common for manic depressive children to blame others for their own mistakes.

Returning to Washington after his first electoral defeat was devastating and threw Johnson into months of depression. He described that period as "...the most miserable in my life. I felt terribly rejected, and I began to think about leaving politics and going home to make money. In the end, I just couldn't bear to leave Washington, where I at least still had my seat in the House."[10] Not even an encouraging phone call from the President lifted Johnson's depression.[11]

By the time the Japanese attacked Pearl Harbor on December 7th, Johnson was in his usual form and joined the Navy the next day.[12] Despite his lack of training, he was made a Lieutenant Commander. He helped to write his own orders, which permitted him to pursue politics and go to parties in Hollywood for the first 5 months of his service.[13]

Finally, it became politically embarrassing for him to stay in the U.S., so FDR sent him to the Pacific to observe one mission and then brought him back to spend the war safely at home. Johnson flew on that one bombing raid as a passenger who saw no more than 13 minutes of action. He was brave enough during his encounter with the enemy, but it was a brief one.

He was an observer in one of the bombers when the 22nd Bomber Group left Port Moresby, Australia to make a short run to New Guinea and drop some bombs on a Japanese air base there. Before reaching the air base, Johnson's plane developed engine trouble, jettisoned its bombs, and turned back. It was then attacked by Japanese fighter planes that kept shooting at it while the gunners in the bomber returned fire. One Japanese plane was shot down. The pilot's evasive maneuvers tossed Johnson around in the radio compartment. The bomber landed at Port Moresby badly shot up, but no one had been injured.[14] That was the modest foundation on which Johnson was later to erect a castle of fantasy. Although his only contribution to the raid was to remain unruffled, General MacArthur, no slouch at politics himself, gave the Congressman, and only the Congressman, a Silver Star.[15]

Later, when asked if he'd been in combat, he replied: "Yes, I was. I was out there in May, June and part of July." He embellished this: "I lived with the men on fighting fronts. I flew with them on missions over enemy territory. I ate and slept with them and was hospitalized with them in the Fiji Islands." He had contracted pneumonia, which he changed to the more exotic dengue fever, and his 25 pound weight loss became 40 pounds. The 20,000 miles he had flown in total grew to 60,000. His embroidery continued: "During the months we were there, we must have talked to 10,000 men, flown to hundreds of bases...."[16]

The drama of his mission also increased. He said he gave the plane's only parachute to a friend. One Japanese plane had been shot down, but not in LBJ's version: "I saw 14 of 'em go down in flames right in front of me." He even bestowed upon himself the nickname "Raider Johnson" which he claimed the men on his plane had, moved by admiration for his courage, given to him.[17] Later he referred to "the horrors I experienced against the Japs in the Pacific" and said that an admiral called him "one of the bravest men I have ever fought with in my entire life." During his 1948 senatorial campaign he falsely claimed to be "the only candidate with a fighting war record."[18]

It took years for the story to reach its final epic dimensions, but it eventually rivalled "Gone With the Wind." He even developed a fictional prologue. While campaigning unsuccessfully for the Senate in 1941, LBJ had repeatedly promised to "be fighting in the front line, in the trenches, in the mud and blood," a promise never kept. He also declared that he asked the White House to send him into active duty. In actuality, he only asked for "something big" in Washington, although mud and blood were hard to find there.

Then there was the medal. After the one raid, it was given to *him*, although the pilot of the plane whose evasive action saved everyone, and the gunner who shot down the pursuing Japanese plane, received nothing. Some of the crew members, despite flying 25 missions, never received a medal, but of course, they were not congressmen. Later, LBJ said he deserved more medals, but a genuine war hero, Joe Kilgore, commented: "...to hear the man complaining that he had gotten only the Silver Star for an experience that thousands of people had was almost irrational."[19]

Brown and Root, Johnson's largest contributor, drew the attention of the I.R.S. in July of 1942. In September of 1942, the I.R.S. began to investigate Brown and Root for, allegedly, several hundred thousands of dollars of illegal campaign contributions to LBJ's 1941

Senate campaign.[20] These were disguised as employee bonuses, which were tax deductible. The books of that company also revealed a series of suspiciously large "attorney's fees" and bonuses to the firm's officers. The investigators discovered that the final destination of the money was Johnson's 1941 campaign.

Whereas the Corrupt Practices Act limited a candidate's total campaign expenditures to $25,000, Brown and Root had funneled hundreds of thousands of dollars to Johnson. Were this to become widely-known, the Congressman's career could crash in flames of scandal. A year later, the I.R.S. was prepared to charge Brown and Root an additional $1,062,184.87 in taxes plus a fraud penalty of $531,002.45. On January 13, 1944, LBJ and Alvin Wirtz met with President Roosevelt. After they left, the I.R.S. investigation of Brown and Root's campaign contributions was terminated.[21] All prosecution was dropped and Brown and Root only had to pay, in total, $372,000 to the government for back taxes.[22]

With such friends in Washington, Brown and Root were able to commit additional illegalities during LBJ's next Senate campaign.[23]

Johnson, by the time he entered the Texas Democratic Primary of 1944 for his congressional seat, seemed to have developed the grandiose delusion that he was now somehow above lowly politics. Even after winning, he saw himself as a victim, claiming that his opponent had done a "hatchet job."[24] This amused people who heard the kind of scurrilous lies Johnson would spread against his opponent in his next try at the Senate.

Two years later another congressional contender attacked Johnson for using his influence with the New Dealers to get rich. It was exactly what Johnson was doing, but he felt that his nine years of service to his constituency should exempt him from criticism. Furthermore, he was shocked that anyone in his district could be so ungrateful as to oppose him in any way, but especially to run against him.

Johnson again considered quitting the game of politics, and continued to doubt whether he should stay in it during 1947 and

1948.[25] These were years when depression played a larger part in his life than it ever had. Many manic depressives experience more frequent, longer, and more severe depressions as they get older. For Johnson, the worst was yet to come.

He was devastated by the death of FDR on April 13, 1945. Johnson wept, stopped taking phone calls, and took to his bed on the day of the funeral. Grief turned into a depression that hung on into the summer. Johnson was mourning more than the loss of a powerful patron. After his defeat in the senatorial race of 1941, he was mourning the loss of hope that he could ever win a seat in the higher chamber. And this was a man for whom ambition was his life's blood. He left it to his staff to care for his constituents, and, as a legislator, just coasted.[26]

In the first days of 1946, Johnson was hospitalized in Austin for the usual "flu," the "nervous exhaustion" that was really another incapacitating depression. The details of his illness were treated like state secrets during the month he spent in the hospital. When he returned to Washington he was still unable to face the world and stayed in bed at home.[27]

Johnson played truant from the House. In 1948 he told other Texas congressmen that he was ready to quit and return to Texas to make money if he failed in his next try for the Senate.[28] Having gotten what he wanted from the F.T.C. to upgrade his radio station, he was giving half his time to this now thriving business.[29]

At the end of his congressional career, Johnson became a turncoat, not only abandoning the New Deal principles of FDR, but working assiduously to defeat legislation that he previously would have supported.

Manic depression can be expressed in such varied ways that, once its genetics and neurochemistry is better understood, it will probably be described as a group of related disorders with overlapping symptoms. On several occasions, Johnson has been shown being dishonest, cruel, and breaking laws, with mania being credited for his behavior. He was not by any means representative of all manic depressives. He was typical of what one might call the tyran-nical manic, but that is just one of several varieties. Many others, even predominantly manic personalities, are considerate and trust-worthy.

During the period 1947 through 1949, he was to demonstrate how much he was willing to throw overboard in the pursuit of power. In 1947, President Truman introduced his Fair Deal, designed to benefit the kind of people Johnson had worked for just ten years earlier. The Fair Deal contained a higher minimum wage, national health insurance, federal money for education, for higher Social Security benefits, and for the first time in decades, legislation to defend the rights of Blacks. All of this and more would eventu-ally be offered to the nation as part of LBJ's Great Society. But now conservatives held the reins of power in Texas and Johnson needed their help in the upcoming Senate race. He not only voted against Fair Deal legislation, he broke his customary congressional silence and gave speeches against the bill.[30]

At home he kept the union out of his radio station. In Washington he voted anti-Black and anti-labor. In an interview he said that the only part of the New Deal he favored was that favor-ing the construction of dams (contracts for Brown and Root) and the development of other natural resources (such as oil, for his friends in that industry).[31] He began making accusations that peo-ple who opposed him were Communists or Communist-influ-enced.[32] If history has its little jokes, one was now in the making. The labeling of people as Communists that was initially done for political profit eventually became the content of Johnson's most paranoid nightmares.

The 1948 campaign for the Senate was a desperate one for Johnson. It was his last chance. He could only run for one office; going for the Senate sacrificed his congressional seat. He had decid-ed that if he failed to win, he would retire to private life.

In March he fell into an immobilizing depression and could not get his campaign started. To make matters worse, a popular and highly respected former governor of Texas, Coke Stevens, entered the Primary. Finally, what roused Johnson to action were some supporters' requests that he help John Connally to run in his place.[33]

That depression was just the beginning of Johnson's troubles. A few days before he announced his candidacy on May 12th, he felt the premonitory pains and nausea of kidney stones. Surgery and six weeks of recuperation would leave Johnson only three weeks in which to wrest victory from a man who was running ahead of him three to one.[34]

That was unacceptable. A rally on May 22 was scheduled to launch the campaign with a speech by Johnson. By that day he was a sick man, gagging and vomiting, doubled over with pain. His doctors, fearing that delay would cause irreversible kidney damage, wanted to operate immediately. Johnson refused, determined to pass the stone as he had done in the past. He failed to do this, but nevertheless managed to deliver a rousing speech in Austin. He held out for a few days longer, before agreeing to go to the Mayo Clinic for tests. He arrived with a 104° temperature. Gasping from the pain, and he vomited all over himself in the wheelchair that took him to his room.

His mania returned, despite his discomfort. John Connally reports: "On his being admitted to the Mayo Clinic, Lyndon almost immediately became its star patient and leading pain in the ass.... He demanded and got three telephones in his room; he had two radio sets...he made 64 telephone calls in one 24-hour period."[35] A nurse complained that Johnson insisted on making a long distance call while she was trying to treat him. The hospital staff was out of their element with a patient who turned his room, the waiting rooms, and even the nurses' central station into campaign headquarters.[36]

Three days passed but the kidney stone did not. John Connally told the press that the candidate was in the hospital. Johnson declared that he was withdrawing from the campaign: "If I can't control my own campaign, I certainly can't control the Senate" (that left no doubt about his intentions) "and if I'm not in control, I'm much better off in Johnson City, where no one can hurt me." Lady Bird saw to it that the resignation was not delivered to the press.[37] The following day Johnson had the stone removed by cystoscopy and a week later returned to the campaign riding his high mood again.[38]

When he was manic, his campaign style was manic too. The daring and pursuit of novelty so characteristic of manics was evident in his campaigning in the first helicopter ever to cross Texas skies.[39] Like a deus ex machina, he would descend from the "Johnson City Windmill" on a small Texas town, where people would gather, if not to hear him, to see the helicopter. This was the perfect vehicle for a manic campaigner; it allowed him to appear in 30 towns in a day.

Johnson was running on only three hours nightly for sleep. The morning began with a 5 AM broadcast to farmers. Even if he got to bed by eleven, he was up until two AM, running his campaign on the telephone.[40] He was the fastest candidate in Texas, and not only because of his mode of transportation. A newsman furnishes this description of the candidate's hyperactivity: "While talking, he may, among other things, move from chair to chair around the room, pace the floor, puff cigarettes endlessly, rub salve on his hands, take a digestive tablet, gulp water, and use an inhaler in his nose. He's just too nervous to remain still."[41] This is the level of activity seen in manic patients who are ill enough to be hospitalized.

For the most part, Johnson was in a state of irritable, not euphoric mania. While hovering over a town, Johnson's announcer would call to the voters with a loudspeaker: "Come to the speaking, come to the speaking." If the response was tepid, the candidate would angrily bellow at them: "Come on out to the speaking!" And if the audience was not perfectly attentive to his speech, he would stop talking.[42]

On one occasion he arrived at a meeting where, he had been told, all he had to do was shake hands. Once there, he was informed that he was expected to deliver a speech. Oblivious of the audience, he screamed at his advance men, "I thought it was just gonna be coffee, doughnuts and bullshit!"[43]

His temper showed quickly in hotel lobbies where even slight delays in registering him or collecting his bags would result in the candidate screaming, while astonished guests stared. Every meal delivered to his room triggered a barrage of complaints. Horace Busby, then his press secretary, says that it was unbearable to witness Johnson's verbal assaults on waiters and waitresses. That was something Johnson could get away with in the privacy of his room. But the candidate did not stop there. Despite admonitions from his political daddy, Alvin Wirtz, and his campaign manager, that his efforts were being sabotaged by his behavior, he could not contain himself even in front of the local political leaders he was trying to impress.[44]

They had to witness "...explosions, tirades," noted Busby. He continues: "Especially explosions against the women who worked for him: 'Everyone in this outfit is against me!' That kind of thing. ...His behavior was hurting him with local politicians...." The wives seemed especially upset by the way Johnson treated the women who were his secretaries.[45]

Johnson's overt sexual pursuit of his secretaries, who were seen emerging from his bedroom at indiscrete hours, also became widely known and damaged the candidate's reputation.[46]

Indiscretion is a manic trait that characterized much of Johnson's behavior. He often left his hotel bedroom door open to get a breeze. But he neglected to close the bathroom door when he was seated on the toilet in full view of some voters. When a room full of supporters and their wives lingered too long for Johnson, he simply started stripping his clothes off.[47] A naked politician spiced up the campaign considerably.

The candidate was as reckless in his lies as he was in his conduct. He claimed that he had wanted to run for the Senate in 1942 "But when that election came around I was in the jungles of New

Guinea." He was never near a jungle of any kind. More pernicious were his lies about his opponent, Coke Stevens. Texas was an anti-union state, so when Tommy Corcoran, Jim Rowe and Willy Hopkins funneled labor money to Johnson for his campaign, it was done secretly. Then the A.F.L. endorsed Stevens. Johnson claimed "Labor leaders made a secret agreement with Calculating Coke that they could not get out of me." One of Johnson's speech writers admitted to feeling ashamed because he knew that he was writing a lie.[48]

Johnson was so "high" that even longtime friends remarked that they had never seen him quite like that. His aide Warren Woodward said "The minute we woke him up, he hit the ground running....Charging from morning to night." Johnson, now euphoric, would not just shake hands with little old ladies, he would fling them by. Two of his aides positioned themselves where they could catch any that were thrown too far.[49]

By late June, Johnson's mania gave him dangerous delusions that victory was assured, and that no runoff would be necessary. He would get his audiences to chant with him: "Ain't gonna be no runoff." But Stevens was still ahead of Johnson in the polls by 11%.[50] On Election Day, Coke Stevens' lead had narrowed to 6%. Still, a runoff had not been avoided. It was scheduled for August 29.

This time, Johnson ran like a man pursued by the hounds of hell. If he couldn't win the election, he was determined to buy it. His people started paying local political leaders $1,000 each for their support. At that time, this was a lot of money.

Ralph Yarborough, Senator from Texas from 1957 to 1970, was amazed at what was going on: "They were spending money like mad. They were spending money like Texas had never seen. And they did it not only so big but so openly.... And they were brash about how they spent it, and they were utterly ruthless. Brown and Root would do anything....they didn't have a chance using conventional political methods. Coke Stevens had that race sewed up."[51] In addition to Brown and Root, Johnson was getting funding from oil, rubber, and aircraft companies, all of whose executives expected a good return for their dollars.[52]

Some of the money was being spent to pay for platoons of liars. These were Johnson's "Missionaries," local people with influence among particular groups of voters. In addition to lies that Stevens was in the pocket of labor racketeers, they spread the false accusation that he was sympathetic to Communism. Johnson made the same smear on the radio and in an August mailing to 340,000 voters: "Communists favor Coke."[53] Even with all this, Johnson expected to be defeated, and after August 9, his chief aide, Walter Jenkins, said that he had never seen him more depressed.[54] However, this was not one of Johnson's immobilizing depressions. He was running scared, but he was running.

Johnson bought votes all over Texas, including votes from the graveyard, but not even those were enough to give him a victory. It fell to George Parr, the "Duke" of Duval County, to save the election for him. Parr reported a 99.6% turnout from that county, a result that would have done honor to Stalin. Over 24 hours after the polls closed, an additional 425 votes for Johnson were delivered from Duval. Six days after the election, with Stevens still leading by 351, Parr reported enough additional Johnson votes to give him a lead of 87.[55]

One of the men who added 200 votes to a closed ballot box later admitted doing it. According to Luis Salas, Johnson met with Parr and told him: "If I can get 200 more votes, I've got it won." Parr instructed Salas to add the votes. Salas agreed. According to Salas, without having it spelled out, Johnson knew his problem was going to be solved."[56]

After the election, Federal Masters in Chancery began to investigate, and although they looked at only three counties before they were interrupted, they found that a high percentage of the 7,279 votes for Johnson were either not cast at all or were cast for Stevens. William R. Smith, who had presided over the hearings concerning Precinct 13, (where Luis Salas had done his work), said: "...I think

Lyndon was put in the U.S. Senate with a stolen election, and I think he and everybody else knew it."[57]

So, of course, did Coke Stevens. He charged that Johnson had committed vote fraud. He told Federal Judge T. Whitfield Davidson of the U.S. District Court for the Northern District of Texas: "We expect to lay before this court testimony that will affect thousands of votes in this election." The judge, as a compromise, suggested that both Stevens' and Johnson's names go on the ballot in November.[58]

The legal elite of Texas, some ten lawyers, was unanimous in advising Johnson to take the offer and avoid a trial. Johnson was furious and he refused to do it: "This is a free country! I won it fair and square, and you want me to trade it away!" He refused to discuss it further.[59] This was a man who never could admit even to himself that he had done something wrong. The delusional part of his outburst was not his refusal, but his claim of innocence.

He was ready for another throw of the dice, rather than face certain defeat. Consummate politician that he was, Johnson may have realized that the dice were loaded in his favor. He went to President Truman and said that Stevens would win the court challenge. Whatever his reasons, Truman apparently reached Supreme Court Justice Hugo Black, who that same day sent a telegram ordering the stopping of the investigation by the Masters in Chancery.[60]

Johnson was in.

CHAPTER 6

TYRANNY IN THE SENATE

Johnson began in the Senate as he had in the House, by being friendly to everyone. He needed a sense of humor to do it. He would offer a handshake, saying, "Howdy, I'm Landslide Lyndon." And his campaign of flattery commenced at once. He had his staff phone every other Senator to request autographed photographs of them.

If anyone had the right equipment for the Senate, it was Lyndon Johnson. He had intellectual gifts and social assets of the highest order. He combined these with an extraordinary capacity for work and a relentless will to obtain and exercise power. The resulting man was one of the most effective politicians to perform in Washington, and, eventually, one of the most dangerous.

By the 1950s, Johnson was wealthy enough to go on manic shopping sprees and return with loads of presents for friends and staff.[1] The mark of a manic shopper and giver is ordering a few—say—gold charms as Christmas gifts and ending up buying 152, which he did one year.[2]

His offices filled during the Christmas and Easter seasons with hundreds of boxes of candy for the people who kept Capitol Hill running: telephone operators, janitors, waiters, elevator boys, etc. He believed these attentions would pay off, and usually they did.[3]

When it came to generosity, Johnson didn't neglect himself. He wasted no time in grabbing amenities available to senators: he acquired four rooms and phones instead of three, and a special parking space.[4]

Johnson was not the same enthusiastic, unscarred young man he had been during his early days in Congress, and the attractive attributes of mania were not now much in evidence. The ugly manic had arrived. His Gargantuan ego was always on display.

According to Bryce Harlow, who was then the Special Assistant to President Eisenhower, Johnson was a disrupting presence in committee rooms. He would sit, stand up, talk to his neighbors, and set off the alarm on his wrist watch. Harlow said that the alarm was used by Johnson to get people's attention whenever he felt neglected. Harlow adds that Johnson insisted on everyone doing what he wanted and he usually got what he wanted.[5]

Johnson was unblushing about putting his own welfare first, particularly his political welfare. He told Bobby Baker: "Labor's not much stronger in Texas than a popcorn fart.... I'm for nearly anything the big oil boys want because they hold the whip hand and I represent 'em. Hell, half the people from Texas are against me."[6] If the recent election was any indication, it was more than half.

LBJ was known as a master at manipulation. *Washington Post* Editor Benjamin Bradlee underwent the Treatment. "...when you got the 'Johnson Treatment' you really felt as if a St. Bernard had licked your face for an hour, had pawed you all over. When he was in the Senate, especially as majority leader, it was like going to the zoo. He never just shook hands with you. One hand was shaking your hand; the other hand was always someplace else, exploring you, examining you. And of course he was a great actor. He'd be feeling up Katherine Graham and bumping Meg Greenfield in the boobs. And at the same time he'd be trying to persuade you of something; sometimes something that he knew and I knew was not so, and there was just the trace of a little smile on his face. It was just a miraculous performance."[7]

Not only was LBJ a massage parlor of persuasion, he often came armed with memos and other papers supporting whatever he wanted you to believe. Hubert Humphrey called it "...an almost hypnotic experience. I came out of that session covered with blood, sweat, tears, spit—and sperm."[8]

Johnson gave Humphrey the following cynical advice on getting bills passed in Congress: "You have to take it slow and easy, working your colleagues over like gentlemen—not on the floor but in the cloakroom...always letting them see what's in it for them. Then when you're sure...and you know you have the votes buttoned up in your back pocket, you come out statesmanlike on the Senate floor and, in the spirit of democracy, have a little debate for the people."[9]

It is not inevitable that politicians behave this way, and indeed, many do not. Humphrey made a comparison between the Great Manipulator and his exact opposite, Senator Mike Mansfield. Humphrey said that LBJ tried to find out everything about his fellow senators, especially anything reprehensible, and would use this information to control them. Mansfield, by contrast, was a man of integrity who never relied on coercion or punishment or reward, who was not manipulative, but respected the convictions of others, and who succeeded as a leader because he was trusted.[10]

Winning was what mattered most to LBJ too. According to Bobby Baker, he could be very nasty about it. Johnson, drunk or sober, liked to brag about manipulating and deceiving and stomping all over people. Baker adds that sometimes Johnson's boasts were repeated to his victims, who became furious with him.[11]

LBJ was the man to stomp on you. With his towering height and over 200 pounds of weight, he came to resemble a huge grizzly bear rearing up on its hind legs, a political carnivore for whom everyone was prey. Humphrey said: "He'd come on just like a tidal wave sweeping all over the place. He went through walls. He'd come through a door, and he'd take the whole room over. Just like that. Everything."[12]

Senator George Smathers said LBJ affected the Senate like "...a great, overpowering thunderstorm that consumed you as it closed in around you."[13] It appears that in his later Senate years, LBJ was not merely intimidating, he was frightening.

Domination became his style. He was the worst of backseat drivers, constantly spouting criticism and orders to whoever was behind the wheel. When he was doing his own driving, he cursed other drivers for daring to share the road.[14] As a passenger in the front seat, with his wife, daughters, or secretaries in the back, he treated the women like personal property. He would tell them to apply a new coat of makeup and comb their hair. If he did not approve of their hairstyles, he insisted on changes.[15] So Johnson was not only obsessed with wielding power in public life, there was domination at the personal level, where he developed the lifestyle of a Roman emperor. He expected and got other people to bathe his feet and dress him.[16]

On January 2, 1951, "Landslide Lyndon" became the Senate Whip, the assistant floor leader. That spring, he was interviewed by a journalist who became his biographer, Alfred Steinberg. The journalist's plan was to cover all the congressional leaders but Johnson wanted "...a whole big article on just me alone." Steinberg was getting the "treatment," with Johnson grasping his lapels and going nose to nose. Steinberg asked: "What would the pitch of an article on you be? That you might be a Vice Presidential candidate for 1952?"

Johnson replied "Vice President—hell! Who wants that? ...President! That's the angle you want to write about me....you can build it up by saying how I run both houses of Congress right now!" This required an explanation and Johnson provided it: "Right here in the Senate I have to do all of Boob McFarland's work because he can't do any of it....Then every afternoon I go over to Sam Rayburn's place. He tells me all about the problems he's facing in the House and I tell him how to handle them. So that's how come I'm running everything here in the Capitol."[17] This unblushing display of manic indiscretion, egotism, and grandiosity showed Johnson was in manic territory again.

Even before he reached the White House, LBJ's approach to foreign policy was as aggressive as his conversational style. President Eisenhower attested that, while Sam Rayburn, the Leader of the House, appreciated the importance of negotiation, Senator Johnson preferred actions that would demonstrate the armed strength of the United States.[18]

LBJ's own words to the Soviet Union, in November 1951, confirm Eisenhower's take on him: "The next aggression will be the last....We will strike back, not just at your satellites, (he meant countries—this was before Star Wars) but at you. We will strike back with all the dreaded might that is within our control and it will be a stunning blow." He also said: "There's an old saying down in Texas, if you know you are right, just keep coming on and no gun can stop you."[19] That attitude was reflected in his escalation of the Vietnam War.

If power did not corrupt Johnson, who was already corrupt by any legal definition, power certainly gave him the opportunity to display his aggressiveness. During the Korean War, in a February 1952 newsletter, the Senator gave a foretaste of his Vietnam style: "We should announce, I believe, that *any* act of aggression *any*where, by *any* communist forces, will be regarded as an act of aggression by the Soviet Union.... If *any*where in the world—by *any* means, *open* or *concealed*—communism trespasses upon the soil of the free world, we should unleash all the power at our command upon the vitals of the Soviet Union."[20] It seems that he did not then quail at the thought of launching an atomic war.

Johnson's obsession with power was more blatant than ever. Having stolen his way into the Senate and flourished, he seemed to have become completely cynical about democracy as it existed in the United States. It appeared that his only interest was to get all that he could as fast as he could. Since the voters didn't want him, the voters be damned. A fellow senator reported that Johnson no longer talked about his father's defense of the underdog, and seemed to be devoted only to the pursuit of power.[21] Johnson later recalled: "I began to feel that I was growing in size as well as importance....I took great pleasure in the position I was building."[22]

The Minority Whip became Minority Leader in January, 1953. That was also the year that Johnson ran for reelection. On the campaign trail he was the usual terror to his staff. Nothing went right in his eyes, and everything that went even slightly wrong enraged him. He screamed at his staff: "You couldn't even pour piss out of your boot" and "You can't even reach your ass with your right hand." Then he demanded that his speechwriters produce something "that will make me seem goddamn humble."[23]

The election not only returned Johnson to the Senate, a majority of Democrats came with him, making him the youngest Majority Leader ever, and soon to be the most powerful.

His first use of power was a benign one; he organized the Senate to bring down Senator Joseph McCarthy. It wasn't exactly Saint George against the dragon. More like Tyrannosaurus Rex against the dragon. But McCarthy, who was rapidly succumbing to alcoholism and paranoia, had finally become too much of a menace to the Washington establishment. He was painting the town of Washington Red. As KGB records reveal, there were real Soviet spies in the U. S. government, but McCarthy's scattershot accusations were all off target. He called Richard Nixon, among others equally unlikely, a pawn of the Reds.[24] What Johnson did was to handpick the hearing committee that censured the Senator and stripped him of his seeming invulnerability.[25]

As Majority Leader, Johnson could indulge his pressure of speech with telephones at hand wherever he was or went.[26] In 1955 it was very few who had telephones in cars, but he did. At the ranch he even had a telephone wired from a tree. A favorite manic occupation is to make long distance phone calls at three AM. Johnson did this regularly.

The following anecdote, though trivial in itself, is an illustration not only of manic acquisitiveness, but also of Johnson's superb political skills and his use of his official powers to pursue private ends. One day, he visited Grover Ensley, the executive director of the Joint Economic Committee, in Ensley's office. The following day, Ensley was informed that the Majority Leader had to have his office. Ensley, who did not want to move, appealed to the Democrats on the committee. In order to secure their agreement, Johnson had already seen each one. John Sparkman was promised another hideaway office for himself, Paul Douglas was promised the chairmanship of the committee, and William Fulbright was promised the chairmanship of the Senate Foreign Relations Committee.[27]

He was possessed of remarkable techniques for persuasion. These he augmented with what amounted to a skilled seduction of those he wanted to use, if not at once, then later on. He sent the objects of his political affection on trips as delegates to prestigious conferences abroad. He arranged increased funding for his favorite subcommittees. He sent cooperative senators his staff's research on bills of interest to them. Not a birthday, not a wedding, not a funeral in a senator's family went by without some generous and appropriate response from Johnson.

More importantly, the Majority Leader helped those he favored increase their own political capital by getting their legislation passed. Senator Stuart Symington attested, moreover, that Johnson was able to deliver dams, military installations and the like for whatever senator wanted one badly enough. Later, the Majority Leader came around to collect a return favor or two. Senator William Fulbright, who was not a fan of Johnson, said: "He was the manager of the Senate. He could make it function. He got action!"[28]

Bobby Baker, who observed Johnson at close hand, thought the Majority Leader had a special intuition about people and could sense exactly what to use and how much it would take to manipulate that person, be it money, federal projects, vote trade-offs, or naked flattery.[29] Johnson did not rely on intuition alone, however. He hoarded information about his colleagues as though it gave him the combination to their safes. Senator Hubert Humphrey observed that when Johnson reached the Senate, he had already done a thorough investigation of each senator and had learned what would motivate that person to do whatever Johnson wanted.[30]

It was aide Gerald Siegel's opinion that Johnson knew his fellow senators better than they knew themselves. He also brought to bear upon his targets his formidable talents as an actor. He was a master mimic who could imitate the people who were the subjects of his funny anecdotes. The senators he amused with his performances were often the very ones who fell victim to his deceptions. Siegel adds that Johnson could become the kind of person with the kind of message that would most appeal to each individual. Demure with one, he'd swagger with another, play the populist with one senator, be a model conservative with another.[31]

People who are not interested in power rarely pursue political careers. The question is—how much power and over whom? Even to his fellow senators, who were not lacking in ambition themselves, LBJ appeared obsessed with a hunger for power. Senator Paul Douglas commented: "Johnson was an intensely ambitious man, anxious to get power and hold onto it...."[32]

Johnson had not forgotten one of the lessons of his college years: that it pays to court those who have power. Richard Russell, Chairman of the Senate Armed Services Committee and also of the Senate's Southern Caucus was one of the leading members of the Senate. Here, like Sam Rayburn, was another lonely bachelor ripe for the picking. Johnson made him a member of the family and had the Johnson daughters call Russell "Uncle Dick." Before long, Russell was joining the Johnson household every weekend for meals. These were followed by long car rides during which the host squeezed his guest for the latest political intelligence.[33]

Johnson employed the power of appointment principally to

augment his power. He kept Senator Albert Gore off the Judiciary Committee to thwart Gore's presidential ambitions. He placed Warren Magnusen, a "drinking buddy," on the Appropriations Committee to help Johnson control the Senate's "purse strings." James Murray went on the Democratic Policy Committee because Johnson looked on the Senator as his personal "rubber stamp."[34]

When political institutions stood in Johnson's path, he reduced them to empty shells. One of these, the Democratic Policy Committee, had a function that the Majority Leader wanted to exercise himself. The committee was supposed to set the Senate Democrats' legislative goals and priorities. Johnson confined it to scheduling when bills would reach the floor. Even in this limited capacity, the committee became the glove to his hand, and he called it "my cabinet."[35]

He also castrated the Caucus of Democratic Senators, which was supposed to be a sort of Politburo, a body within the Senate doing the real governing. He prevented it from meeting except infrequently, and all it was left to do was to ratify his continuation as Majority Leader and affirm his choice of people for lesser offices. He also transformed into his personal tool the Senate Democratic Campaign Committee which provided money and help in Senate elections.[36]

Johnson was like a great black hole sucking up all the power within the reach of his gravity. He did what no Majority Leader had done before: dispense office space, set the schedule for legislation to be brought to the Senate floor, and determine who got on what committee. He also sufficiently undermined the seniority system so that he could determine the pecking order in the Senate.[37]

When he could not eliminate the positions that others held, he usurped their functions. Senator Mike Mansfield, then Democratic Whip, said: "Lyndon attempted to be the whole show. Instead of letting committee and subcommittee chairmen handle their bills on the floor...he demanded that they fill him in quickly on the subject and he would serve as floor manager....about the only thing I did as Whip was to pull on his coattails when he was talking too long and beginning to lose votes because of this."[38]

As Majority Leader of the Senate, LBJ cared more about exercising power than what was done with it. When a bill came to be voted, his eye was on the head count, rather than on the bill's purpose. He was willing to whittle the bill away to get a larger head count.[39] Columnist Tom Wicker said that for Johnson what mattered was proving that he could get any bill he wanted passed, and he did not much care what was in the bill.[40]

When all else failed, Johnson resorted to tricks. On one occasion, he wanted Senator Fulbright to miss the voting on a bill scheduled to be voted at two PM. Johnson arranged a luncheon in the Senator's honor for that day and made sure it was too far away for Fulbright to return in time.[41]

There was no way to get things done without Johnson, who had the manic's love of meddling in every detail. Senator George Smathers noted: "Lyndon involved himself in every petty Senate matter as well as the important business."[42]

One observer claimed that LBJ's approach to arriving at a consensus was: "Come let us reason together, you little chickenshit." According to Senator Fulbright, LBJ's interest in politics was a thinly veiled hunger for domination. "Johnson is an extraordinary man, and he goes to extraordinary lengths to convert people, and if not, to neutralize them. It is all personal, because he has never shown any interest in issues or substantive matters."[43]

Where legislation was involved, the Majority Leader's principal concern was to avoid the personal embarrassment of a defeat. Bobby Baker observed that Johnson was fearful of losing a vote on a bill.[44] For the Majority Leader, that was public humiliation. He would rush or delay, twist and eviscerate legislation, do whatever it took to get a bill passed and to protect his ego.[45]

However, he delighted in deflating the egos of his colleagues. The Senate floor was often the arena for LBJ's acid playfulness. Once he was sure that he had the votes to defeat the Republicans, he would say to their leader, William Knowland: "Bill, you know you don't have the votes, don't you? You just don't have 'em! I can tell you what the vote's gonna be if you'd like to know." Baker adds that Johnson, who often did imitations of Senator Knowland, did not dislike the man, but merely enjoyed displaying his power over him.[46]

We have seen LBJ's penchant for cruelty at work on his employees. In his early years in Washington, Johnson confined his sarcasm and bullying to the people in his office because they could not afford to respond.[47] As LBJ accumulated more power, there were fewer people in a position to fight back. When he became Senate Majority Leader, he would attack men who in earlier years would have received his courtesy. After hearing some particularly inept remarks, he tore into the man who had just delivered them. One of his aides reminded him of the politeness due a fellow Senator. LBJ's response was: "But he's a stupid bastard."[48]

On July 2 of 1955, six months after becoming Senate Majority Leader, Johnson gave a very public display of exactly what *he* was. At a supposedly pro forma news conference, Johnson was asked questions he didn't want to hear, much less answer. He started giving sarcastic responses. John Chadwick of the AP persisted in asking a question about the McCarren Walter Immigration Act. Johnson cursed the reporter so offensively that the other reporters present sprang to their colleague's defense. Then they were attacked too by Johnson with obscene language. The offended reporters stormed out of the room.[49]

In the autumn of 1955, commentator Dan Rather, then a radio reporter in Houston, collided with Johnson's contempt for the press and his growing paranoia. Rather arrived at the ranch in the early morning for an interview. By lunch time, Johnson had neither appeared nor sent any message. Rather used the telephone in the den to inform his boss that he hoped to see the Senator in the afternoon. As he was speaking, Johnson loomed up from behind, grabbed the phone, and said to Rather's boss that the reporter was a liar and bad mannered on top of it. Then Johnson told Rather to get off his property. As the reporter was getting into his car, Lady Bird invited him back to the house for a drink. "As you know," she explained, "that's just the way Lyndon is."[50]

Johnson's ego was like a huge, bulging aortic aneurism. Any puncture would bring death by hemorrhage of self-esteem. He couldn't even bear the pricks that are part of the rough and tumble of politics. His fury was aroused on any occasion when he felt the press paid him inadequate attention. Actual press criticism was intolerable.[51]

Rowland and Evans add that Johnson's thin skin was not limited to how the press treated him. "...with less than a year as Democratic floor leader under his belt, Johnson was developing an imperious sensitivity to criticism from his fellow Senators that would cost him dearly in his last two years in the leadership."[52]

Gradually, Johnson assembled a list of senators who were too independent for his taste, or who offended him in some other manner. These became not people to be courted, but rather targets for vengeance. First, he would try to enforce his hegemony by sheer intimidation. According to Senator George Aiken, "Lyndon would go around and try to change votes by pounding his finger into your chest and yelling at you, 'You better vote the other way!' If you got in bad with him, he punished you by never calling your bills off the calendar." Or, as Senator John Williams attests, Johnson would punish a senator by waiting until the man had left the Senate Chamber, and then calling the senator's bill for discussion and vote. Assiduous in wooing those who would cooperate, Johnson was equally thorough at cutting the rebels off at the knees. Senator Russell Long noted: "He...could not bear to have anyone operating outside his camp. When he saw this developing, he would either reconcile or isolate them. As for Senate loners, he could make their lives miserable."[53]

LBJ came from a part of the country where taking vengeance was woven into the history and the culture. Attacks by Indians were answered with violence. In the hill country where the Johnsons had taken root, neighbors would feud and fight like the Hatfields and the McCoys. This section of Texas became vigilante country. And violence was part of the family tradition for LBJ, whose grandfather once set out to fight a duel.[54]

Threats and vengeance were a regular part of LBJ's political modus operandi. The mildest punishment he meted out was to stop speaking to people who had offended him, which may have been a relief to some of them. Sam Rayburn received the silent treatment in 1956.[55] That same year, LBJ displayed his ruthlessness at a Democratic State Convention. Among his choice remarks were: "You tell those Mexicans from Laredo I'll break their legs if they don't vote for us." He screamed at another: "If you don't help me get rid of her and put Mrs. Bentson in, you ain't never gonna get to be a federal judge!" Finally, he bellowed, "Woodrow Bean, I'm gonna give you a three-minute lesson in integrity. And then I'm gonna ruin you."[56]

Men and women who make it to the Senate are not pushovers. Consequently, Johnson's autocratic rule over that august body spawned resentment. The first to voice this was Senator William Proxmire, who did not appreciate the methods of the king-size Napoleon. Proxmire called Johnson "dictatorial." He added that the extent of Johnson's power grab had made Senate history: "The typical Democratic Senator has literally nothing to do with determining the legislative program and policies of the party." He called the annual party caucus a "sham."

Senator Richard Newberger warned Proxmire that he was biting the hand that fed him and that Proxmire owed everything that he had in the Senate to Lyndon Johnson. That was a curious defense of the Majority Leader. Proxmire remarked later, "Senator Newberger made my point. Senator Johnson sure did make the committee appointments, he did indeed decide what legislation would come up and...everybody in the Senate knew that if you wanted things to get done, you had to do it through the leader or he could stop you."

Several senators privately expressed agreement that Johnson was tyrannical, but the senators expressing it to Proxmire did so in telephone calls to Proxmire's home, for fear that Johnson had all the Senate phones tapped and taping. Senator Russell compared Proxmire to "…a bull who had charged a locomotive train. That was the bravest bull I ever saw, but I can't say a lot for his judgement."

Johnson was upset enough by Proxmire's criticism to threaten to resign the Leadership unless the party caucus gave him a vote of confidence. He later decided to refuse to make any response to Proxmire on the grounds that liberals were using the Senator to sabotage Johnson's coming try at the Presidency.[57]

There was no evidence of this. Paranoia was becoming a well entrenched member of Johnson's staff. This was the man that columnist and friend Stewart Alsop called: "…the second most powerful man in the nation; perhaps even the most powerful man, because he loves to exercise power and Eisenhower does not."[58]

CHAPTER 7

THE HEARTBREAK HOTEL

★ ★ ★ ★ ★ ★

Johnson may have had his eye on the Presidency, but he was actually running for a heart attack. Since becoming Majority Leader he had been in overdrive, working sixteen-hour days, including Saturdays, and coming to the office on Sunday as well. He would retire to bed with packets of reading material. Sleep evaded him, and staffers received instructions by phone at two, three, four AM. Some nights Johnson didn't come home or sleep at all, but roamed the Senate's halls, talking to anyone he found there.[1] If he did make it home, often at around ten or eleven PM, he brought guests for dinner, with whom he continued the business of the day.[2]

The manic speed had returned too. Booth Mooney, who was working for Johnson then, described his employer as a man who was never still, who would literally run from the Senate Office Building to his car. Johnson would race back and forth, talking on the phone, not pausing to sit while he wolfed down a hamburger for lunch. He was smoking sixty cigarettes a day, drinking heavily at night and, noted Mooney, the Majority Leader's temper was worse than ever.[3]

Intense mania does not allow one to rest, and Johnson was incapable of relaxing. Senator George Smathers tells the story: "I took him on a fishing trip to Florida, but he refused to go fishing once we got there. He would just get mad and sulk in the house when the rest of us went out on the boat. He wanted us to stay around and talk politics all the time." For the Majority Leader, talking politics was not a form of amusement, it was how he worked.[4]

As June wore on, Johnson felt tired, but it was not the fatigue of depression. On July 2 he had a serious heart attack. He had lived as though he were immortal. He began his convalescence thinking about his father's dying of a heart attack at age sixty. Depressed and frightened now, Johnson worried about his own survival.[5] He thought that continuing in politics might kill him. Aide Walter Jenkins recalled that Johnson was given medication for his depression, but whatever it was, it did not work. Johnson was in a retarded depression that left him lying like a corpse on the bed. In his more lively moments, he would sit up, staring blankly at the world.[6]

The depression lifted sufficiently for Johnson to make plans to retire from politics. He told Bobby Baker: "I had a close call, and I may be forced to resign from the Senate." "Then he asked, If I did, would you resign and go home with me to run a radio station?"

A few days later, the depression was gone and with it all thoughts of leaving the work he loved.[7]

Johnson thought he could survive if he moderated his pace. "I've thrown away the whip," he said.[8] But he could no more "throw away the whip" than he could throw away his head. Being manic was not an offer that he could refuse.

His days of convalescence fell into a rhythm. One day he was depressed, a good boy submissive to his mother and wife as they took care of him, and he was ready to resign from politics. The next day he was running his office from his bed, telephoning endlessly, seeing too many visitors, and defiantly refusing suggestions to rest from his mother and wife. Anxiety is a common thread in both mania and depression. Johnson said: "I knew then how awful it was to lose command of myself, to be dependent on others. I couldn't stand it."[9]

One of the worst periods of abuse that Lady Bird endured was in the days following LBJ's heart attack. On the fourth day after the attack, the doctors told him what he had to give up if he wanted to live much longer: cigarettes, fattening foods, and most of the alcohol he was accustomed to consume every day.

George Reedy noted that whenever Johnson was forbidden to smoke, he fell into a rage and dumped his anger principally on his wife. One of the doctors wanted to abandon the Senator because Johnson's treatment of Lady Bird was so insufferable. On one occasion, LBJ decided that his wife had given him too much watermelon. Although the room was full of people, he accused her of "trying to kill me" with the extra calories. Lady Bird told a friend: "When Lyndon is out of danger, I want to go off alone somewhere and cry."[10]

Having returned to the ranch to recuperate. Johnson endured a gloomy Autumn, during which he spent a week on a reclining chair in his living-room.[11] His silence and immobility reached the extremes seen in the deepest states of depression.

Johnson returned to the Senate on January 3, 1956. "He was absolutely tormented," George Reedy said. "He believed he'd missed out on something in his youth—I think he thought it was love—and he was determined to find it now."[12]

Tormented or not, Johnson was always ready to play the con man and impose his will on others. James Rowe had the works thrown at him when LBJ wanted to hire him. He got most of their mutual friends to tell Rowe that he had to help poor, sick Lyndon out in his hour of need.[13] Finally, LBJ moved in for the attack, which began with tears: "You know I am going to die, and nobody cares. You don't care. It's typically selfish. Nobody cares." This finally was too much for Rowe, who agreed to take the job. Rowe adds: "And within seconds the tears were gone. He straightened up in his chair and said, 'All right, but just remember I make the decisions, you don't!'"[14]

One of the obvious problems that LBJ had as an employer was that he lacked, as we have seen, any sense of limits. While a senator, he decided that his staff would send a letter of congratulation to each Texas high school graduate that year, and the 50,000 letters could not be form letters in case the students compared them.[15] That was a typically manic project, involving as it did, an extravagant expenditure of effort far in excess of any possible benefit.

Everyone around LBJ was supposed to imitate his pace. On the Senate floor he was usually in high gear and could not wait for a page to deliver a paper to the clerk's desk. LBJ would snatch it out of his hands and deliver it himself.[16] The impatience contributed to his irritability. He would get angry if one of his aides were in the shower when he called and he had to wait for the man to come to the phone.[17]

Manic contagion, the taking up of a manic's enthusiasm, optimism and objectives by others, continued to be part of Johnson's arsenal. According to Sam Houston, his brother's manic energy could definitely become infectious: "...Lyndon was...the most energetic man in Washington, heart attack or no heart attack, and some of that energy seemed to pour into the rest of us."[18] LBJ was considered the hardest working man in Washington.[19] He also tyranized the hardest working staff.

Meddling is a manic behavior. It comes from a manic's delusion that no one can do anything as well as he can and from his desire to control everything that happens around him regardless of how trivial, or from paranoid suspicions that without his close supervision he will be sabotaged.

Manic meddling often does not confine itself to the employee's work. The secretaries were told what colors to wear and how much hair spray to use.[20] According to journalists Richard Harwood and Haynes Johnson, LBJ even sent his secretaries to New York to learn how to apply cosmetics. Harwood and Johnson observed: "Lyndon's attempts to dominate the people around him are legendary."[21] One can also see here in grownup form, the manic child's

lack of awareness of the boundaries of others and of their entitlement to dignity and privacy.

LBJ's harassment of his employees helped to maintain his dominance over them. Criticism, no matter how gently put, can be
painful. People will learn to do anything to avoid it. LBJ's criticism
was not gentle. Some of those who worked for him simply crum-
pled under the onslaught. A staffer reports that the boss would
drop not so subtle hints like: "Well, I see we're putting on a few
pounds, aren't we?" Or if he thought the secretary had gone too
long without having her hair done, "Well, it's getting a little windy
out there, isn't it?" Merely to walk away from him was to undergo
a thorough scrutiny, and woe betide the woman with a run in her
stockings.[22] This constant critical attention is typical behavior for
many manic personalities.

But the Boss's demands always went further than that.
According to George Reedy, LBJ "...was notorious for abusing his
staff, for driving people to the verge of exhaustion—and sometimes
over the verge; for paying the lowest salaries for the longest hours
of work on Capitol Hill...."[23]

When the wives of his employees complained about the long
hours, he put them to work too.[24] Long hours for low pay did not
suffice for LBJ. He insisted that his employees be available by telephone 24 hours of the day, seven days a week, wherever they
were.[25] It was nothing unusual for him to call someone at 3 AM with
a long list of things to be done before coming to the office. Staff
members learned to keep a pencil and pad by the bedside.[26]

When he wanted to hire John Hicks to work at the Johnson
radio station, he informed him: "...I expect total loyalty. If I call you
up at two o'clock in the morning and tell you to be somewhere, I
want you on that horse." Oddly enough this did not appeal to
Hicks, who refused the job, LBJ never forgave him.[27]

LBJ's blindness to his own faults was so overriding that he could
not understand why anyone would want to leave his employ.
Columnist Hugh Sidey noted: "No man could leave Johnson grace-

fully, because Johnson found in every departure a bit of disloyalty."[28] LBJ tried to hold people not because they were indispensable but to protect his own ego. He put on an astonishing performance to hold the would-be deserter. Flattery, avowals of love, promises of money and advancement, and insistence that the person could not be spared were all part of it. He promised one man that the reward for staying on was to become chief of staff, constantly working directly with Johnson. It was a mistake to believe any of this, because shortly thereafter, LBJ would treat the employee worse than before and none of the promises were kept.[29]

The subservient became servants. And bartenders. When the boss was done for the day he would hold out an empty glass expecting a secretary to fill it instantly with Cutty Sark.[30] Staff members had to be on call for baby-sitting duties.[31]

LBJ's furies stopped just short of violence. One of his staff members thought that LBJ's rage could easily have overcome all self-restraint: "I've seen him practically whip members of his staff... if he'd had a whip in his hand I'm sure he'd have given them a couple of lashes."[32] On one occasion there was no whip available, only a glass. A new secretary, unaware of LBJ's alcoholic requirements, on being asked for a drink, gave him sherry and water. One taste told him it was not Cutty Sark. He yelled "You've poisoned me" and threw the glass across the room.[33]

LBJ did not allow people to take vacations if he could talk them out of it. When he was Senate Majority Leader, a newspaper report about this finally made him give his staff some time off.[34] Even LBJ's brother Sam thought the staff was overworked: "... some of his staff members were apt to develop into nervous, humorless drones, plodding along with a wary eye on the boss, afraid to displease him, certainly afraid to criticize him. Small wonder that he has often been surrounded by scared-assed sycophants...."[35]

Lady Bird became a specialist in damage control. Only her kindness kept many of those who worked for LBJ willing to endure him.[36] Booth Mooney states that his employer was unable to apologize for anything and other sources corroborate this.[37] Lady Bird made the apologies for him. "I will not take on Lyndon's animosities or quarrels because I don't want him to lose any friends."[38] Many times she telephoned the victim of LBJ's wrath with words of appreciation and perhaps an invitation to some social event.[39]

His cruelty to his wife could be life threatening. As they were preparing to go riding one day, LBJ helped his wife onto her horse and then startled the animal with a hard blow on its flank. It took off like a rocket, with Lady Bird barely hanging on. She managed to get the horse under control and return to the stable. This time she told him what she thought: "Damn you! Don't ever do that to me again. I could have been killed." He treated what he had done as a joke and never apologized.[40]

With the flood of sexual harassment suits, the manic boss today may think twice before groping his female employees. But LBJ did his groping before women had much legal recourse. As a new congressman he already had what observers called a "harem."[41] According to George Reedy, Johnson had a preference for young girls, especially those who were good humored, easy to influence, and appeared to dislike him. He enjoyed a challenge.[42] He wooed them by telling them he trusted them and needed them to work directly under him. He told them "You remind me of my mother." That dubious compliment was supposed to be the clincher and it often was.

While effecting their political conversion to whatever he espoused at the moment, he would see to their physical transformation. He wanted them to slim down to movie star proportions, to make up their faces and style their hair like fashion models, and he replaced their wardrobes with his idea of what was attractive. He demanded that they worship him, and he got at least superficial compliance. Some actually did.

The reward for what Reedy called "the reigning favorite" was (besides looking glamorous a la LBJ) sharing the upscale social life of the Johnsons, accompanied by an innocuous male escort for cover. Then there was her greatly magnified influence over the office and the boss, which other aides quickly learned to recognize and use.

LBJ made no effort to hide his liaisons. Senior aide Walter Jenkins would filter the orders of the reigning favorite so that the stupid demands had no consequences. For the several weeks that these affairs lasted, LBJ would shower favor on the lady of the moment at the expense of everyone else and Lady Bird would try to comfort the wounded. During this period of "turmoil," Reedy says, "...workable routines would be upset; morale would fall to all-time lows; efficiency would go out the window," and Mrs. Johnson would carry on heroically.[43]

Except for these recurrent weeks of obsession with one woman, LBJ spread his sexual harassment around liberally. When he was a senator, for example, he couldn't keep his hands off a secretary while helping her get out of a car. "As I leaned over to get out, he took the opportunity to feel me up," she said. "It happened so fast I didn't even have a chance to complain."[44]

Then there was Madeline Brown whom LBJ met in 1948 at a party in Austin. According to Brown, LBJ considered Lady Bird just the "official" wife. Brown's son Steven was born in 1951. LBJ made monthly payments to support mother and child. In 1987, Steven Brown sued for a share of the Johnson estate, thus making public his mother's affair with LBJ. Steven Brown failed to appear in court, so the suit was dismissed.[45]

Bobby Baker reported that among LBJ's many affairs were one with a newswoman and one with a congressman's wife. LBJ later asked President Kennedy to give the congressman a federal position at a distant city because of complications that had arisen, and Kennedy complied.[46]

LBJ's Senate office became known among newsmen as the "Nooky room." He sometimes had affairs running with two or more women at the same time. Obviously, it was not LBJ's nature to be faithful to his women in or out of marriage.

In 1955, not long after his heart attack, he announced to his doctors that what he liked most in life was sunshine, whiskey and sex.[47] George Reedy repeats this remark and adds: "He collected women like some men collect exotic fish."[48] LBJ is probably the only man to occupy the White House who enjoyed bovine pornography and instructed his photographer to take pictures of cattle mating at the ranch.[49]

The sexual pressures of mania encourage people to reveal their bodies and the manic's lack of inhibition makes them strip in the wrong places and at the wrong times. LBJ, obsessed with sex as he was, was already an exhibitionist in college. He introduced his penis to people as "Jumbo."[50] He was still at it in his senate office. When an old friend came up from Texas for a visit, LBJ pulled "Jumbo" out of his pants and asked: "Have you ever seen anything as big as this?"[51]

His sexual appetite was not the only one that he indulged without stint. He was a man who could deny himself nothing. He was a phenomenon even at the dining table. Senator George Smathers called him "...the biggest eater I ever watched. He would eat two large meals and gulp them down as if he were starving. Nobody could slow him down."[52] Without a moment's embarrassment, LBJ would grab food from other people's plates.

No one could reign in LBJ's appetite for space and luxury and service either. His senate offices consisted of 20 huge rooms ostentatiously decorated, with another room off the Senate gallery and a seven-room suite. Greed, hypocrisy, and extravagance made a heady cocktail for LBJ during his Senate years.

While parading as a watchdog over government spending, he took over the quarters of a seven-man committee for his sole use and spent over a million taxpayers' dollars to bring it up to his standards.[53] His offices were known as the "Taj Mahal." His inner office was the "Emperor's Room." He insisted that three elevator operators spend their Sundays at the Senate Office Building to run the automatic elevators for him.[54]

Senator Barry Goldwater asked: "How could a man, almost

penniless, come to Washington and die a man worth over $20 million?"[55] It was a good question, and LBJ would have had an even greater fortune if he had not loved to spend money. When depressed, he would announce that he was leaving politics to go out into the world to make his fortune. The truth is that, from 1941, he never stopped making money, lots of it. In 1941 he had under $11,000.00 in the bank. Seven years later he told his friends that he had become a millionaire.[56]

The secret of LBJ's success (and it wasn't exactly a secret) was not his hard work so much as his influence over the Federal Communications Commission. He denied, of course, that he ever influenced it in any way, but he got seats for himself and his friend, Senator Smathers, on the Senate Interstate and Foreign Commerce Committee, which oversaw the budget and status of the personnel of the FCC.[56] Moreover, one of the Commission's members was the nephew of LBJ's political daddy, Sam Rayburn.[57] The favorable rulings followed thick and fast.

First, KTBC instantly became more valuable when it received permission to increase the strength of its signal, to be on the air 24 hours a day, and to become affiliated with network radio stations.[58] Less than 20 years after LBJ bought it, KTBC was worth seven million dollars.[59] And this was just the core of the Johnson media empire. When the FCC distributed the nation's TV channels, LBJ got the only one in Austin, with the unique privilege of selecting what programming he wanted from all three TV networks. He also demanded and got NBC to pay him national advertising rates for broadcasting its commercials even though the audience was too small to qualify. Furthermore, although Austin was small, it was the largest city of its size with only one TV station, a monopoly by courtesy of the FCC.[60]

LBJ destroyed other TV stations by getting the FCC to rule against them. Then he would acquire full or part ownership of them at low cost, in one case, for no money down, and have the rulings reversed. He bought station KRGV-TV for $100,000 and sold it the following year for a $1,300,000 profit.[61] LBJ also used his influence with the Civil Aeronautics Administration to make it accept a tower he wanted built that it had previously ruled a danger to air traffic.[62]

Secrecy and deception helped the Senator amass his fortune. A former friend admitted that LBJ erected "false fronts everywhere."[63] But Johnson's reliance on lies and deception began to work against him. The Washington bureau chief of the *New York Times*, Arthur Krock, observed while LBJ was still a Senator, whatever Sam Rayburn said was accepted at face value, but his fellow Texan was considered a doubtful source.[64]

When it came to drinking, the Majority Leader was no slouch. Two of the men who spent a lot of time with LBJ repeatedly saw him drink heavily. Bobby Baker relates that on one occasion they were so drunk when they left LBJ's Senate office that they had trouble walking. Baker slipped and pulled LBJ down with him. The Senator said: "Goddam, Bobby, help me up before the goddam Republicans see us."[65] George Reedy, who was not a drinking buddy, records that Johnson would often swallow one scotch and soda after another, passing into a stage of rage and invective, and eventually, stupefaction.[66]

Journalist Russell Baker describes LBJ drinking like an alcoholic at a Washington dinner party: "…pouring down Scotch whiskey like a man who had a date with a firing squad….all the while talking nonstop…." Johnson launched into one of his monologues while ignoring the food. Baker concludes: "I had seen people smoke and drink dinner before," however, Lyndon "…did it like a man trying to kill himself."[67]

After his heart attack LBJ was warned to reduce his consumption of alcohol, but such warnings rarely deter alcoholics. It merely made him sneaky. When he flew from Washington to the ranch, he ordered one of his secretaries to get a couple of bottles of Cutty Sark on board without letting Lady Bird see them.[68] By the end of the fifties, his drinking was as heavy as ever, though well hidden from the public.[69]

It was not hidden from presidential historian Theodore White, who saw that from December, 1959 through February, 1960 "…he could outdrink almost anyone around him."[70] According to Reedy, the graph of LBJ's alcohol consumption was on a rising curve during 1960 and the Majority Leader was breaking his own records during his drinking bouts.[71]

It appears that being Majority Leader was not good for Johnson's mental health. Whether the stresses of his position increased his alcoholism could be debated, but it is clear that having so much power encouraged his inclination towards megalomania. The manic may be deluded about his attractiveness, his talent, intelligence, wealth, social status and power. If he is far enough into his mania, he may believe he has the kind of powers usually ascribed to divinities. LBJ traveled the entire manic road, from ambition and arrogance to delusions of unlimited power.

John Kennedy saw something in his fellow senator in 1958 that inspired the following joke. Kennedy said that in a dream God promised him he would be the next President. When he told his dream to Senator Stuart Symington, Symington said he had the same dream. When they both related their dreams to LBJ, he remarked: "That's funny. For the life of me I can't remember tapping either of you two boys for the job."[72]

Perhaps Johnson, who by now had had many romantic affairs, yearned for love not from an individual, but from multitudes. In 1956, the Presidency was very much on his mind, and he was afraid that his heart attack had put it out of reach. He told Baker: "…every night when I go to bed I'm afraid I'm not going to wake up. When I get tired I have terrible chest pains and I really live on an hour-to-hour basis." He was caught in a vicious circle. Depression focused his thoughts on death (though in depression-free intervals, he returned to his reckless lifestyle), dying meant he would never get to be President, and that realization increased his depression.

Baker said that Johnson kept turning on and off his intention to run for the Presidency. However, for more than a year, Speaker Sam Rayburn and Johnson's leading staff members were running a sub rosa campaign committee, with volunteers and a paid staff, which was never disbanded by the non-candidate. Baker concludes that, despite LBJ's vacillating course, his presidential ambitions never abated.[73]

The strategy that LBJ adopted was the same one he would use in 1960, despite its proven failure in 1956. It had, for LBJ, the irresistible advantage that it would, in the process, if not in the result, spare his ego the agony of rejection. He would not enter primaries or openly campaign in any way, but would wait for the Democratic Convention to stalemate and then turn to him with his phalanx of southern and southwestern delegates.[74]

The first that journalist Sam Shaffer heard about it was the first day of the Democratic National Convention on August 13, 1956. Johnson held a press conference to announce that he was a candidate for President of the United States. Shaffer says: "We were all flabbergasted.... Outside of the Senate, who was he?" It was indeed a grandiose thing to do.[75]

Once at the Convention, LBJ fell into a euphoria that clouded his normally superb political judgement.[76] He convinced himself, if only himself, that northern labor would flock to his support despite his repeated, effective efforts to defeat civil rights laws. Tommy Corcoran exclaimed: "Hell, as long as he wasn't with them on civil rights, they were *never* going to support him!"[77]

LBJ's euphoria was, as usual, unstable, and was frequently replaced by depression, bringing with it anxiety that he would fail to be nominated. In that mood, he retreated to his room, refused to meet with four state delegations, and insisted that party leaders who wanted to see him had to come to *his* headquarters. His explanation for his diffident campaign was "I didn't come here to be humiliated."[78]

This was a man unequaled in his ability to assess the sentiments and predict the votes to be cast for or against laws in the Senate.

How could he fail to anticipate, not just the magnitude of his defeat in the Convention, but the fact that he never really had a chance? According to Tommy Corcoran, "He wanted it (the nomination) so much he wasn't thinking straight."[79] Desire alone did not separate LBJ from reality. His oscillations between an optimism born of high mania and fearful anxiety born of dark depression dismantled his common sense.

When Johnson belatedly accepted that he had lost, he notified Adlai Stevenson that he was available for Vice President. Stevenson politely refused the offer.[80]

By 1957, Johnson had recovered from his presidential disappointment and was starting a legislative campaign that would show he was "Presidential timber." To weaken the power of the Southern senators, he inserted liberals on key committees, and then masterminded the passage of the first civil rights legislation in this century.[81]

By January, 1958, Johnson seemed to have forgotten his heart attack. Journalists noted: "He is a man of frenzied activity and intensity." "Rest and relaxation seem to be painful to Johnson." Even when not at work, Johnson's manic pace amazed observers. Another journalist wrote: "He will stride into a Washington cocktail party...a whirlwind of movement.... LBJ lives his life at top speed."[82]

This manic period came to an end when Johnson's mother died on September 12, 1958. Lady Bird thought he hit an unprecedented low. Johnson drank more heavily than ever. His threats of resignation were more frequent.

This depression hung on. Without mania, Johnson had lost his magic touch as Majority Leader. He was like a great orchestra leader who becomes deaf in the middle of a concert. Many of Johnson's bills went down to defeat, and his enemies were increasing.

Despite the anguish of these days, Lady Bird described the period her husband spent in the Senate "...the happiest twelve years of our lives."[83]

His theme now, when he drank too much, was that he would

not only leave politics, he would leave his family and go out there to get rich.[84] He did nothing of the kind. Instead, he spent the next year confounding his staff and friends with his continuing vacillations about running for the Presidency.

At the start of 1959, his friend and advisor, Jim Rowe, told him it was high time to start the campaign. Johnson refused, insisting that the nomination was out of reach. This must have been one of his depressed days. "He wanted the thing," Rowe recalled. "I think he wanted it so much his tongue was hanging out. Then this other part of him said, 'This is impossible. Why get my hopes up? I'm not going to try. If I don't try, I won't fail.'"

Rowe was right about Johnson's fear of failure and his ambivalence. Presidential ambition and the expectation of being rejected by voters in primaries across the country were riding the seesaw of Johnson's mind. That spring, the stealth candidate saw to it that Texas election laws were rewritten to move the primaries from July and August to May and June, and, hedging his bets, to let him run for the Senate and any other national office simultaneously.[85]

George Reedy describes his boss's contradictory attitudes and behavior: "As for the forthcoming presidential election, his expressed attitude was simply, 'Fuck 'em all. I want no part of it!' ...It was a period in which he put on one of the greatest Jekyll-Hyde shows in history. He would authorize the establishment of a campaign headquarters and then refuse to allow it to do anything. He would authorize his staff to draw up campaign proposals and then forbid any action, even to contacting potential supporters."[86] At the same time, Johnson was turning down those who offered help.[87]

In early January of 1960, liberal Democrats mounted a revolt, proposing to take back some of the power that Johnson had arrogated for himself. They wanted the Democratic Senate Policy Committee to actually make policy again and they wanted all the Senate Democrats to appoint the members of the committee instead of having the leader keep that privilege. Johnson said: "Screw 'em all, I'm sick and tired of this kind of nonsense....This is

nothing but a reflection on me. ...I don't think I ought to be subjected to this kind of torment." He wasn't. The resolution was
defeated 51 to 12.[88]

Johnson's wild oscillations of mood and direction continued
through the spring of 1960. When a more positive mood replaced
his depression, Johnson had Walter Jenkins organize a state-by-state
campaign, talking with local party leaders. There were already
"Johnson for President" clubs set up by Jenkins in many states.[89]
The clandestine candidate was also meeting with dozens of men he
had sent across the country to round up delegates, while stubbornly refusing to admit that he was a candidate. This charade annoyed
Sam Rayburn, who remarked: "Lyndon's using his friends to raise
money and count delegates and he's making them as well as himself look silly by declaring himself a non-candidate. He ought to
shit or get off the pot."[90]

The secret candidacy was no secret. Even such an outsider as
the business editor of *Time* commented that Johnson should be
open about his candidacy.[91] Telling the people what he was doing
was one thing Johnson refused to consider, and that refusal would
prove a fatal flaw during his prosecution of the Vietnam War.

Another flaw that he would maintain as President was his reluctance to hear, much less believe, bad news. Delegates to the previous Democratic National Convention had been polled the previous
year, with the result that Kennedy would get 409 votes, Senator
Stewart Symington 259 1/2, Adlai Stevenson who had already been
defeated twice would get 244, and Johnson would be given only 195
1/2, with other possible candidates trailing.

Even this did not motivate him to campaign openly.[92] In the
spring of 1960, Johnson was informed by Dick Berlin that
California Governor Pat Brown was going to deliver his state's delegation to Kennedy. Johnson refused to take the warning seriously.
Berlin said to Jenkins: "You know Lyndon—he believes what he
wants to believe."[93] The problem with Johnson was that manic
depression gave him the wrong priorities. The first one was to pro-

tect his ego from the unbearable agony (for him) of rejection. The second priority was to shield from all challenges his grandiose delusion that his power as Majority Leader would deliver the nomination at the convention.[94] Dealing with the realities of a rapidly moving national Presidential campaign came a distant third. And Johnson's delusions distorted his view of those realities.

Johnson felt that being from a Southern state put him at a considerable disadvantage across the country, vis-à-vis the Northern candidates. He once told a Northern reporter: "...you think we all have tobacco juice on our shirts."[95]

Johnson often ignored political reality. For example, Senator Vance Hartke said that Johnson could have easily won the Indiana Primary. He should have known; it was his state. John Kennedy, who worked so hard to win in West Virginia, thought Johnson would have beat him there.[96] But the protection of the Johnson ego required that he not even be tempted to run in a primary. So he had to discount any positive news about his prospects in the primaries.

In order to maintain the delusion that his allies in the Senate and Sam Rayburn's allies in the House would deliver their delegates, Johnson invented an explanation for this unlikely occurrence. He convinced himself that Kennedy, Stevenson and Symington would be so damaged at the convention that he would emerge as the only person capable of leading the party to victory. To maintain this fiction, Johnson ignored the bad news that came to him as soon as he reached the Convention City of Los Angeles. When his advance men told him that Kennedy had this or that state locked up, Johnson fired them and called them "defeatist." This is the way Stalin behaved when being told that the Wehrmacht was rolling across the borders of the Soviet Union. And, as with Stalin, Johnson's men stopped telling him bad news.[97]

It came as a terrible shock to him when Kennedy won almost two-to-one on the first ballot. This was just the beginning of Johnson's troubles. The emperor of the Senate was about to become a nobody.

CHAPTER 8

HELL IN SECOND PLACE

★　★　★　★　★　★

Lyndon Johnson was not jubilant when he told reporters at the Democratic National Convention that he would be Kennedy's vice president. And he became deeply depressed soon after the announcement was made. Perhaps saying it aloud forced him to survey the blighted landscape of his presidential ambitions. When Lynda Bird could not be located in time to play her part as a smiling member of the happy Johnson family on the convention platform, her father fell into an all too public rage, embarrassing even to Sam Rayburn, who had seen these outbursts before.[1]

After accepting the nomination as Vice President, Johnson said "Power is where power goes."[2] He wanted to maintain his hold on the Senate, and to assume as much of the President's job as Kennedy would allow. He knew enough history to realize how irrelevant his predecessors in office had been.

In July, Johnson took 37 Texas reporters and editors on a plane he chartered to visit JFK at the Kennedy compound in Hyannisport. While Johnson was giving a press conference, his pressure of speech turned the volume all the way up, so that people wandering by on the street could hear what was meant to be off the record. He went on a two-day talking jag. During a joint press conference with JFK, Johnson could not restrain himself from rushing out answers to questions addressed to the presidential candidate before Kennedy had a chance to respond.[3]

During the same visit, Johnson met with JFK's Press Secretary, Pierre Salinger. The topic was how to increase the Senator's appeal to the electorate. Johnson must have been in the euphoric, optimistic phase of his mania. At that moment, he was not seeing himself as a poor, despised Southerner. He interrupted Salinger's advice to make perhaps the most grandiose suggestion ever made to a press secretary by a vice presidential candidate. Johnson wanted to be presented to the nation as a flesh and blood Western hero. The one he had in mind was the one from the television show "Gunsmoke." "You know," he said, "...like Marshal Matt Dillon ...big, six-foot-three, good-looking—a tall, tough Texan coming down the street."[4] He was indeed six-foot-three.

As the campaign pressed on, Johnson played host to a group of reporters at his ranch. Midnight was long passed and everyone else was sleeping the sleep of the exhausted campaigner, when Johnson and three reporters settled in hammocks around the pool. With endless energy the candidate kept talking, never noticing that no one remained awake to hear him.[5] Manics have been known to talk to blank walls if no more sentient audience is available.

Mania not only kept the candidate awake and talking, it made him unrealistically optimistic. At such times, he saw himself as a President who would be better than Kennedy. Of course, when depressed he insisted that the campaign was more than his injured heart could take.[6]

While giving a brief talk at a hotel during a reception for voters, the candidate cordially invited the crowd to visit him in his Washington office: "The coffee pot is always on...and sometimes Lady Bird bakes a bunch of little cookies in the shape of the state of Texas to go with the coffee." Later, in the elevator, he admonished his aide for setting up the talk.[7]

Combine manic impulsivity with quick and extreme changes of mood, and the result is the kind of chaos that governed Johnson's campaign. Columnist Hugh Sidey noted: "His schedules made no sense, his speech subjects were infrequently pertinent."[8] Stopping in New Orleans, Johnson had an aide order a grand dinner for the staff at the finest restaurant in town, and told him to reserve rooms in a good hotel for everyone.

The hotel Johnson wanted was already fully booked because two conventions were being held in the city. He flew into a rage when told no rooms were available. The terrified hotel manager hustled a whole floor of guests out of their rooms to accommodate the candidate's people. Suddenly, Johnson declared that New Orleans was "sin city," and hurried his exhausted entourage onto a plane to fly back to his ranch before they could even have that dinner.[9]

His staff was trying to win the Olympics on a field full of land mines. The candidate sabotaged his own campaign time and again, often canceling speeches after a large crowd was already gathered to hear him. Or he would suddenly be inspired to give a speech where none had been scheduled and it was too late to get a crowd.[10]

Impulsivity also made Johnson appear to be less than honest as he would hand out to reporters the texts of his speeches before standing at the podium and then go on to say something quite contradictory. Moreover, reporters caught him in what was undeniably duplicitous behavior. They heard him promise Southern politicians that the platform's civil rights plank would never be acted upon.[11]

Johnson's domineering behavior when he campaigned in Texas was a forerunner of the suffering that was ahead of his staff in Washington once he was without power or influence. He was unrelentingly imperial in his home state, turning the congressmen of Texas into campaign assistants and their staffs into his serfs. Which meant that he treated the staffs very badly, battering them with criticisms and screaming orders at them.[12]

The kind of trivia that Johnson found insupportable is shown in the complaint that he yelled at an assistant: "Who was that redhead son of a bitch set two chairs down from me? Whoever he was, I don't want the goofy s.o.b. setting in the same room with me. Ruined mah whole night."[13]

By the end of a day of campaigning, Johnson was usually drunk and brutish. This was the most alcoholic campaign that he would ever make. He was drinking to the point where anything could and did happen. One night, after hours of drunken rambles up and down the corridors of his hotel, he invaded the room of one of his secretaries and climbed into her bed like a child seeking the warmth of its mother.

The mornings were nightmares for his staff, who had to haul him out of bed and pump his arms to help him breathe.[14] Then they did what little they could to sober him up for the day's appearances.

Johnson appears to have been caught in a 24-hour cycle of mania, rage, and depression. During the plunge into depression he would drink and talk about resigning. While buoyed by mania, he was inexhaustible and could deliver as many as 18 impromptu speeches a day as his train stopped at small towns.

Members of the press could not have been unaware that something was wrong with the candidate. Johnson was so out of control that he exploded in a crowded hotel lobby. On one occasion he accused his staff of arranging a press conference that he insisted he had not agreed to. Finally, he held the press conference, and on hearing a question he did not like, he yelled furiously "That's it! Thank you, boys!" and left.[15]

At times paranoia took over the candidate. He claimed that liberals, labor leaders and political bosses from large cities wanted to sink him because he came from Texas and lacked a Harvard education.[16]

The victorious end of the campaign brought no relief. The victory was a bitter one for him. He was locked into a job he considered a badge of failure and mediocrity. Journalist Margaret Mayer observed: "The night he was elected Vice President ... I don't think

I ever saw a more unhappy man....Lyndon looked as if he'd lost his last friend on earth, and later he was very rude to me, very rude...."[17]

When Johnson returned to the Senate to finish his term, he could feel his power draining away. Bobby Baker described him as listless, discouraged, visibly sad at having become a lame-duck leader.[18]

Whatever he may have expected, Johnson's stint as vice president would not be a period of unrelieved misery. But he was about to become one of the more "peculiar" vice presidents to cross the threshold of the White House.

A month before his inauguration, the depression lifted. Bobby Baker observed that LBJ became high-spirited. What cheered him was a scheme he devised for regaining some power. He told Baker: "...I'm workin' it out with Mike and Hubert to attend meetings of the Senate Democratic Caucus. Maybe even preside over 'em. That way I can keep my hand in. I can help Jack Kennedy's program, and be his eyes and ears."

Baker was amazed that Johnson could be so naïve. The Senate was always alert to protect its power from the executive branch and would never tolerate interference from a vice president. Moreover, Tsar Johnson had tread on too many toes to find a welcome among his former subjects. Baker tried to warn him that he might be rebuffed, but Johnson would not listen. He also ignored Baker's later reports that senators were not favorable to the plan.[19]

We see here a repeat of Johnson's refusal to take seriously any information that posed a threat to his ego. For a man of Johnson's political astuteness, who gathered political intelligence as though he were J. Edgar Hoover and the nation's security was at stake, this behavior seems irrational. But, as he did during his stealth campaign for the presidency, Johnson would stubbornly blind himself to whatever could disappoint him. Hubert Humphrey noted another distorting factor in Johnson's reading of Senate reality: "It was too much for him to leave that center of power. He was just very reluctant to give up those reins...."[20]

He did enlist the help of Democratic Majority Leader Mike Mansfield. The new Vice President attended the meeting on January 3, 1961, of the Senate Democratic Caucus. Mansfield offered a rule change that would allow the Vice President to preside. This was not well received. Although the 17 votes against the measure were not enough to defeat it, they were sufficient to make Johnson feel unwanted.[21] Like the child who took his ball away when he was not chosen to be pitcher, Johnson refused to attend any further meetings of the Caucus. He also refused to help Kennedy's programs gain Senate votes.[22]

One might say paranoia ushered Johnson into the vice presidency. On January 3, 1961, when he was opposed in his plan to preside over the Senate Democratic Caucus, Johnson saw a conspiracy: "Those bastards sandbagged me. They'd plotted to humiliate me, all those goddam red hots and troublemakers."[23] This was easier for him to believe than the truth that many senators resented his dictatorial treatment of them when he was Majority Leader.

Johnson had hoped to rule from behind the throne. He said more than once: "If there is only one man the President can turn to, I want that man to be me."[24] There was one such man, but it was the President's brother, Robert.

Johnson had witnessed the closeness of the brothers. Undeterred, he sent one of his aides to the President with an executive order to make Cabinet members and many agency heads report to the Vice President as well as to the President. The executive order would also have given Johnson responsibility for NASA and several other important areas of government. The executive order wasn't signed by Kennedy. Johnson lost his last hope for power as Vice President.[25]

Johnson was totally uninhibited and sadistic. While driving around the ranch with two male staff members in the back seat and a female friend in the front between LBJ at the wheel and Lady Bird by the door, he slipped his hand under the woman's skirt and enjoyed himself while his wife looked on in silence.[26]

In his manic state, the man who was a heartbeat away from the Presidency was more domineering than ever. Like Emperor Napoleon, he was unwilling to have his will thwarted even by nature. He ordered his pilot to take off from the Austin airport in a fog declared too thick for flying. The pilot objected. Johnson, who was not going to be a passenger himself, gave the man an overwhelming tongue-lashing. The pilot and copilot died in the ensuing crash.[27]

Johnson continued to crack the whip over his staff. There was, in his book, no excuse whatsoever for missing work as long as one was physically capable of reaching the office. When loyal Walter Jenkins absented himself to attend his mother's funeral, LBJ remarked: "And tomorrow it'll be his grandmother's funeral and the week after that it'll probably be his aunt's funeral."

A bit of depression would have toned Johnson down and made him a safer advisor during the Cuban missile crisis. Instead, the Vice President showed enough aggressiveness to have started World War III with nuclear weapons, had he sat in Kennedy's seat.

The Soviet Union had placed some of its nuclear missiles in Cuba, as American high altitude photographs had revealed. Kennedy demanded the missiles' removal and put American nuclear forces on alert. Then he proposed a blockade of Cuba. Johnson opposed this, endorsing instead an unannounced bombing of Cuba.[28] Fortunately for the world, his advice was not taken and Kruschev withdrew the missiles without further confrontation.

During mania, Johnson was a loud, nonstop talker. When the Vice President managed to attend legislative or Cabinet meetings, depression rendered him silent.[29] Kennedy commented: "I cannot stand Johnson's damn long face. He just comes in, sits at the Cabinet meetings with his face all screwed up, never says anything. He looks so sad."[30] Johnson rarely volunteered opinions and when asked what he thought about something, would speak so quietly that he was all but inaudible. His appearance was typical for a person in depression: complexion bloodless, facial muscles sagging, body in a tired slump. At these times, he felt that he would "shrivel up."[31] Depression made him lose interest completely in what was happening on Capitol Hill. In addition, it caused him to interpret whatever Mr. and Mrs. Kennedy did as social rebuff, which made him feel even worse.[32]

George Reedy thought that the Vice Presidency was "a nightmare." Johnson's drinking, self-pity and paranoia reached new levels, levels that his staff tried to hide from outsiders. Reedy says: "To the maximum extent possible, they acted as a buffer between him and the world, and some of them were afraid that if they left, the withdrawal of the buffer would expose the rest of the country to a very peculiar Vice President indeed."[33] The Vice President drank while depressed and holed up in bed. Reedy noted that Johnson also spent a lot of time looking up at his bedroom ceiling, and would speak harshly to anyone who entered the room.[34]

However, even during this agonizing period for both Johnson and his staff, there were days of manic relief, at least for him.

Travel often alleviates depression, and the presence of adoring crowds was always a powerful antidepressant for Johnson. During the 35 months of his Vice Presidency, he visited 33 countries. His travel requirements said a lot about the man: dozens of cases of Cutty Sark for him and hundreds of boxes of pens and cigarette lighters to give away.[35] He drank heavily in the course of his travels and, while in Taiwan, ordered a military plane to fly from Hong Kong just to bring him a case of Cutty Sark.[36]

His first journey took him to Senegal. He returned through Europe. The embassy staffs were overwhelmed by his sudden schedule changes. His wife had to fill in for him with the President of Senegal while, buoyed by euphoria, Johnson ran through the streets passing out pens, and making speeches in English, which the crowds did not understand.[37] Armored by manic confidence, he did not care what risks he was running as he hurled himself into the crowds.

On May 5, 1961, cheering crowds made Johnson euphoric

again.[38] But four days into the trip, euphoria made a quick transition through irritability and into rage. Without having done anything to provoke the Vice President, speechwriter Horace Busby became the victim of Johnson's fury. "You're fired!" Johnson roared. "Get the hell off this plane!" They were flying over the Pacific at the time, so Busby objected. "I don't give a fucking damn! You're fired. Get off this plane," Johnson yelled.[39]

Exaggeration is something that comes naturally to manics, LBJ's staff realized what he was doing. One of them, Frank Cormier, says: "We learned very early that you could put yourself in peril if you always accepted LBJ's pronouncements at face value."[40] Cormier, Booth Money and Bill Moyers used the same word to describe their employer's conversation: "hyperbole."[41]

Exaggeration, like indiscretion, also entered into LBJ's foreign policy. He met Ngo Dinh Diem, the leader of South Vietnam, during one of his Vice Presidential Asian tours and called the autocrat "The Winston Churchill of Asia," claiming that he had "the qualities of George Washington," "the courage" of Andrew Jackson, and the "astuteness" of FDR.[42] When asked by a reporter if he really meant it, the Vice President replied: "Shit, Diem's the only boy we got out there."[43] Hugh Sidey spoke for the press when he said that "...the persistent exaggeration chipped away at the reliability of the White House word."[44]

The Vice President went into campaign mode in Saigon, shaking hands, distributing pens and lighters, and also passes to the Senate Gallery, as he said: "Get your mamma and daddy to bring you to the Senate and Congress and see how the government works."[45] In his manic enthusiasm he lost sight of the facts that most of these people did not speak English and those few who did were unlikely to reach the United States. Impulse set his agenda, and the haggling he did with shopkeepers, to the point of offending those who witnessed it, further complicated all attempts to keep him on schedule.[46]

In May of 1961, when Vice President Johnson toured the cities of America's Asian allies, he identified with the nationalist leaders he met. He saw the Thais, Philippinos, Taiwanese, and South Vietnamese as members of his team, almost as though they worked in his office, bravely keeping their fingers in the dike to hold back the tide of world Communism. Even after South Vietnam's leader, Diem, was assassinated by the South Vietnamese military opposition, LBJ said: "...let no day go by without asking whether we are doing everything we can to win the struggle there."[47]

LBJ treated manipulation as though it were a form of swordsmanship, and kept his performance sharp by continual practice. Political columnist Marianne Means observed that for Johnson manipulation and confrontation were as natural and as necessary as breathing.[48] There are manics so obsessed with power that they can only relate to people as manipulators and every conversation with them contains a struggle for dominance. For example, LBJ, during his Vice Presidential travels, would haggle with impoverished native craftsmen for their wares just for the hell of it.

Another manic behavior, impulsivity, appeared in Bangkok, where Johnson jumped onto buses to shake hands and pat children on the head, although he had been informed that touching the bodies of strangers was a severe breach of etiquette in Thailand. To Chinese-speaking crowds he gave speeches in English, without the assistance of a translator.[49]

The usual scheduling chaos prevailed. How do you schedule an earthquake? In Bangkok, the Vice President called for a press conference at two AM, which he held in his pajamas. The next day a trip to the water markets was scheduled for seven AM But reporters were called in the middle of the night because the trip was canceled. They were next awakened at six AM only to be informed that they had missed the trip.[50]

Travel did not improve Johnson's manners. In addition to being as uninhibited as a two-year-old, he failed to recognize that others had rights, not even to the food on their plates. He would reach

119

over and lift the butter from someone's plate, or dig his spoon into someone else's ice cream.[51] He stole a piece of chocolate cake from the plate of a journalist when she wasn't looking, and took a piece of meat from the wife of Australia's Prime Minister.[52] His utter disregard of others was demonstrated when, at a State Department reception, he got salt on his hands from eating nuts. He wiped his hands clean on the backs of the tuxedos of men who were standing near him.[53]

Lady Bird had an opportunity to watch another form of outrage when she accompanied her husband to a NATO meeting in Paris. A dinner party was held at Maxim's. After some inappropriate attention from the Vice President, the wife of a State Department official moved onto LBJ's lap and the two treated the tableful of people to an exhibition of grope and grab.[54]

Johnson was not an euphoric, but rather an irritable manic during his trip to Berlin in August, 1961. He hotly berated the mayor of Berlin. In Copenhagen he took hours out of his schedule to scold a painter about the prices of the paintings he was offering. The Vice President fell into a rage in Stockholm because he missed a fashion show.[55]

For all the traveling that the Vice President did, the most dangerous road he took was the path to paranoia, and Johnson was well on his way. A fundamental difference between having suspicions and being paranoid is that paranoia becomes the lens through which the paranoid person views the world. Everything that happens which is unpleasant, frightening, or diminishes the ego, is attributed ultimately to the machinations of one's enemies. Evidence to the contrary is disregarded.

Attendance at meetings of the Cabinet made Johnson accutely aware that he was merely an appendage to the Presidency, a position that was intolerable to a man who so loved power. He usually appeared sad and withdrawn during these meetings. Depression rendered the normally loquacious Johnson silent, but paranoia also contributed to his reticence. He told Bobby Baker: "If I speak one word of disagreement with the Cabinet and White House staff looking on, then they'll put it out to...everybody that I'm a damned traitor."[56]

As Johnson was to make clear in when he occupied the Presidency, he came to look on disagreement with his policies as treason, so this delusion was a comfortable fit for him. George Reedy said that the Vice President interpreted everything that involved him with the administration as evidence of plots against him.[57] Johnson would plaintively ask those close to him: "Why does the White House have it in for me?" He held as an article of faith that those around Kennedy wanted him out, and that Robert Kennedy and the Justice Department were trying to smear him with Bobby Baker's illegalities even though there was no evidence to support that suspicion.

Johnson became euphoric during his trips abroad. However, with the exception of the trip to Berlin, the Vice President always set out on his travels under a cloud of paranoia after putting up considerable resistance to going.[58] He thought that his May, 1961 trip to Asia was a plot by Bobby Kennedy to subject him to the same mob harassment Vice President Nixon had endured in Venezuela. JFK innocently sent his sister Jean Smith and her husband Steve on the trip with the Vice President, and Johnson thought that they were there to spy on him.

The Vice President was in Cypress in August of 1962 and paranoia was packed in the luggage. Richard Nixon's disastrous trip to Venezuela was again on Johnson's mind, but this time his suspicions fell on the press. In a nearly incoherent rage he screamed: "That God-damned press has lied about me enough! They have been trying to 'get me' ever since we started this trip. I am not going to let them do to me what they did to Dick Nixon!"

He believed that the press was under the control of Robert Kennedy. George Reedy adds that Johnson insisted on having a 'showdown' with the press, which certainly would have made the Vice President appear irrational to the very people who could destroy his reputation. It was with the greatest difficulty that Reedy talked Johnson out of staging this disaster.[59]

As the months of impotence wore on, Johnson expressed often his fear of being dumped. One might expect him to rejoice at the prospect of leaving a job he hated, but he could not bear rejection by anyone. By the autumn of 1963, his friends were aware of his deep despondency.

A bullet in Dallas was about to bring LBJ more power than he knew how to use.

Part Two:

LBJ Becomes The Most Powerful Man In The World

CHAPTER 9

THE ACCIDENTAL PRESIDENT

★ ★ ★ ★ ★ ★

L BJ recalled that on the plane returning from Dallas with the corpse of John Kennedy, he: "…made a solemn vow: I would devote every hour of every day during the remainder of John Kennedy's unfulfilled term to achieving the goals he had set."[1] This was no sudden reverence for the man he had envied and mistrusted. In dying, Kennedy had become a greater hero than he'd been in life. LBJ was seeking ways to legitimize himself and acquire some of the fallen President's popularity.[2]

According to LBJ: "…for millions of Americans I was still illegitimate, a naked man with no presidential covering, a pretender to the throne, an illegal usurper.…And then there were the bigots… and the Eastern intellectuals, who were waiting to knock me down before I could even begin to stand up. The whole thing was almost unbearable."[3] His illness had crossed the borders of sanity into the dark territory of paranoia.

The first night of his presidency was hard on him. He expected the country to sink into mourning and feared that the national mood might trigger one of his own immobilizing depressions. He was so anxiety filled that he insisted Horace Busby spend the night watching him sleep, even though Lady Bird was there. When Busby tried to tiptoe away, LBJ called him back.[4]

LBJ retained most of Kennedy's staff. In view of his paranoia about people loyal to Kennedy, one might well wonder why.

"I needed that White House staff," he said. "Without them I would have had absolutely no chance of gaining the support of the media or the Easterners or the intellectuals. And without that support I would have absolutely no chance of governing the country."[5] While he was correct about the importance of the news media to any presidency, his assumption that the Eastern establishment was against him stemmed from paranoia, not fact.

Then there was the jealousy factor. Robert Kintner, a special assistant to LBJ, observed that Johnson always felt painfully outclassed by the suave, popular, eloquent Kennedy.[6] Moreover, Kennedy had been handsome, had possessed a beautiful, stylish, patrician wife, a rich, influential family, an aristocrat's education, and an enviable war record. Before he had spent two months in the White House, LBJ called together his top government public affairs officers to complain: "You're not getting my picture on the front page the way you did the Kennedys."[7] Again the President assumed that the press was at his beck and call.

Most of the time, LBJ's ego suffered when he compared himself to the Kennedy family. Joseph Califano, who became his special assistant, says: "His envy for the glamour that surrounded the Kennedys in life and the adulation that attended them in death was Shakespearean. He yearned for appreciation from the Ivy League intellectuals whose ideas he had turned into law, from the young to whom he opened the doors of higher education; from the poor and the black."[8] But this became unattainable because these were the people who either opposed the Vietnam War or were sent to fight it.

LBJ was not the only person measuring the new President against the previous one. One of the people who compared LBJ to Kennedy and found the former less impressive was the Secretary of

State who served both of them, Dean Rusk. He thought LBJ was a crybaby, whereas Kennedy maintained a quiet stoicism even when the stresses of the presidency were at their highest. Whatever came, said Rusk, be it success or failure, Kennedy kept his equanimity.[9]

Some of the differences that Rusk found are the differences between a markedly manic depressive and someone who is not. The difference is in emotional intensity. "Whereas John Kennedy's approach on issues such as civil rights was often intellectual, Lyndon Johnson's just gushed out of him like lava from a volcano."[10] Rusk's next observation was that Johnson, unlike his predecessor, could never be content with a modest objective.[11] Here we have LBJ's megalomania. Last, Rusk contrasts Kennedy with the dominating, overpowering LBJ: "...John Kennedy was in no sense an overwhelming personality. There was no 'Kennedy' treatment comparable with the 'LBJ' treatment...."[12]

Completion of Kennedy's program was insufficient for LBJ, who was determined to surpass it. For example, believing that the public had considered Kennedy's administration spendthrift, LBJ insisted on presenting a smaller budget.[13]

We are all creatures of moods, but except on rare occasions, such as periods of mourning, our moods do not dominate our lives the way they do those of manic depressives, nor do our moods change with astonishing speed. LBJ's emotional liability caught the eye of historian Eric Goldman: "He was given to jubilant enthusiasm and deep gloom, and he could go from one to the other in minutes. He made little effort to control these moods."[14] Whether LBJ tried to rein himself in or not, we cannot know: intense moods are not easy for anyone to control, and his were usually at the far end of the scale. He seemed to go through life carried by his moods like a man on a runaway horse.

"Mercurial" is a term that journalists commonly apply to public figures who behave like manic depressives but are undiagnosed or unacknowledged to have that disorder. "Labile" is a psychiatry's term for the same behavior.

Mania drives the mind to work at top speed. LBJ had that speed. He also was blessed with an extraordinary memory. He sopped up information from reports and briefings, made sense out of piles of facts and statistics and, most important, remembered almost all of it.[15] His friend Abe Fortas called him "a pack rat for information. And he was very, very intelligent."[16]

LBJ had the kind of memory that successful politicians need. It is a memory for people's names and for personal details about anyone who could possibly be useful or make trouble.[17] What is less common for politicians is the ability to recall the minutia of legislation. People in government often rely on their staffs to act as walking memories for that kind of detail. LBJ's mind was a legislative encyclopedia.[18]

In addition to his megabyte memory, LBJ could summon what very few manics can command: great powers of concentration. This was an essential element of his talent for politics. He could analyze a problem, think through to a solution, and carry it out to completion without being distracted by the multitude of demands on his time.[19]

It may be enough for a philosopher to out-think his peers, but a politician also has to out-work the competition—or be very lucky—if he is to rise to the top. Mania provided LBJ with enough energy to excel at whatever he undertook, and age had not diminished that energy when he reached the White House. Author and political observer Theodore White wrote: "Of the man it may be said that he could not stop....An unbelievable physical vitality fueled him."[20] LBJ for the most part made use of that energy. He was alert and would begin working the moment his eyes opened. Before he left his bed, he read whatever material remained from the previous night.[21]

Here is his account of the kind of grueling schedule that was typical for him as President: "I awaken… every morning at 6:30 and immediately review the intelligence reports from 130–odd countries… the cables that have come in overnight, the reports from the commanders in the field, the engagements of our troops; I look at the losses we have suffered and the developments that have taken place during the night. And, the last thing I do before I go to sleep is to finish the night reading...."

That task might not begin until midnight and would take him two or three hours. He would read and make decisions on some hundred or so documents before he was done.[22] In this instance it was the Vietnam War that occupied him, but previously, only the subject matter differed. The schedule was the same.

For a politician, what a priceless asset that energy was. Economist John Kenneth Galbraith thought that the President never went to bed and never stopped working.[23] That was an exaggeration but it was customary for LBJ to sleep only four or five hours per night with perhaps a nap in the afternoon.[24] He was as intolerant of others' need for sleep as he was oblivious to their need for rest. He thought nothing of calling his Secretary of State or Defense at any ungodly hour of the night and never offered an apology for waking the man.[25]

LBJ behaved as though convinced that the night owl got the worm. His post-midnight activity may not have been terribly valuable, but the total output of work that his energetic insomnia permitted was impressive.

With his bottomless energy, he rarely had to stop because of fatigue. He was often seen watching three different television news shows at a time, while simultaneously talking on three telephones.[26] Perhaps because of his virtually unlimited energy, LBJ had a poor sense of limits in other areas too. Like a woman who pours on the perfume, he never seemed to know when enough was enough.

The President's mind, in mania, was a car with an accelerator stuck to the floor and no brakes. His physical restlessness and unceasing thought processes made him uncomfortable when he had nothing to do. George Reedy noted: "Relaxation was something he did not understand and would not accord to others."[27]

A characteristic often seen in mania was LBJ's penchant for gift-giving. According to his son-in-law, Patrick Nugent, LBJ gave to everybody: "He was in the habit of giving people something or other whether it was a pocketknife or a cigarette lighter, and it always had his name on it....he'd pull something out of his pocket and say, 'Here, I want you to keep this as a momento of your visit to the Ranch; but for God's sake don't embarrass me by leaving it in a whorehouse someplace."[28]

His generosity could be as profound and impulsive as it was extensive. Driving near the ranch one day he passed a family of six living in a one-room cabin. He had two more rooms added on.[29] As mentioned above, LBJ's staff kept track of birthdays, anniversaries, weddings, etc., and sent appropriate gifts, all of which increased his political capital. However, trying to buy loyalty wasn't the whole story. He seemed to have a genuine compassion for misfortune. When a reporter needed expensive medical care, LBJ secretly offered him financial help.[30]

Political gifts are like boomerangs: the benefit returns to the giver. LBJ went even further than most. According to attorney general Ramsey Clark, "Johnson was a compulsive giver. He just wanted to give something always. I don't think I have ever gone by that he didn't wind up giving me something.... I think I've got four or five copies of *My Hope For America*, (by LBJ).

When he was President, LBJ liked to give his aides gold: gold tie clasps and cuff links, gold buttons for jackets, a gold cigarette lighter, all bearing the Presidential Seal.[31] On occasion, gifts for the staff were substantial, and ranged from top-of-the-line cameras and expensive clothing to luxury cars.[32] However, says George Reedy, the suit, the jewelry, whatever, "...was always followed by an outpouring of irrelevant abuse ... and a few members of his staff noted that the gift was inevitably tax deductible on his part. Furthermore, some of the most lavish presents frequently went to members who had performed no services other than adulation."[33]

The President was suspicious of Latin Americans, but he felt they were winnable, and that made them suitable subjects for American largess. His manic generosity kicked in when he had the U.S. Treasury for a pocketbook.

According to Dean Rusk, "LBJ was especially interested in the Western Hemisphere. He used to tell us, 'This hemisphere is our home. If we can't make it work here, where we live, how can we expect to make it work anywhere else?'"

LBJ was particularly lavish with gifts of photographs of himself. The President's gifts had little relevance to what the recipient could use, and, as Ramsey Clark indicated, he often gave the same LBJ-labeled gift over and over to the same person.[34] In this triumph of ego over generosity, manic assets were becoming detriments.

LBJ's generosity was reversible. When a cameraman, Moe Levy, admired one of the Johnson goats during a tour of the ranch, LBJ gave it to him. Subsequently, in order to take pictures, Levy had some furniture at the ranch moved without LBJ's permission. Outraged at this insubordination, the President yelled "Moe, get your goddam equipment out of here right now—and bring back the goddam goat!"[35]

A sense of humor is, these days, almost an entrance requirement for a politician, and mania provides it. Those who are not genuinely witty rely on speechwriters to supply them with ready-made humor. LBJ sometimes did this, but he also had his own stories. The following joke may or may not have originated with him: "Every time Grandma got pregnant, they took her to the plains so the Indians could attack her."[36] The vulgarity sounds genuine.

Dean Rusk and many others considered LBJ to be "a very funny man." Rusk delighted in the Johnson impersonation of Dean Acheson testifying before a congressional committee.[37] The LBJ version of Harry Truman was considered equally "hilarious," as was his imitation of Eisenhower delivering a vacuous, rambling paragraph to the press.[38]

LBJ became particularly adept at denigrative mimicry. George Reedy says that the Johnson versions of people for whom he had little use—Bobby Kennedy, Adlai Stevenson, Estes Kefauver, and Richard Nixon, were very funny. However, Reedy insists that his boss was not truly witty: "He had no other form of humor—except for the practical joke—and whatever wit was found in his speeches invariably came from a ghost." Reedy thought that LBJ's humor was chiefly inspired by latrines.[39]

A good humorist fits his performance to his audience. In his later years, at least, LBJ would tell offensive stories in the presence of people who did not want to hear them, and he would tell the same story to an audience who had heard it many times before.[40] By the time he had reached this stage of self-absorption, his comic gifts were no longer the asset they had been.

Mania as extreme as that of LBJ eventually gave him a corrosive personality. One could feel, in his presence, that one had walked into a fog of acid, with little stings everywhere. His jokes often involved teasing: his sense of humor had a wide streak of cruelty in it.[41] He enjoyed ribbing others, playing practical jokes on them, and seemed to find their discomfort hilarious.

After he bought an amphibious car, he took his elderly cousin Oreole for a ride without telling her about the vehicle's capabilities. Then he drove into the Pedernales River while she screamed. During a visit to the ranch by two Cabinet members, LBJ took them for a ride in a golf cart. He ran at top speed at a cameraman kneeling in the driveway and barely missed the man. While Lady Bird screamed "Honey, don't!" LBJ made a second pass at him.[42]

The exuberance of the manic, so attractive when appropriately expressed, also began to spoil in the heat of LBJ's egotism. While leading a tour of the ranch for reporters, LBJ climbed into a pigpen to show off its residents, then chased some steers across a field. During the chase, the President was flapping and whooping like a demented crane. He also put his hat on a bull's head, a comparison he should not have invited.[43] On another occasion, LBJ took a strong liking to someone. Hugh Sidey describes what happened to one unsuspecting guest. LBJ's "...exuberance often bubbled over, like the time he dragged poet Carl Sandburg from Mansion to Cabinet meeting and then held a press conference from the Truman balcony, shouting to the reporters on the lawn...."[44]

A manic depressive may be raised to heights of eloquence by mania, but more commonly, it merely makes him annoying. Mania increases the speed, loudness, and quantity of his conversation, and these alterations, in themselves, tend to render his verbal output less tolerable. Mania can also reduce the quality of his conversation by making it disorganized and eliptic, and consequently hard to follow. All of these faults appeared in the talk of LBJ, particularly the problem of excess. Theodore White, a chronicler of presidents, considered this one the most talkative.[45]

LBJ was certainly no Calvin Coolidge. In fact, his pressure of speech was reminiscent of an open fire hydrant. He had enough flow to give 22 speeches in one day. The private backgrounders he gave to the press often lasted three hours and once ran on for four hours beyond that. Nothing he said received proper emphasis because he inundated people with information and ran nonstop at high speed.[46] Even in private conversation he gave monologues lasting over three hours without pausing or permitting a pause for the listener to make a trip to the bathroom.[47]

Moreover, he did not want to let anyone else talk. Bobby Baker observes: "When Lyndon Johnson was in a manic mood, conversation with him turned into a soliloquy; in a 90-minute conversation he might dominate 88 of those minutes and then drum his fingers impatiently while the other fellow claimed his allotted two minutes."[48]

It is bad enough to be an uninterruptable talker. To be jealous of anyone else who tries to talk is over the top. LBJ's guided tours of his ranch were all accompanied by his monologues. When he took two fellow Texans for a ride, one of the men, Ed Clark, a millionaire banker who was also a lawyer, insisted on interjecting a sentence here and there. LBJ screamed at him to shut up seven separate times, to no avail. Finally the host seized the leg of his other guest, Allen Duckworth, a political columnist, and ordered: "If Clark won't stop talking, you quit listening to him."[49]

Manics are known for making long distance phone calls, especially in the wee hours of the morning. LBJ made those calls all day long, sometimes three calls at a time. On one occasion, Horace Busby had to rendezvous with his boss at the National Airport and found him hoarding three telephone booths. LBJ said: "Horace, don't try to use any of those three phones. I've got long distance callin progress on all three."[50]

LBJ could average 80 calls a day, many of them inessential.[51] Another sign of telephone addiction was his supply of phones. He kept them in his bathroom, bedroom, dining room, living room, theater, and in all his cars, boats and planes. At the ranch they hung from trees, sprouted around the pool, and sat on a raft. He also had them around the White House pool. His shortwave system allowed him to phone anyone in an LBJ car that was within 20 miles of the ranch. And, Big Brother style, the ranch had 13 loudspeakers to carry the master's voice.[52]

Of course, his speeches were subject to a certain amount of discipline by his speechwriters, although LBJ would depart from the text. But his conversation was pure LBJ and when he wasn't revealing the dirty secrets of fellow politicians or telling smutty jokes, he liked to brag about his wealth.[53] The exception was when he was talking to the press. He told Henry Luce, the Editorial Chairman of *Time*: "...I'm worth three or four hundred thousand, and that's that."[54]

Johnson frequently boasted about his sexual prowess. This was an LBJ tradition that began when he was in college.[55] As President, LBJ wanted it known that he *exceeded* the sexual exploits of his predecessor. He insisted that he "...had more women by accident than Kennedy had on purpose."[56] As he had done in college, LBJ told his male friends not only about the women he bedded, he went into anatomical detail and pornographic description of the action.[57]

In a performance that must have made his wife cringe, LBJ perfectly blended bragging with indiscretion. When he took people on a tour of the ranch house and reached his bedroom, he would wave at the bed, saying: "Ah've had hundreds of women in my life, but let me tell you, nobody is better in bed than Lady Bird."[58]

Special assistant Jack Valenti said that the President was too frank in his press interviews.[59] LBJ's indiscretion became an element in his foreign policy. In March, 1964, the Organization of American States expressed disapproval of the way LBJ handled the crisis in Panama. The President's public comment about the O.A.S. was: "It couldn't pour piss out of a boot if the instructions were written on the heel."[60] This remark was a typical response to criticism.

LBJ was greedy about information: he could not have enough of it, and his generosity did not apply to this commodity. We have seen how unwilling he was to share power in any form. That was true for information too, when he was not carried away by the indiscretion of mania. He made Nixon's concern about leaks look almost nonchalant. No one at the White House, not even Cabinet members, was permitted to give out any information without LBJ's go-ahead. If word got out anyway, say, about some project, LBJ would pull the plug on it regardless of the consequences. His commissions and task forces were also muzzled.[61]

Information could leave the LBJ White House only with his permission, and he did not give it often. The information that he guarded most jealously was information about himself. It had long been his policy to hide his motives. Special counsel Harry McPherson observed that LBJ would not reveal his own opinion on an issue until he knew where the other person stood and he had decided how to manipulate that person.[62] That was a direct translation of information into power.

LBJ once commented, "A man in a tough situation rarely reveals the real reasons why he does something."[63] Perhaps for him all situations were tough. He was especially proud of his ability to pull the wool over the eyes of the press: "...the damn press always accused me of things I didn't do. They never once found out about the things I did do."[64]

LBJ was not a man you would want to know your own secrets because he would use them against you. When he was in the White House, he had the FBI taping anyone who might possibly make trouble for him at the Democratic National Convention of 1964, where he was virtually unopposed. The FBI also obligingly planted bugs in embassies and private homes to collect information about Nixon's campaign in 1968. Nixon was not the first in the White House to tape the unwitting. LBJ secretly had more than 10,000 telephone conversations recorded and taped conversations with people in the Oval Office.[65]

At this stage of his life, what had LBJ's mania done to his character and career? The career had reached its pinnacle: the man's character was becoming monstrous. By contrast, Secretary of State, Dean Rusk, said. "Although some would not agree, I found Lyndon Johnson to be a man of great personal kindness."[66] The two always got along well, particularly since Rusk wholeheartedly endorsed LBJ's Vietnam policies. But special assistant Joseph Califano expressed the majority view: "I watched him...humiliate those he loved as well as those he hated."[67]

LBJ's mania, whatever benefits it brought to him, made him a dangerous man to be around. It turned him into a dictator in the office and in his own home. Mania, like a cruel god, gave him big dreams and drove him to failure; it gave him an extraordinary career, then sabotaged it; and finally, manic paranoia rendered him unfit for office.

1963

Soon after being sworn in, LBJ dismissed three out of his four military aides because they "get in my way." This brought much protest from the Pentagon. LBJ's response was: "...tell the admiral and tell the general that if their little men like to believe they can pressure their Commander in Chief on what his strategy ought to be in war or what his decision ought to be in peace...they don't know their Commander in Chief."[68]

That was just his first salvo. He did not seek the opinions of the Joint Chiefs of Staff, nor did he let them know what he was going to do.[69]

According to Secretary of Defense Robert McNamara, Kennedy had requested planning for a total withdrawal of U.S. forces in 1963. The Secretary, on September 3, formally approved the plan to start by returning 1,000 men by the end of the year.[70] On October 2 of that year, Kennedy announced that he expected U.S. advisors to have finished training the South Vietnamese and the U.S. forces would begin leaving within three months, withdrawal to be completed in 1965.[71] Whatever the Cold War meant to Kennedy, he was reluctant to fight it in Vietnam with American armed forces.

LBJ was another story. An eager Cold Warrior in his Senate days, he wasted no time taking on the Communists of Vietnam. Kennedy was barely in the ground when the new President agreed to a large-scale program of clandestine warfare.[72] Nevertheless, LBJ wanted it to appear that, as he finished Kennedy's term, he was merely continuing JFK's policies in Vietnam. He wasn't. In late 1963, LBJ, while declaring the opposite, began to depart from Kennedy's withdrawal plan for Vietnam.

On December 2, Senator William Fulbright warned him to get out of Vietnam: "...I'll be goddamned if I don't think it's hopeless. ...You don't want to send a whole lot more men in there, I don't think."[73] Nevertheless, LBJ quickly approved a plan for open-ended, full-scale war to make South Vietnam strong and non-Communist. On December 21, his administration gave an open-ended pledge of support to the leaders of South Vietnam, canceling Kennedy's target for bringing most American troops home by the end of 1965.[74]

Meanwhile, the President was also lying about something more personal. While Bobby Baker worked for him in the Senate, LBJ had nothing but words of high praise: "He's my strong right arm, the last man I see at night, the first one I see in the morning."[75] On one occasion, LBJ told Baker: "If I had a son, Bobby, I would want him to be just like you." He told others that Baker was "one of my most trusted, most loyal and most competent friends."[76] In 1960, LBJ had maintained: "That Bobby Baker is the greatest man who ever worked for me." The Bakers and Johnsons saw each other socially. LBJ gave Baker cattle which were cared for at the ranch, and Baker named two of his children Lynda and Lyndon.[77] Rarely did LBJ lavish such praise and sentiment on anyone.

Baker became rich while working in the Senate. In nine years, his net assets rose from $11,025.00 in 1954 to $2,166,866.00.[78] He hadn't won a lottery and the money was gotten too quickly to have been acquired legally.

On October 7, 1963, Baker resigned as secretary to the Senate majority. LBJ suddenly was saying that he barely was acquainted with the man.[79] When asked about Bobby, he maintained that Baker was "no protégé of anyone."[80] Eventually, on January 5, 1966, Baker was indicted and then sentenced to three years in a federal prison for, among other crimes, conspiracy to defraud the government, theft, misappropriation of $100,000 in campaign funds, as well as income tax evasion.[81]

The President was concerned that the story remained in the news longer than he thought it should. He believed that it held people's attention because, he insisted, Bobby Kennedy delivered daily briefings to the press about it.[82]

Despite the pressures and frustrations of his job, LBJ's dream had come true. He was the President, the People's choice, he had climbed to the absolute top. This made him more than happy, it made him manic. There weren't enough hours in the day and he begrudged those from 2 AM to 6 AM that had to be surrendered to sleep. His version of rest was merely a change of activity.[83]

Pressure of speech glued him to the telephone. Senator Everett Dirksen complained that LBJ calling him six times in one day made it impossible to get any work accomplished. Senator Humphrey testified to LBJ's flights of ideas: "I've had 10 calls from the man today. He has a new idea every 30 minutes and he calls me about it.

I can't do anything he wants done because I don't have time to get going between calls."[84] Neither of these men moved at LBJ's pace.

Luci said about her father: "I can't ever tell what he is going to do. He can't either."[85] That was because her father was frequently ruled by whim. His behavior rarely was constrained by consideration for others. He not only appeared where he was uninvited and unwanted, but when he accepted invitations, no one could rely on his actually showing up. During his presidency, he never gave the Secret Security agents enough notice to adequately prepare for his comings and goings.[86]

LBJ's impulsive demands created confusion and uncertainty for Lady Bird and the staff when he was President. One morning he was in the mood for a party and said: "Let's have Congress down this afternoon." The harried White House staff had suddenly to provide music, food, and drink for more than a thousand guests.[87] Liz Carpenter observed that the staff began to look on the President's sudden and often impractical demands as a sort of game, a challenge.[88]

Special assistant Joseph Califano recalled: "Life at the ranch would always be unpredictable. We never knew when we would work or play....lunch could be anywhere from 1 to 4 o'clock; it might be at the LBJ ranch, on the boat, or at one of the Johnson's other ranches. The President usually took a nap, which could last anywhere from 30 minutes to a couple of hours. Dinner might be at 8 or midnight and its location was just as uncertain. On Sundays we had no idea whether we would return (to Washington) that evening or Monday morning, afternoon, or evening, and we often departed on less than an hour's notice."[89]

LBJ's impulsivity, whether it was deliberate sabotage or not, came to appear like harassment to the press he tried so hard to win over. The White House press corps was accustomed to Kennedy's well-prepared press conferences, which were held in the State Department Auditorium and announced well in advance. LBJ, on the other hand, held his wherever caprice prompted and whenever the mood struck.

The press corps could only deal with this uncertainty by always being around in case the President summoned them. They could not afford to go home to their families until late at night. This constant being on call, plus the need to dash suddenly across the country following LBJ, was wearing for all of them.[90]

The first holiday-season that LBJ spent in the White House as president was a time of great euphoria, perhaps the happiest time of his life. His poll ratings were high. He was still wooing the press, taking them not only to his ranch, where he gave them all LBJ ashtrays, but to visit Texas Governor John Connally at the Texas State Mansion and to go hunting at the A.W. Moursund ranch.

He was so uninhibited that he grabbed his unmarried daughter's dress to show the reporters she was not pregnant. He was so beyond restraint and good sense that he said to a Secret Service Agent: "Damn it, I don't want you tailgatin' me. Now you keep that wagon back outta sight or I'm gonna shoot out your tires!"[91]

The new President made the 65-mile trip from his ranch to Austin to join the White House press at their New Year's party.[92] He went to 4 parties on New Year's Eve, including the aforementioned press party, and did not get home to Lady Bird until morning.[93]

CHAPTER **10**

SEX, LIES, AND LBJ

★ ★ ★ ★ ★ ★

George Reedy assessed the period before LBJ's own sweeping election to the Presidency as one when "there was no trace of the ugly arrogance which had made him so disliked in so many quarters." However, the boss was still cracking the whip over his staff in his own inimitable way, and one other factor had not changed; LBJ's temper was as unpredictable and terrifying to his staff as ever.[1] The "ugly arrogance" gave a command performance in the White House.

The President continued to be an extremely erratic person to work for. He was also, at times, the most considerate of employers. Aide Frank Cormier brought his parents to the White House to be introduced to the President. LBJ gave them a personal tour, and told them: "Miz Cormier, your son is in a critical position at a critical time in our nation's history. He's in a job where he could make lot's of mistakes—but he doesn't make very many!" Limited though the praise was, it delighted Mrs. Cormier. LBJ also gave the Cormiers a presidential medallion with the presidential head on it and a warmly autographed photograph of himself.[2] On another occasion, the secretaries were the recipients of LBJ's consideration. He thought it would be a treat for them to meet and have dinner

141

with royalty, and so invited them to the White House dinner given for Princess Margaret.[3]

When there are no rules to the game except those the boss makes up as he goes along, it is natural for employees to feel insecure and, if they stay long enough, to grow emotionally dependent on him. He becomes the sun in their sky, his good opinion is what they hope and pray for. They become as cowed and submissive as the worshippers of a vengeful god. However, most of them are unaware of what is happening to them and would deny it if it were pointed out.

An exception was special assistant Harry McPherson. "I was in danger just like everyone around him of capitulating to what you might call the Valenti syndrome, which was to judge myself as a person by his judgement.... When I was in favor, I was on top of the world; when I was out of favor, I was in the dumps. And that struck me as ridiculous. I made a number of efforts to pull back from...an intense relationship with him. It saved my sanity and my judgement...."[4] LBJ's scrutiny was continuous and no detail was too trivial. The President would make his male employees stand in a line for inspection and freely criticize what he saw.[5] Even Joseph Califano's tie came under the lens of LBJ's criticism as the boss, adding insult to criticism, declared: "That four-in-hand knot looks like a limp prick."

What it boiled down to was that people who worked for LBJ in the White House were not allowed to have private lives. Their master became enraged when, on one occasion, he could not reach Joseph Califano, his domestic affairs advisor, by telephone. LBJ insisted that Califano's office bathroom have a phone installed.[6] Califano observed that: "He wanted to control everything. His greatest outbursts of anger were triggered by people or situations that escaped his control...." Then came the further demand that when attending Mass, Califano must stay at the back of the church so that his driver could have quick access to him if LBJ called.[7]

The President insisted on knowing where his employees were

at all times. Larry Temple claims that if an employee went to the bathroom, the President insisted that the White House operators be informed of the employee's change of location.[8] Many were the times a staff member eating at a restaurant was summoned to the telephone to be asked by LBJ what he was eating and: "Now have you salted and peppered it?"[9] Horace Busby was once called to the phone only to be ordered back to the office to have lunch with the boss.[10]

LBJ resented members of his Cabinet taking time off. Even though it was the weekend, he would order the Secretary of Commerce, John Connor, to get off the golf course and come to work. Other Cabinet members were called back suddenly and needlessly from vacations.[11]

Any sign of activity that showed initiative on the part of someone else was intolerable to LBJ by the time he became President. In April of 1964, Under Secretary of State George Ball took steps, following LBJ's policy, to recognize the new government of Brazil. This made the President furious because he had not been told in advance: "Don't ever do that again," he yelled. "I don't care what hour in the morning it is, I want to know. I'm not saying what you did wasn't right, but after this I want to know."[12] In other words, if you worked for LBJ you were wrong even when you did the right thing if he had not pulled your strings first.

For this President, the world was divided into those he could control and those he could not. One of the latter was William Lewis, a young man that LBJ wanted to place in the Justice Department. LBJ announced that the job was waiting and told Lewis: "Bill, I have been observing you very closely, I have decided to make you an LBJ boy." Lewis refused the job and for the following 25 years LBJ scolded him every time they met: "Remember, Bill, you had your chance."[13] LBJ took it for granted that the only chance in life worth having was that of working for him.

Long before he seems certifiably psychotic, a manic may take risks that appear insane. This was true of LBJ, who drove his speedboat in dangerous high-speed turns while waving his arms at the scenery.[14] He was no safer on dry ground, roaring along the high-ways of Texas at just under 90 miles per hour, passing on hills in the wrong lane and forcing other drivers off the road while he hid the speedometer with his hat, so that his passengers could not see it.[15] That Spring, on one of those 90 mile an hour days, he must have been intensely manic. He had 4 reporters riding with him, 3 of them women whom he regaled with colorful descriptions of his bull's sex-ual prowess. He was drinking beer as he roared down the road.[16] Anyone else would have been arrested. It should surprise no one that recklessness also characterized some of LBJ's foreign policy.

In the White House as previously, his needs had to be satisfied at once, whether the demand was for peanut brittle, a particular kind of shirt, or a type of pen. The domestic staff, eager to avoid his rages, tried to stock up on whatever he might desire.[17]

George Reedy attests that: "...when his personal desires were at stake, he had absolutely no consideration for the situation in which other people found themselves. They were required to drop every-thing to wait upon him and were expected to forget their private lives in his interests. He even begrudged one of his top assistant's telephone call to his wife on their wedding anniversary."[18]

LBJ had no master plan to crush people into submission, he just did it naturally. Assistant Booth Mooney saw him constantly cutting down people who were already giving 110% of themselves.[19] One of these was Jack Valenti, who asserts that LBJ "...was a mean bully when he wanted to be and he could humiliate you, both publicly and privately. He would castigate you for being one millimeter off in what you were doing."[20]

Such an incident happened in the presence of Congressman Tip O'Neill and the Massachusetts delegation at the 1964 Democratic National Convention. LBJ wanted Valenti to bring him a recent favorable poll. The aide was not in sight, so LBJ screamed "Where's Jack Valenti?" Valenti appeared moments later to be greeted with "Where the hell were you?" The answer was that he was getting a cup of coffee. LBJ screamed again "You asshole! I told you never to leave my office!" The raking of the loyal Valenti continued for some time in front of the astonished delegation.[21]

Theodore White calls him "a President who yelled and snarled. ...He would snarl at the telephone operators at the White House switchboard and berate them until one burst into tears; he could be harsh and threatening to the members of his Secret Service protective escort...."[22] White observed that the first months of the Presidency were a time when LBJ's "harsh, almost brutal treatment of his people reached a peak," and "the President was consuming astonishing amounts of liquor without showing signs of inebriation".[23]

Mania continued to inflame every aspect of LBJ's life, including the sexual. President Johnson earned his own nicknames: the "Dancing President", the "Kissing President" (he always aimed for the mouth and gave women a good feel, if not a good feeling), and a few thought of him as the "Porn President."[24]

It seems that LBJ never missed an opportunity to place a hand on an attractive woman and if opportunity was lacking, he created one. At a state dinner at the White House for Harold Wilson, LBJ gave a demonstration of how he seduced England's Prime Minister. He grabbed the wife of *Washington Post* correspondent Chalmers Roberts and demonstrated his technique on her as a crowd of guests watched.[25]

One day Vice President Hubert Humphrey heard the President's voice come over the intercom in Jack Valenti's office: "Jack, you listen to me. The next time you come in here, you knock. How do you know who I'll be fucking?"[26] And he wasn't kidding. The White House logs from 1965 on were notable for frequent unspecified 45-minute or one hour intervals. LBJ made it no secret that he was having sex in the Oval Office with several different women.[27]

The Presidency did as little to dampen LBJ's ardor as it did to JFK's. A White House staff member claimed that the man must have "extra glands."[28] One White House secretary recalls having sex with the President on a desk.[29] Another one was not so accomodating. She asked then Ambassador Carl Rowan to help her transfer away from the White House. She explained that when she was at the ranch, where no doors had locks, LBJ woke her up one night with the beam of a flashlight and said: "Move over, this is your President." Rowan had her transferred to the State Department.[30]

When David Brinkley and his wife were invited to visit the Johnsons at the ranch for a weekend, he was unable to attend, so she went alone. Mistake. LBJ kept trying to get her to go to bed with him.[31]

Mania appears to weaken internal censors of language and what emerges can be quite raunchy. LBJ used some of the ugliest language heard in the White House: "I may not know much, but I know the difference between chicken shit and chicken salad" was a favorite saying.

His remarks were often censorable: "Ford's economics is the worst thing that's happened to this country since pantyhose ruined finger-fucking."[32] His jokes continued to be redolent of the outhouse and his anecdotes still featured prominent politicians in compromising situations.[33]

The following is a demonstration of his connoisseurship of bovine pornography. He was asked what kind of civil rights conference he wanted. He answered by describing his prize bull, "...the biggest, best-hung bull in the hill country. In the spring he gets a hankering for those cows and he starts pawing the ground and getting restless. So I open the pen and he goes down the hill, looking for a cow, with his pecker hanging hard and swinging. Those cows get so goddamn excited, they get more and more moist to receive him, and their asses just start quivering and then they start quivering all over, every one of them is quivering as that bull struts into their pasture. Well, I want a quivering conference."[34]

Dean Acheson, who had seen a generation of politicians come

and go, said: "Let's face it, Mr. President, you just aren't a likeable man."[35] Acheson was being polite: this was an X-rated President.

George Reedy, who knew fewer politicians than Dean Acheson, but knew this one very well, agreed that it was not pleasant to be with LBJ, whose manners were insufferable, and sometimes purposely offensive.[36] At times it may have been true that LBJ deliberately used his own bad manners to humiliate and assert his dominance over others. But his publicly scratching his scrotum, picking his nose wherever he was, and belching at table could just as easily arise from his manic's lack of inhibition.[37]

In the office, LBJ would pull down his pants and underwear to show his hernia in the presence of the women who were his secretaries. Reedy noted: "He gloried in exposing his body...and constantly sought flimsy excuses for doing it."[38] At home, the President would strip for a backrub no matter how many women were in the room with him.[39] Walking around the house, he would lower his pants to examine a boil, or stand naked, brushing his teeth while he gave orders to Califano.[40]

LBJ's sudden, uninvited, and frequent intervals of nakedness failed to enhance his reputation with the press. During a press conference in Saigon, he did a complete change of clothing while the foreign correspondents watched.[41] He did the same thing on Air Force One in the presence of the press pool.[42] He insisted on nude swimming in the White House pool with a group of newspaper publishers and editors. This did not improve his treatment by their papers. LBJ also stripped in front of Katherine Graham, the dignified owner of the *Washington Post*.[43]

It was customary for LBJ to converse with his staff or give dictation while he was defecating in the bathroom with the door open.[44] Sometimes he didn't bother with the toilet, but opened his fly and peed into the sink, again with the door open.[45] In 1964, after the election, he took reporters around the ranch, and, stopping at the family graves, opened his pants and peed on the graves to make a point.[46]

In earlier centuries the crowned heads of Europe held court while they were still in bed. LBJ surpassed them, giving dictation in the presence of a room full of women, including a network reporter and daughter Lynda Bird, while he was receiving an enema.[47] His Secretary of the Treasury, C. Douglas Dillon, after being treated to a bathroom conference, resigned rather than endure more of them.[48]

After his 90 mile an hour drives in Texas were reported in *Time* magazine, LBJ screamed his outrage at the editors and later lied: "I am unaware that I have ever driven past 70."[49] He also had a letter sent to all U.S. highway officials requiring them to start a campaign against speeding: "We cannot tolerate this terrible...loss of life."[50]

Meanwhile, LBJ's reputation for dishonesty was growing. Most of the lying that the President did while in the White House concerned Vietnam. Here are a couple of examples: LBJ insisted that Richard Goodwin, who coined the phrase "the Great Society," never wrote speeches for him.[51] And despite announcing his candidacy for the Presidency, LBJ later insisted: "You folks who think I'm power-hungry may not believe it, but I never wanted this job for a minute."

What was so baffling about many of LBJ's lies is that they were so easily disproved.

When LBJ moved into the White House, he was not satisfied unless he felt he was in complete control of the press.[52] He insisted: "Reporters are puppets. They respond to the pull of the most powerful strings....There is no such thing as an objective news story....If you don't control the strings...you'll never get good coverage no matter how many great things you do for the masses of the people."[53]

One way that the President tried to control his press coverage was by pretending to be what he thought reporters wanted him to be. He said that he would appeal to Stewart Alsop as an historian, would talk about "backroom politics and political intrigues" with Evans and Novak, would appear dominating to Mary McCrory, and with Doris Fleeson would "sound like some impractical red-hot liberal."[54]

As President, he tried both bribery and threats: "I'll tell you everything. You'll know everything I do. You'll be as well informed as any member of the cabinet. There won't be any secrets except where the national security is involved. You'll be able to write everything." That was the carrot, here was the stick: "If you want to play it the other way, I know how to play it both ways too, and I know how to cut off the flow of news except in handouts."[55]

Aide Frank Cormier noted: "No other President ever spent so much time with so many newsmen, and on terms of such personal intimacy."[56] LBJ kept inviting reporters to the ranch and would send his own plane to get them.[57] He had long lunches at the White House for members of the media, paid visits to leading journalists and editors, gave private interviews to 40 of them, sent them gifts, called them on the phone, and held frequent press conferences.[58]

Inevitably, a backlash developed. Journalists were reluctant to write anything nice about the President for fear of appearing to have been corrupted. Once LBJ called Phil Potter of the *Baltimore Sun* to request a particular story. Potter told him to call the advertising department and hung up on him.[59]

President Johnson continued to abuse alcohol. He would, at lunch, drink several cups of coffee laced with bourbon.[60] At dinner, his usual quota was six scotch-and-sodas.[61] As LBJ reports it, Lady Bird told him he must run for President in 1964 because "…she told me that if I went back to the ranch then, I might get to drinking too much."[62] That sounds like a delicate way of expressing concern over his current levels of drinking. At the very least, it was an accurate prediction. According to Frank Cormier, during the 1964 campaign, "…a tumbler of Cutty Sark often was close at hand."

The press, so despised by LBJ, protected him throughout his presidency, keeping silent about his drinking marathons and his sexual exploits. But the lies eventually became insufferable. And the biggest assault on the truth was his pretending to be a peace candidate.

CHAPTER **11**

THE PEACE CANDIDATE

★ ★ ★ ★ ★ ★

1964

Vietnam was not the only enemy that LBJ wanted to attack. There was poverty. LBJ thought a war on poverty would be a springboard into the golden pages of history. He was certain it could get him elected in 1964 if he could make people believe that taxes would not go up to pay for it. He was ready to promise to deliver a slum-free America where everyone was healthy, happy, and well educated and it wouldn't cost a dime extra.[1]

On January 8, 1964, he said in his State of the Union address: "This administration today, here and now, declares unconditional war on poverty in America. I urge this Congress and all Americans to join me in that effort....It will not be a short or easy struggle, no single weapon or strategy will suffice, but we shall not rest until that war is won."

Behind the brave façade there was no plan, no prepared legislation, no idea of what administrative structure would be necessary.[2] It was a typically manic undertaking: long on hype, short on commitment. On January 20, LBJ said: "We know what must be done, and this nation of abundance can surely afford to do it."

George Reedy, who became press secretary, adds: "Neither statement, it would turn out, was even remotely true."

On February 3, LBJ was already feeling misgivings about the war in Vietnam, and said: "Anytime you got that many people against you that far from your home base, it's bad."[3]. Nevertheless, he informed the French and British that he would not negotiate until the enemy met all his terms. That is equivalent to requiring complete surrender even before the negotiations begin.[4]

The President had not completed his third month in the White House when he decided to see how the public would respond to bringing the war to North Vietnam and perhaps later to China. The media reacted as though he were offering the country another Korean War, which it could have been. An apparently chastened President instructed the Secretary of State to reassure the country that the U.S. would not become involved in military action outside of South Vietnam.

Meanwhile, LBJ gave orders for the U.S. Navy to participate secretly in South Vietnamese raids against North Vietnam.[5] That same month, the President directed American bombers to make secret raids in Laos.[6] When the Chinese reported the raids, LBJ denied them, even after 2 American planes were shot down in Laos.[7]

The Presidency acted on LBJ's already monstrous ego like a growth hormone. As he personalized every opposition to the war, turning it into a quarrel with himself, so he personalized every foreign event that involved the United States. There had been disputes with the Cuban government over the rights of Cuban fishing boats in U.S. waters. Castro retaliated by cutting off the water to the U.S. Naval base at Guantanamo Bay. In February, LBJ ordered the Navy to make the base self-sufficient in its water supply. He explained: "I had no doubt about Castro's purpose. He had decided, perhaps with Soviet encouragement, to take the measure of the new President of the United States, to push me a little and see what my response would be."[8] The new President was determined to demonstrate valor.

Despite his prevailing euphoria, there was a note of discouragement evident when the President addressed a group of educators on March 1, 1964. He said, with typical depressive discouragement: "I don't know what will be written about my administration. Nothing really seems to go right from morning 'till late at night."[9]

While the President kept telling the American people he was winning a war he refused to admit was taking place, he imposed a different set of deceptions on the American military. On March 4, 1964, the Joint Chiefs of Staff told the new President that there were only two choices in Vietnam: get out, or to win regardless of the cost. They felt that gradual escalation was not a winning strategy. However, LBJ was unwilling to get out, and equally unwilling to wage a visible, expensive war that would interfere with his expensive and visible Great Society program. So he kept his intentions hidden from the men who had to carry them out.[10]

In time, the JCS realized what was happening and kept written records of their disagreement with "the Asian Bay of Pigs," as they called gradual escalation, but they were unable to change LBJ's policy.

Senator Mansfield made a case for neutrality for Vietnam. On March 20, 1964, LBJ declared his opposition to neutrality "wherever it rears its ugly head."

In April, commentators Richard Harwood and Haynes Johnson saw an "ebullient" LBJ drop in without warning at a private party for journalists and editors. The President gave one of his great performances, featuring insider stories complete with mimicry of the politically powerful. Hubert Humphrey was there, and as LBJ discussed possible running mates for the '64 election he, as a guest put it, "played Hubert on a pole like a bait with a trout." He was staggeringly impulsive that night, telling a man he had just met that he was going to appoint him to the Civil Rights Commission. One guest remarked after LBJ left: "He was so exuberant, so high, that some of us wondered about his mental stability."

The euphoria did not last past the President's departure at two AM. Driving home, he voiced his anxiety and paranoia to Harwood and Johnson, who report the President's lament: "The Kennedy crowd and the intellectuals...were never going to accept him as President of the United States....They would cut him to pieces because of his speech, his mannerisms, his Southern origins....He knew his education would never qualify him in the eyes of the Ivy League; knew...most of his fellow Southerners would never forgive his demands for black rights and knew many blacks would never fully trust him for being Southern.... 'You just wait' he said. 'and see what happens when I put one foot wrong.'"[11] That same month it was a grim LBJ who hosted *Washington Post* editors at a White House lunch. The President found it hard to smile, his charm was in short supply, and he kept grumbling about press criticism.[12]

The Secretary of Defense, Robert McNamara, was recruited into LBJ's circle of deception. On May 15, before the campaign had begun, McNamara was ordered to report what he knew to be untrue: that American soldiers were not fighting, on land or in the air, but were merely training the South Vietnamese.[13] McNamara later explained that the President believed it was necessary to deceive the voters in order to prevent a Goldwater victory, which would be a threat to world stability.[14]

Charles Roberts, a contributing editor for *Newsweek*, rode in the plane with LBJ on May 22, 1964. "...that was what I would call the president in his manic phase," Roberts said. "He was a compulsive talker mostly when he was in this buoyant, euphoric mood after giving a speech or when things were going right for him."[15]

Then a depression set in a few days later, and brought with it pessimism about Vietnam. Privately, the President said on May 27, to national security advisor McGeorge Bundy: "...it looks to me like we're getting into another Korea. It just worries the hell out of me....I believe that the Chinese Communists are coming into it. I don't think that we can fight them ten thousand miles away from home. I don't think it's worth fighting for and I don't think that we can get out....what the hell is Vietnam worth to me? What is Laos worth to me? What is it worth to our country? No, we've got a treaty, but hell, everybody else's got a treaty out there and they're not doing anything about it."[16]

Bundy told him two days later that ninety percent of Americans were against going to war in Vietnam.[17]

So LBJ campaigned for the Presidency as a peace candidate against Senator Goldwater, an avowed hawk. James Reston of the *New York Times* was told by the President: "We won't abandon Saigon, and we don't intend to send in U.S. troops."

Did Johnson really believe that victory was impossible, and if so, why did he send in the troops? We have seen that Johnson, as a senator and Vice President, was an ardent cold warrior who believed that American military might could solve any problem. He did not begin to doubt this until he saw, in 1964, that the political situation in South Vietnam made a winning war effort by the South Vietnamese dubious. Yet he kept sending in the troops. Time and again, he said that he had no choice. His illness and the delusions that it engendered indeed left him no choice.

Mania returned that spring. Four times, a euphoric President took tourists along on his walks on the South Lawn of the White House. He said to each group: "All you ugly men get up front and all you pretty girls come back here with me."[18] His aide Frank Cormier recalled: "...rarely has he displayed such high good humor."[19]

LBJ's moods continued to zigzag. In May, despite the fact that his legislation was moving rapidly into law, depression struck again, with its attendant anxiety. LBJ always could find real things to worry about: his health, the dismal performance of South Vietnam's army, race riots in the cities. He reiterated his paranoid insistence that the Eastern press would never accept a Southerner despite assurances that he had the backing of such press luminaries as James Reston and Walter Lippmann. He asked several of the people closest to him whether he should run or not, and unanimously they answered yes.[20]

Congressman George Smathers informed LBJ on June 1 that no one he had spoken to in the House believed that "we ought to fight a war in that area of the world. To start committin' more and more is just got everybody really worried!"[21]

The President and his top Vietnam advisors met in Honolulu from June 1 to June 3, 1964, to make plans for escalating the war. LBJ also asked for a rough draft of what later was called the Tonkin Gulf Resolution so he could have a free hand with Congress. Special assistant Joseph Valenti recalled: "He wanted something in writing at some point. He wanted to go to the Congress and get the Congress to approve and authorize the Southeast Asian adventure."[22] On June 23, the President said again, "...the United States seeks no wider war."[23]

People around the President, for their own reasons, continued to advise him to run. Disregarding their advice, on June 12, the President dictated a statement declaring he would not run for election. He was wounded by press criticism and by claims that he was power hungry. He showed the announcement to his wife, who argued against it.[24] That same day, he told senior aide Jack Valenti that he wanted to resign. Valenti recalled: "...he said to me that there was such a general disregard, even distaste for him, that no matter what achievements were made, no matter how far toward a more decent and abundant life he could bring the disadvantaged and the dispossessed of this nation, ...there would remain this exposure to the raw breath of relentless critics."[25] Although this would become an accurate prediction of what LBJ and his war would bring to pass, it was his depression and paranoia speaking at that time, for his popularity was high.

Frustrated by the press, LBJ, was still able to find amusement during the summer in playing with the ambitions of his former colleagues. Teasing, though it masquerades as humor, usually inflicts pain and asserts dominance. The President indulged in it repeatedly during the summer of '64 by dangling the Vice Presidency before three Senators: Thomas Dodd, Eugene McCarthy, and Hubert Humphrey.[26] LBJ was too politically savvy not to guess that he was earning their enmity, but mania makes one feel invulnerable, and act recklessly.

The summer was not a period of unalloyed joy. Euphoric mania often evolves into irritable mania, as it did for the President. He began treating members of the media like yoyos, alternately caressing and cursing them.[27] Periods of depression also clouded his days, bringing the usual fears of being rejected by the voters, and, following his pattern, LBJ talked about not running.[28]

For LBJ, mania and anxiety were often intertwined. His latest worry was that Robert Kennedy had only to appear at the Democratic National Convention to be nominated by acclamation. LBJ's first step to diminish the Bobby Kennedy threat was to tell him he would not be chosen as Vice President.[29]

The prelude to the campaign drama was cruelty and a lie. After LBJ told Robert Kennedy, on July 27th, that he would not be the Vice Presidential candidate, the President invited three influential Washington correspondents to lunch at the White House. He kept them there for four hours, giving one of his manic performances. The high point of it was his reenactment of his rejection and humiliation of Kennedy. He did it, he said, because "There was a little group that felt the Attorney General (Robert Kennedy) was God...." Later, LBJ swore to Kennedy that he had not leaked anything about their meeting. It was obvious that this was a lie, and Kennedy said so.[30]

On July 31, 1964, American "advisors" had participated in a South Vietnamese attack on two North Vietnamese islands, Hon Nieu and Hon Me.

Two days later, in retaliation, three North Vietnamese torpedo boats exchanged fire with the U.S. destroyer Maddox. The Maddox fired first. The North Vietnamese responded by firing three torpedos at the Maddox. Two missed and one was a dud.

LBJ lied again when he said on August 4, that the destroyers Maddox and Turner Joy had been attacked by North Vietnamese torpedos. McNamara eventually wrote that there was no attack on either ship on August 4.[31] Later, LBJ said: "Hell, I think we might have fired at a whale."[32] In retaliation against this never-happened attack, the U.S. sent 64 planes against 4 North Vietnamese targets, damaging or destroying 25 ships.[33]

The President limited the American response to one bombing raid so that he could, for the duration of the presidential campaign, continue to wear the feathers of a dove. While plans were being made for the bombing of North Vietnam, he exclaimed on August 29: "I haven't chosen to enlarge the war." On September 25 he insisted: "There are those that say you ought to go north and drop bombs.... We don't want our American boys doing the fighting for Asian boys."[34]

Actually, he was preparing to do all of it, as he indicated in a cable he sent to General Taylor: "...it seems to me that what is much more needed...is a larger and stronger use of...appropriate military strength on the ground and on the scene...."[35]

After the second, but nonexistent, attack on American destroyers in the Gulf of Tonkin, LBJ hurried over to the office of his National Security Advisor, McGeorge Bundy and said that he was going to make a national speech announcing retaliation. He added that he needed backup from Congress. Bundy interrupted, suggesting that they "think it over." LBJ retorted: "I didn't ask you that. I told you to help me get organized." [36]

In this artificial crisis atmosphere, the Tonkin Gulf Resolution was quickly passed by Congress in August. It authorized the President to respond to aggression in Southeast Asia. However it was not intended as a substitute for a declaration of war, or an authorization to increase 16,000 military advisors in South Vietnam to an army of 550,000, though LBJ eventually used it for those purposes.

There was an election to win, and the anticipation of a successful campaign was lifting the spirits of LBJ. Theodore White described the rising mania of LBJ in the days preceding the Democratic National Convention: "For days his sense of euphoria and goodwill had been building. Master of all he surveyed, stage manager of his own Convention; he faced the appetizing prospect of a campaign against Barry Goldwater...."[37]

On August 25, LBJ told George Reedy that he would not accept the nomination: "And I don't want this power of the Bomb. I just don't want these decisions that I'm being required to make. (Decisions of any kind are hard to make in a depression, which also diminishes self-esteem.)...And I know that I'm *not* the best in the country."[38]

He continues with his chief aide, Walter Jenkins:"And I do not believe I can physically and mentally carry the responsibilities of the bomb and the world and the Negroes and the South....Now there are younger men and better-prepared men and better-trained men and Harvard-educated men. And I know my limitations."[39]

The following day the mania was back and the President walked a pack of reporters around the South Lawn of the White House. It was 89 degrees in the shade. He led them around for an hour and a half, talking cheerfully all the while. One reporter told his bureau chief: "We're dropping like flies. It's a death march!"[40]

The still energetic President continued with a full schedule for the rest of the day, including phone calls to 70 senators and congressmen, 30 governors, and innumerable business and labor leaders.[41]

At midnight, LBJ asked George Reedy to walk with him on the South Lawn, but this was different from the manic morning walk. He told Reedy again that he would withdraw from the presidential race. He was going back to his ranch. Reedy tried to talk him out of it, saying that if he withdrew Goldwater might win, but LBJ countered that a Goldwater victory was preferable to a 4-year fight with Bobby Kennedy.

The President told Reedy to write a withdrawal speech. Reedy refused, but LBJ insisted and the speech was written. It said: "After 33 years in political life most men acquire enemies, as ships accumulate barnacles. The times require leadership about which there is no doubt and a voice that men of all parties, sections and color can follow. I have learned after trying very hard that I am not that voice or that leader."

It took Lady Bird hours to persuade her husband not to deliver the speech.[42]

The following day, the 27th, LBJ was riding the up escalator again when he reached Atlantic City. Senator Humphrey noted: "He was very 'high' that weekend; I think that convention, which he'd managed every minute of, every movement, every motion, every gesture, everything; that was the greatest time of his presidency and I think of his life."[43] Humphrey well understood that for LBJ, control was everything.

The day after the convention, according to Humphrey, Johnson was still exuberant, and ordered his running mate and Mrs. Humphrey to go flying off with him to the ranch. It did not matter to the President that the Humphreys had their own plans, When the plane was about to takeoff, LBJ saw Katherine Graham, owner of the *Washington Post*, standing nearby. He insisted that she also come to Texas with them. Ignoring her objections, he practically carried her off. Humphrey adds: "If the plane had run out of fuel in midair, President Johnson's frenetic energy and excitement would have kept it flying."[44]

Having dragged Humphrey to Texas, LBJ found the opportunity at the ranch to humiliate him. He dressed the Senator in cowboy clothes that were too large and put him on a rambunctious horse as though he were a clown act for the press to photograph.[45]

In the autumn, U Thant got the North Vietnamese to agree to open negotiations with the U.S. in Rangoon, Burma. LBJ insisted that no discussions be held until after the U.S. presidential election. Following the election, U Thant renewed the offer of talks but he was rebuffed. The administration expressed concern that the South Vietnamese government would become upset by the prospect of negotiations.[46] By the autumn of 1964, there was no government in South Vietnam that deserved the name. One coup followed another.

There was nothing about this campaign to depress the President. Political sophisticates declared that the nomination of Barry Goldwater must have been the expression of a Republican death wish. LBJ's campaign took off at high altitude, with 22-hour days and 20 speeches a week. He was euphoric and inexhaustible well into October.[47] By mid-October, however, LBJ found a downer in his belief that he was getting support only because people were afraid of Goldwater. He was feeling unloved again and asked people how to improve his image.[48]

LBJ continued to terrorize his staff on the campaign trail even though he was always more exposed to critical observation when traveling than he was in the privacy of his office. Kenneth O'Donnell, a member of JFK's team, commented on the President and his staff: "He treated them awful." O'Donnell also witnessed LBJ shouting at Lady Bird that she was "working for Goldwater."[49] When LBJ was angry, accusations of treason, however ridiculous, sprang to his lips.

Enthusiastic crowds always made LBJ euphoric, and despite what had happened to his predecessor, turned him into a death-defying candidate. While his motorcade drove down city avenues, he would climb on to the roof of his limousine and yell, assisted by a bullhorn: "Y'all come to the speakin.'"[50] As he had done during his Vice Presidential travels in Asia, he charged into crowds, kissing babies and shaking hands. By the end of the campaign, he showed off his swollen, bleeding hand to reporters, exclaiming: "Have you ever seen anything like that?" The campaign was a harrowing experience for his Secret Service team.[51]

Plans were made and instantly unmade as the President's whim drove his campaign back and forth across the country.[52] The speeches were often inappropriate for their audience, but, as Goldwater was frightening the country with bellicose talk, it didn't matter.[53]

Nixon's team was not the originator of "dirty tricks" in politics. LBJ sent his people to Goldwater rallies to hold anti-Goldwater signs in camera range and cause as much uproar as opportunity permitted.

This may have been the most manic campaign LBJ ever experienced. Certainly, he never was received so enthusiastically before.

Even at the end, said Reedy, "I've never seen anything like it. The cheers and applause were like new blood in his veins."[54]

But danger signs were also manifest. The President's egocentrism took center stage in Denver when he climbed onto the trunk of his car to yell: "I'm just here to appoint you—all to look after me."[55]

There was no such thing as too much applause for LBJ. He boasted that one of his State of the Union speeches had to be stopped for applause 80 times.[56] His response to applause was "Oh, boy! Listen to that! It even beats screwing."[57] LBJ made a point of telling people that his speech got more applause than Kennedy's.[58]

One sign of his burgeoning grandiosity was LBJ's decision to scrap his campaign strategy of concentrating on the most important sections of the country and go for everything. Theodore White noted: "...it seemed like a storm assault on the whole nation."[59] The President gave a grandiose interpretation to his reception by the voters: "Those Negroes go off the ground. They cling to my hands like I was Jesus Christ walking in their midst."[60]

On October 28, 1964, LBJ told the American people: "The only real issue in this campaign, the only one that you ought to get concerned about, is who can best keep the peace."[61] Three days before the election he said: "We know there are 200,000,000 in the Chinese Army.... No sir! I don't want to fight them."[62] Again, he was blurring the distinction between his own identity and that of the United States.

The President was convinced of his omnipotence at home. On one of his plane trips he told the press corps: "You-all know a good bit about the Republicans in Congress and there must be a few of them that *you* think deserve to be defeated. Give me some names and either Hubert or I will try to get into their districts in the next few days and talk against 'em." Frank Cormier said it was "a proposition that seemed rather astounding at the time and still does." And the press corps was left dumbstruck by the President's attempt to co-opt them.[63]

The country was accustomed to campaign promises not being kept, but those offered by LBJ were so grandiose it would have been impossible for anyone to keep them. He said: "So here is the Great Society. It's the time—and it's going to be soon—when nobody in this country is poor.... It's the time...when every slum is gone from every city in America, and America is beautiful. It's the time when man gains full dominion under God over his destiny. It's the time of peace on earth and good will among men."[64] These were noble ideals that everyone could wish for, but to promise their realization without considering the obstacles in the way or the resources available went beyond optimism into delusion.

What was the role of depression in LBJ's life? Because of the secrecy that did and still does surround the mental problems of politicians, it is difficult to tell when LBJ was physically ill, depressed and ill both, or just depressed. The confusion is compounded by the fact that depression often made him physically ill.

Physical illness coincided with the stress of political campaigns. During the congressional campaign of 1937, he had an appendectomy. He was hospitalized with what was referred to as "pneumonia" during the losing senate campaign of 1941. His service in the Navy, though hardly stressful, saw him come down with at least half a dozen bouts of pneumonia.[65] He was hospitalized in January, 1946 with what was pneumonia and/or depression, and in March for an attack of kidney stones, and in October for a bronchial infection.[66]

The senate campaign of 1948 was interrupted by a hospitalization to remove a kidney stone. Another stone was removed early in 1955. On July 2 of that year, LBJ had a major heart attack. He was Vice President for only three days when he was hospitalized with a "cold," but he was taken to the hospital in an ambulance. In October of 1965 he had a kidney stone and his gall bladder removed. He reentered the hospital in November of 1966 for surgery again. December of 1968 saw him back in the hospital.[67] For all his toughness, this seemed a fragile man.

His career had a certain fragility too. His press secretary, Horace Busby, noted: "You have to understand that across a long span of Lyndon Johnson's career, one expected at least once a year to go through one of those sessions in which he was going to quit public life."[68] There is nothing unique about wanting to quit one's job and longing for a completely different existence. But not many people announce that they are going to take the nearest exit every year.

LBJ's letter to his mother, written when he was thirty, indicates that the urge to quit had been coming over him for decades: "Your thoughtful letter...I shall remember when I get downhearted and feel like tossing everything out the window. During the years your letters have meant more to me than I can say. They have urged me on even when I have despaired of accomplishing anything."[69] By then he had a successful stint as an NYA director behind him, had married the woman of his choice, and was a newly elected congressman. That was hardly a life cramped by failure.

George Reedy noted that threats to quit "...did not appear to be (in) any relationship between the locale and the episode. It could happen in his Capital office; in the living room of his ranch; in a tourist court on a campaign swing...." But it was "invariably preceded by a wild drinking bout".[70] LBJ wanted to quit when he was depressed, not when he was manic.

The autumn depressions arrived in 1937 after the death of LBJ's father, also in 1941, 1948, 1955, 1956, 1960, 1963, 1964, and 1967. There may have been more, but dates are not always given in the accounts of LBJ's depressions. Clearly these were not all election years.

One of the means that the President unwittingly used against himself was deception of the American people, which was an explosive with a delayed—action fuse. He maintained the fiction of being a peace candidate.

Two days before the election, the Vietcong attacked the Bien Hoa airfield, destroying 5 B-57 jet bombers and damaging 13, as well as damaging other planes. General Taylor and the Joint Chiefs asked for immediate Marine landings at several places and for bombing attacks. The President refused to allow any action at all.[71]

After his landslide victory, he expressed again the grandiose delusion of being universally loved: "Millions upon millions of people, each one marking my name on their ballot, each one wanting me as their President.... For the first time in all my life I truly felt loved by the American people."[72]

LBJ continued his masquerade as a dove in the days following the election. In late November, referring to the current carousel of military dictators in South Vietnam, he insisted that this turmoil had to stop before the U.S. did anything more. He spoke often about the need for America's allies to do more before the Americans would increase their involvement in Vietnam.[73]

On Christmas Eve, 1964, the Vietcong wounded 63 Americans and killed 2 in an attack on officers quarters in Saigon. Again LBJ refused to take action: He was waiting for his Inauguration on January 20. It was after additional attacks by the Vietcong that killed 7 and wounded 109 on February 2, 1965, that the President ordered a retaliatory bombing.

CIA Far East Director William Colby recalled that conditions were already worsening after Diem's assassination in late 1963: "The chaos and anarchy which infected the Vietnamese government at that time caused everything to fall apart. The assessments were very clear that the situation was going downhill very fast during 1964, and our assessment was that the Communists would probably win the war by about the end of 1965."[74] Additional secret U.S. documents informed LBJ in December, 1964, that war in Vietnam was not going well, would drag on for a long time, and still might end badly.[75]

1965 was going to be a terrible year.

CHAPTER 12

"THE ONLY PRESIDENT YOU HAVE"

★ ★ ★ ★ ★ ★

It would profit us to understand the more productive elements of LBJ's Presidency, and the curious way in which his manic depression contributed to his achievements.

One would expect very little in the way of benefit to others from a manic as self-centered as Johnson. His obsession with himself severely limited LBJ's experience of the world. Foreign travel was wasted on him. Hugh Sidey noted: "It is obvious when you travel with LBJ that he...lacks deep interest in those visits. His mind is on (Lyndon) Johnson, not Pago Pago."[1]

We have seen LBJ lavish Senate passes on pedestrians in Asian cities because he was not concerned with what the people there needed or could actually use. With some manics, philanthropy is prompted by egotism. Their giving burnishes their self-esteem. The lack of genuine interest in others may explain why LBJ's behavior was so inappropriate and often offensive to people in the countries he visited. But then, as we saw, he never hesitated to offend people at home, so why be different abroad?

Evans and Novak reported: "...always Johnson has placed himself at the center, with the world revolving around him."[2] This is a typical location for someone as manic as LBJ. Like a corporation advertising itself, he had the Presidential Seal emblazoned on every available surface, including his cowboy boots, ranch jacket and even disposable water cups. At his ranch LBJ treated himself as though he were a national shrine. He took pride in showing reporters his boyhood home, letters he wrote to his mother and grandmother, and his large collection of family photographs, while delivering an hours–long lecture about himself.[3]

LBJ hungered for appreciation and he took it wherever and whenever he could, even when it was not deserved. For years there were jokes about the Soviet leaders who claimed Russians invented most of modern technology. LBJ did something similar, claiming, as his own, every idea generated by his aides in the White House.[4] His favorite party entertainment was to read aloud flattering excerpts from the Johnson biography written by Booth Mooney.[5]

He could not, even for a moment, bear having others get the attention he craved. One sees this behavior in young children and some manics never grow out of it. Always starved for approval and applause, he was upset when people who worked for him received publicity.[6] He prevented John Steinbeck from giving a speech at the White House because, he said, "It's too good. It will upstage my speech."[7]

He was also extremely sensitive to criticism. He interpreted opinions differing from his own *as* criticisms. A writer for the *Wall Street Journal* said the commonest complaints about LBJ were that he "…doesn't really want argument and independent point of view. That he is too preoccupied with his popular image, is too sensitive to criticism, spends too much of his time answering attacks he should ignore. That he tends to whine over his troubles and blame others for his mistakes."[8] This last dynamic is standard for manics defending their delusions of infallibility.

Greed and cheating are often part of manic behavior, and by the time Johnson was innaugurated, he was the richest man to ever become President. His wealth dwarfed the fortune John Kennedy received from his father.[9]

Banks were attractive to LBJ, who bought all or part of four of them. He managed to force out the man who had built up the Citizens' National Bank in Austin and replaced him with Pat Nugent, LBJ's son-in-law.[10] There was also extensive investments in real estate: a mansion in Washington, properties in Austin, and of course, ranch land. By 1960, in addition to many millions of dollars, he had a ranch of some 400 acres. Six years later, it had grown to 50,000 acres and on them had built a world class zoo.[11]

LBJ bought airplanes, so he had to have an airfield at the ranch. Hundreds of thousands of taxpayer dollars were lavished on building one in the name of national security.[12] While he was Vice President, he bought 12,000 acres that he wanted to upgrade, and got the Texas Highway Department to build a $750,000.00 bridge over the Llano River to make his land more valuable.[13]

Many manics ignore rules and they delight in whatever violations they can get away with. LBJ, like Napoleon, could not bear to lose at anything, and, like the French Emperor, regularly cheated at games. The President played his own brand of dishonest dominos with guests such as Henry Ford II, or heads of state like Charles de Gaulle and Prime Minister Harold Wilson, from whom he collected hundreds of dollars of winnings.[14]

With LBJ, cheating was not limited to games. A trust was established by the LBJ business interests for the benefit of employees. But, while it made large profits lending money, and investing in oil, gas, and mines, the employees were not on the receiving end. In 1963, 38 employees wanted to know where the money had gone and had to seek their answers in court. The Johnson Foundation, ostensibly a purely charitable organization established in 1956 to donate funds for charities and the needy, was much better at increasing its assets than at giving anything out. It payed no taxes.[15]

LBJ seemed to some to be a man who was colossally greedy, and who cheated whenever he could. Why would such a person then herd through Congress the greatest portfolio of social legislation seen in the last century? The President was concerned that he lacked his own trademark program, something to compare favorably with F.D.R.'s New Deal, the Fair Deal of Truman and JFK's New Frontier.[16] George Reedy notes: "He had hoped that by suitable public relations, he could persuade posterity to attach his name to what he regarded as 'good' adjectives....His favorite was 'the education president'...."[17]

Never a man to recognize the limits of the possible unless he was depressed, LBJ eventually arrived at the notion of buying the votes of practically every significant interest group in the country. He later lamented: "I asked so little in return. Just a little thanks. Just a little appreciation. That's all."[18] He wanted a lot more than appreciation. Johnson, who knew how to trade federal largess for senatorial votes, was trying to buy the affection of his fellow Americans by offering something to everyone in the form of the Great Society.

Here was a man who had his eye on the future, on the LBJ that historians would present to coming generations, and Johnson wanted that image of himself to dwarf the memory of Franklin Roosevelt. The Great Society would be his monument, the most expensive ever conceived to glorify a single politician.

As President, LBJ drew more legislation from Congress than any man who preceded him in that office. He explained how he did it: "There is but one way for a President to deal with the Congress and that is continuously, incessantly, and without interruption. If it's really going to work, the relationship between the President and the Congress has got to be almost incestuous. He's got to know them even better than they know themselves. And then on the basis of this knowledge, he's got to build a system that stretches ... from the moment a bill is introduced to the moment it is officially enrolled as the law of the land."

Columnist Drew Pearson recorded how the President pursued his quarry: with notes, flattering phone calls to ask their opinions, heartfelt expressions of gratitude for political favors, and finally invitations on Tuesdays and Thursdays to spend the evening with him at the White House.[19]

The years LBJ spent in college being a sycophant and professional son taught him lessons he never forgot. This was his advice on how to prevail at anything: "Don't assume anything; make sure every possible weapon is brought to bear...; keep everybody involved; don't let them slacken."[20]

LBJ excelled at both persuasion and manipulation. Part of his pleasure in getting Great Society legislation passed was the opportunity it gave him to exercise power at the most personal level. Before LBJ selected his Vice President, he had said: "Whoever he is, I want his pecker to be in my pocket."[21] The pecker in his pocket was one of his trademark expressions. Another one that was popular with LBJ was "I want people around me who would kiss my ass on a hot summer's day and say it smells like roses."[22] Sometimes he specified that the kissing should be done in a window of Macy's department store. Beneath the humor, such as it was, is an appetite for the utter humiliation and subjugation of others.

Then there was domination out in the larger world of government. Congress was a challenge to his will. He stated: "In some ways, Congress is like a dangerous animal that you're trying to make work for you."[23] Someone else watching LBJ work on Congress might have seen the President as the dangerous animal, a tiger approaching his next meal.

To make sure that no single individual got the spotlight, President Johnson would announce appointments of groups of officials and swear them in as a bunch. He denied the spotlight to individuals when it came to briefing groups of congressmen. Several officials would have to perform together, and LBJ would keep control over the entire procedure by ending the briefing before questions could be asked.[24]

Sometimes there was only a single opportunity to establish his dominance over someone. This was the case when Roger Blough, the Chairman of U.S. Steel, was summoned to LBJ's office to discuss the inflationary trend in steel prices. Blough was a giant in the business world, but that did not help him. Economist Gordon

Ackley describes the meeting of the titans: "Johnson wanted Blough to hold the line on steel prices. And so he just started working him over and asking him questions and lecturing him. I have never seen a human being reduced to such a quivering lump of flesh....But it wasn't really what he said, it was the way he just leaned over and looked at him."[25]

Robert Strauss spent his life as a political power broker and moreover, he came from Texas, where the game is played hard. He was a connoisseur of political personalities. This is what he had to say about LBJ: "Lyndon Johnson just towered over me and intimidated me terribly....He's the one person who had my number all his life. Even when he was a sick old man, out of office, whenever he called, perspiration broke out on the top of my head. He was the best I ever saw."[26]

LBJ never relied on force of personality alone. When he sat in the Oval Office, he tightened his grip in the Democratic Party by undermining the Democratic National Committee. He reserved for himself the distribution of funds and patronage and used the President's Club, an instrument for fundraising, to siphon contributions into his own political purse. He reduced the staff of the DNC to one third of its former number and shrank its budget by 50%. Then, adding insult to injury, he took away the committee's long distance phone lines.[27]

If the legislators were not cowed by LBJ's domineering manner, there was always the threat of retribution should they resist his demands. He found the White House a perfect place from which to launch his bolts of vengeance.

Here are examples of simple vendettas. After a TV news commentator said something moderately critical about LBJ, the newsman heard from the I.R.S. He recalled: "I was expecting a tax refund from the Internal Revenue at the time, but a few days later I was notified that court action would soon be instituted against me for failure to pay my taxes." His lawyer told him that LBJ had taken action.[28]

The Speaker of the House, John McCormack, was one of LBJ's avenging angels, seeing to it that defiant congressmen were stripped of their seniority on committees. Senators also felt LBJ's whip. Idaho Senator Frank Church opposed LBJ's war policy. During a dinner at the White House, the President demanded to know where Church got his ideas. The Senator said that he followed the views of columnist Walter Lippmann. LBJ replied: "All right, Frank, next time you want a dam in Idaho, you go talk to Walter Lippmann."[29]

An elaborate vendetta was launched against insurance executive Don. B. Reynolds who testified that LBJ insisted on kickbacks when he took out $200,000 of insurance. Reynolds also claimed that when Vice President Johnson stopped at Hong Kong, he drew $100,000 in government money to buy gifts for his friends during a shopping spree.

This testimony was given on November 22, 1963 before the Senate Rules Committee and Senator John Williams of Delaware insisted on the report being made public. LBJ encouraged columnist Drew Pearson to smear Reynolds and sicced the IRS on people close to Reynolds. As for Senator Williams, who had also insisted on Senate action against LBJ's right hand man, Bobby Baker, there was a four-pronged approach. Drew Pearson attacked him in print, LBJ campaigned against him in Delaware, the I.R.S. started an investigation, and the Senator's mail was tampered with.[30]

The President's propensity to meddle could have positive effects. It also contributed to his ability to drive into law an immense and complex program of legislation. Jack Valenti noted: "Attention to detail, minute and usually overlooked detail, became his hallmark."[31]

At the ranch, where LBJ had his own little kingdom, he concerned himself with falling fences, loose gates, and the condition of his cattle, but he also involved himself in menu planning.[32] He told his wife when to replace the curtains and instructed the secret service men to swat flies.[33]

The White House was not his castle, but he regularly checked the condition of White House cars. Late at night he would prowl the West Wing offices reading whatever papers were left on people's desks[34] He determined how the thermostats were set.[35] He called from the ranch with instructions: "Have the janitor clean the red rugs every hour....Keep the ashtrays in my office and in the area where the red rugs are clean....Tell the secretaries that there are to be no conversations in the hall." He oversaw White House menus, guest lists and seating arrangements.[36] If you hear of a top executive doing this, it is not unreasonable to suspect that a manic is at work.

While reviewing the Air Force budget, it was not enough for LBJ to check on the cost of aircraft and atomic weapons. When he came to costs for uniforms, he insisted: "When you buy britches for the boys, make sure they have plenty of ball room."[37] No detail was too trivial.

Finally, without his manic energy, nothing on the scale of the Great Society could have been enacted during a single presidency. Civil rights advocate Virginia Durr observed: "The thing that made Lyndon different from other people, I suppose, was that when he started doing something, he poured every ounce of his energy into it…. He just pounded and pounded on it."[38] LBJ prevailed so often because he did everything humanly possible and would not give up. Such persistence requires an extravagant use of energy.

"The job of the President is to set priorities for the nation, and he must set them according to his own judgement and his own conscience," said LBJ.[39] But even the power of a President of the United States is limited. There are two other branches of government at the federal level, the legislature and the judiciary, and beyond those there are the fifty states of the union, the news media, corporate America, and a myriad of constituencies and interest groups. According to Joseph Califano, LBJ looked on these the way a cowboy feels about the cattle he drives—they are the enemy.

LBJ made the term "consensus" part of the national vocabulary and, in an attempt to appear responsive to the national will, claimed to be governing by consensus. This is how he defined the term: "To me, consensus meant; first, deciding what needed to be done…and, second, convincing a majority of the Congress and the American people of the necessity for doing those things."[40]

Without manic optimism, LBJ could never have guided through Congress the army of bills that mapped out his Great Society.[41] And without megalomania he would not have made so many impossible promises, nor raised the hopes and failed the expectations of so many people. He made it sound as though Santa Claus was on duty full time in the Oval Office. He guaranteed to every child "a good teacher, and every teacher…good pay, and both have good classrooms.…It's time—and it's going to be soon—when nobody in this country is poor."

He assured that there would be "a job for everyone who is willing to work, and he is going to be paid a decent wage." He insisted "poverty and ignorance are the only basic weakness of a free society and…both of them are only bad habits and can be stopped."[42] He affirmed that because "We're the wealthiest nation in the world" it necessarily follows that "We have enough to do it all."[43]

Ronald Reagan was credited with inventing "voodoo economics." LBJ preceded him with magic wand economics. And he was sowing dragon's teeth. But for a while he appeared to be a miracle worker.

The Great Society in all its complexity did not spring like Venus from the head of Zeus, or even from the head of the President. Some of LBJ's legislative initiatives originated with the 40 task forces that he set up from 1964 through 1968 to work on specific issues. The President designated a few individuals as "idea men" charged with reporting directly to him. As always, everyone operated under a cloak of secrecy and only LBJ could determine what information saw the light of day.[44]

Moving the bills through the legislative process was where the President showed his mastery of Congress. Every congressman was invited to the White House to enjoy the Johnson's hospitality. He recruited sponsors for each bill, shepherded the bills through the committees, and then racked up the necessary votes, all the while pushing people as hard and as fast as he could.[45]

Once he kept the congressmen at work until after midnight, insisting that they pass a pet project of Lady Bird's, a highway beautification bill, before he went into surgery for removal of his gall bladder. The speed that he demanded reduced to a minimum not only people's understanding of what the legislation contained, but also any opportunity to argue intelligently against it or to modify it.[46] One result of his blitzkrieg was that he broke records for the number and percentage of his bills that were passed.[47]

So much was written into law and treaty that it is hard to group it into comprehensible categories. Going alphabetically, there were measures for the *arts and humanities*. These included creation of the Corporation for Public Broadcasting (TV and radio) and the National Foundation on the Arts and Humanities, establishing the Hirschhorn Museum and Sculpture Garden, enlarging the National Gallery, and funding what became the Kennedy Center for the Performing Arts.[48]

The *cities* acquired the Department of Housing and Urban Development, the Housing Act, increased community health programs, programs for urban research, the Model Cities program, aid to urban mass transit, and assistance in housing the poor. Juvenile delinquency programs were established. Laws were passed to modernize the government of the District of Columbia and to prevent discrimination in housing.

LBJ sponsored *conservation* measures, including the establishment of 35 National Park areas, conservation belts, a clean rivers law, clean air and waters laws, research for environmental issues, fish and wildlife preservation, and noise pollution laws.

Consumer protection laws were enacted: the Fair Packaging and Labeling Act was joined by laws against flammable fabrics and unwholesome meat, as well as laws providing protection for children from unsafe toys and hazardous substances.

He did indeed deserve to be called "the *education* President." The Higher Education Facilities Act gave money for building classrooms and libraries. The Economic Opportunity Act paid for work-study programs. The Elementary and Secondary Education Act gave funds and loans to students, as well as funds for colleges, equipment, and training for librarians. Additional legislation helped graduate schools, funded the Teacher Corps to get educators involved in their communities, provided funds for centers for international studies, and money for training teachers and administrators from kindergarden through college.

The inadequacies of the *highway system* were addressed with laws to establish a Transportation Department. Safety was the concern of the National Traffic and Motor Vehicle Safety Act and the Highway Safety Act, law was enacted to guarantee tire safety, and there was aid to urban mass transit as well as Lady Bird's highway beautification program.

The *legal system* received attention through the establishment of the Freedom of Information Act, bail reform, antiracketeering laws, a Judicial Center, a National Crime Commission and civil procedure reforms for the courts.

American *medicine* received one of the major overhauls. Medicare gave the elderly access to adequate medical and hospital care, while Medicaid provided health care for the poor and a Medicaid for the military was established. Facilities for research in and the treatment of heart, cancer and stroke disorders were established in every part of the nation. Rehab centers for drug addicts were opened, as was the Deaf-Blind Center. Funds were provided for more medical libraries and mental health facilities.

The nation's *poor* benefited from antipoverty programs, aid to Appalachia, food stamps, rent supplements, vocational rehabilitation, summer youth programs, Social Security increases, increases in the minimum wage, aid to education and better nutrition for poor children, and mine safety laws.

Others were helped with a farm program, aid to small businesses, and tax cuts. Immigration law was reformed, and laws were passed against age discrimination. Benefits for veterans were increased, civil service pay was raised, and the parcel post service was reformed. The Department of Health, Education and Welfare was established.

There were changes in the laws relating to foreign countries. The Asian Development Bank and the InterAmerican Bank were established, the Food For Freedom program, and funds for international education, as well as a foreign investors tax were written into law. Programs to further the exchange of cultural materials and scientific research were set in place. Newly written and passed were the Safety at Sea Treaty, the Consular Treaty, the Outer Space Treaty, the Narcotics Treaty, the Nuclear Non-Proliferation Treaty, and work was begun on laying the groundwork for the SALT Treaty.

The Food for India program was an example of LBJ's attention to detail. India teetered on the edge of famine because of crop-killing weather two years in a row. The Indian government made things even worse. Indian states that had food surpluses did not ship them to states with shortages and the national government would not provide transport for such shipments. It also spent nothing to increase the supply of fertilizers. Nor did it do anything to increase space for food storage, with the result that up to one fifth of the crop was lost each year to rot and pests.

LBJ threatened to stop food shipments if reforms were not rapidly enacted. The Indian government still did nothing, and the shipments were halted, to be resumed only after a remedial program was put in place.[49] LBJ concerned himself with the size of Indian grain stocks, India's rainfall, and the dates of shipments. He controlled the negotiations, not only in this matter but he decided what grants the Agency for International Development would make, something Kennedy had not done.[50]

LBJ's intervention helped to preserve democracy in India, the world's second largest country. Moreover, only the American fleet at that time had the capacity to deliver the food needed. His example induced the Soviets to help as well.[51]

The President was a rebel with a cause, quite a few of them, in fact. Larry O'Brien, Postmaster General, said that the Great Society legislation: "...was revolutionary, and it disturbed a lot of people on the Hill and in the private sector."[52] Trouble had to follow, for many reasons. First of all, LBJ's impatience pushed people to present programs that were rushed and therefore poorly thought out.[53] George Reedy notes: "...his incessant drive for more projects, more proposals, more laws, actually flawed the enormous body of welfare, social, education, and civil rights legislation upon which he based his hopes for a permanent place in history."[54]

To complicate matters, so many social programs were initiated between 1965 and the end of 1968 that the Federal government, state, and local governments could not cope with them. It did not help that often the money needed to implement laws and programs was inadequately provided. What resulted was, as occurred in the Soviet Union when expectations were unrealistic, an epidemic of false statistics about the success of the programs.[55]

Moreover, government agencies weren't given time to comprehend all the changes LBJ imposed on them and the American people were not given either the time to understand all the new laws and regulations nor time to adjust to them. Reedy adds: "...the Johnsonian range of knowledge did not include any respect for the requirements of orderly administration....He was the very antithesis of organized application of the law."[56]

Then LBJ himself began the dismantling process. In 1967 he started cutting the budget for the War on Poverty, limited though it already was. Martin Luther King and CORE's Floyd McKissick assembled an organization to register a million African Americans in the South, but were prevented from doing so when LBJ sent only a small number of registrars to accomplish the task.[57] Poorly funded though they were, the Great Society's programs damaged the American economy by contributing to the coming inflation.[58]

Problems with the Great Society were evident even to LBJ. He admitted to journalist Helen Thomas that he might have tried to do too much too soon to eliminate evils that were at least a century in the making.[59] In his memoir of the Presidency he wrote: "The blue-collar worker felt that the Democratic Party had traded his welfare for the welfare of the black man. The middle-class suburbanite felt that we were gouging him in order to pay for the anti-poverty programs. The black man...began demanding his rightful share of the American promise faster than most of the nation was willing to let him have it....By 1968 it was clear that many people in the nation were tired of being pushed."[60]

In this discussion of the Great Society, LBJ's Civil Rights program has been left for last because it had a long and complicated history, not only in the nation, but in his life. LBJ considered his father to be "a great civil libertarian," and claimed that "I never had any bigotry in me. My daddy wouldn't let me. He was a strong anti-Klansman....The Klan threatened to kill him several times."[61]

However, as we have seen, LBJ decided he would rather be reelected than stick to his father's principles. In 1948, he had reminded Texas voters: "I voted against the so-called poll tax repeal bill" and "I have voted against the Fair Employment Practices Commission...."[62] He presented himself as a foe of any program resembling the Medicare and Medicaid that he would later promote. He also opposed Truman's law against lynching, a law against segregation on interstate transportation, and any protection of the right to vote.[63] He helped Eisenhower to pass a civil rights bill in 1957 but made sure it was toothless.[64]

When LBJ decided to become a civil rights champion, he blandly asserted: "I have always opposed the poll tax" though he had voted for it in 1942, 1943, 1945, 1947 and 1950.[65] Why did he turn around? Those African Americans who were not disenfranchised were deserting the Democratic Party for the Republicans, for one thing. And then there were LBJ's Presidential ambitions, requiring that he present himself to the nation as a man who had overcome the prejudices of his region.

George Reedy thought LBJ had some, albeit limited, sympathy for the disadvantaged: "His feelings for the blacks, Chicanos, dirt farmers were not feigned. He felt their plight and suffered with them—as long as they did not get too close."[66] As usual, self-interest and paranoia also provided powerful motivation. LBJ recalled: "I knew that if I didn't get out in front on this issue, they (the liberals) would get me. They'd throw up my background against me, they'd use it to prove that I was incapable of bringing unity to the land.... I couldn't let that happen. I had to produce a civil rights bill that was even stronger than the one they'd have gotten if Kennedy had lived. Without this, I'd be dead before I could even begin."[67]

The President displayed political courage in asking for a civil rights bill *before* the '64 election.[68] During the campaign he bravely told a New Orleans audience: "Whatever your views are, we have a Constitution and we have a Bill of Rights, and we have the law of the land, and two thirds of the Democrats in the Senate voted for it and three quarters of the Republicans. I signed it, and I am going to enforce it, and I am going to observe it, and I think that any man that is worthy of the high office of the President is going to do the same thing."[69]

Having signed the civil rights act of 1964, LBJ gave an accurate prediction to Bill Moyers: "I think we delivered the South to the Republican Party for your lifetime and mine." He was defeated in five Southern states that November, and four of them had not gone Republican in 84 years.[70] There was a personal loss for him as well. Turning against Southern sentiment cost him friends in the Congress and throughout the region of his origin.[71]

Perhaps the losses in the South dampened his enthusiasm for civil rights. There was no Administration voting rights bill until Senator Mike Mansfield phoned Attorney General Nicholas Katzenbach and demanded that one be written. Mansfield got the bill through the Senate and LBJ took the credit.[72] It is ironic that a man who was so unfair to the people around him would emerge as a defender of the rights of millions of people he would never meet.

Real changes were brought about. The 13th, 14th, and 15th Amendments of the Constitution, which were enacted following the Civil War, had guaranteed rights to all citizens. However these rights were not protected by penalties for their violation until the Civil Rights Act of 1964 was passed. Its eleven titles guaranteed the right to vote, access to public accommodations and facilities, desegregation of schools, and equal opportunities for employment.

Parts of the country found guilty of discrimination would find that the funds for their federally assisted programs were cut off. The Civil Rights Commission was given new powers and the Community Relations Service was established to deal with the problems that would arise.[73]

LBJ moved on other fronts as well, accelerating the desegregation of the armed forces and appointing African Americans to the Supreme Court, the Federal Reserve Board, and the Cabinet. He also appointed the first female African American ambassador.[74] He single-handedly integrated the faculty club at the University of Texas when he brought an African American woman, one of his secretaries, with him to the New Year's Eve party of 1963.[75] All things considered, no American president, save perhaps, Abraham Lincoln, did as much as LBJ to establish and protect the rights of African Americans and other minorities.[76]

Even before his election in 1964, LBJ wanted to establish a record as a promoter of equality for women. He said: "The day is over when top jobs are reserved for men," and made quite a few appointments of women to visible positions in his government. However, although the Equal Pay Act became law on June 11, 1963, it was difficult to enforce, and women's pay forty years later is still not at parity with that of men.[77]

An important fact about LBJ emerges from his involvement with the Great Society and particularly with the civil rights legislation: like many manics, he was a rebel. He confidently ignored the polls which were 47% against or indifferent to changes in the ethnic quota system when he had the immigration laws rewritten.[78]

He did not hesitate to rip up the old Democratic political structure in the South by enfranchising African Americans. His laws concerning health, education, and the environment rode roughshod over states' rights and he expressed no regrets.[79] LBJ was always his own master, and this is something we should remember when seeking the responsibility for the Vietnam War.

What LBJ wanted to do was to leave Lincoln and FDR in the dust. He wanted to liberate African Americans to a degree far beyond anything imagined by the Great Emancipator. He wanted his Great Society to dwarf Roosevelt's New Deal.[80] Even as he sent planes to defoliate Vietnam, he wanted to be the savior of Southeast Asia, to make it more prosperous than Europe.[81]

What disappeared from LBJ's worldview was the horizon. He no longer believed that there were limits to what he could do. During his first State of the Union message he instructed Congress to do "More for civil rights than the last hundred sessions combined" and "to build more homes, more schools, more libraries and more hospitals than any single session of Congress in the history of the Republic."[82]

Joseph Califano testifies to LBJ's megalomania: "There was no child he could not feed; no adult he could not put to work; no disease he could not cure, no toy, food, or medical device he could not make safer; no air or water he could not clean; no discriminatory barrier he could not topple—just as there was no war he could not win and no cease-fire or peace he could not negotiate."[83]

LBJ believed that government, with him at the head of it, could accomplish anything.[84] This is the only mistake he ever admitted to: "...we erred because we tried to do too much too soon, and never because we walked away from a challenge."[85] But there are some challenges only a madman accepts.

The President was an exceptionally persuasive man, which he well knew. But in what follows, he shows that he was losing an essential element of rationality—the recognition that there are inherent limits to one's personal power. He said:"I always believed that as long as I could take someone into a room with me, I could make him my friend, and that included anybody, even Nikita Kruschev. From the start of my Presidency I believed that if I handled him right, he would go along with me."[86] The important thing about his statement is what it reveals about the direction his thinking was taking. He was heading for delusions of omnipotence.

His slide into megalomania is even clearer in this next. "When I first became President, I realized that if only I could take the next step and become dictator of the whole world, then I could really make things happen. Every hungry person would be fed, every ignorant child educated, every jobless man employed. And then I knew I could accomplish my greatest wish, the wish for eternal peace."[87]

Senator Fulbright understood where LBJ was going and called him "a seeker after unlimited power and empire" with a "self-appointed mission to police the world, to defeat all tyrannies, to make...(all) men rich, happy and free."[88] When he gave his acceptance speech for the Democratic nomination for President in 1964, LBJ exclaimed joyously that America's strength "...is greater than the combined might of all the nations, in all the world, in all the history of this planet. And I report our superiority is growing."[89] One would think he had just been nominated to be Emperor of the Earth. No country has ever had that degree of domination of the planet. He saw both the United States and himself through the magnifying lens of delusion.

One more quote from LBJ moves us on to his aspiration for what others might consider to be divine powers. "Control of space means control of the world....From space the masters of infinity would have the power to control the earth's weather, to cause drought and flood, to change the tides and raise the levels of the sea, to divert the Gulf Stream and change temperate climates to frigid....There is something more important than the ultimate weapon. That is the ultimate position—the position of total control over earth that lies somewhere in outer space...and...our national goal... *must* be to win and hold that position."[90] This is science fiction, not science.

Putting that aside, the man is really saying he wants to rule over the earth like Jehovah. Let us move on from his megalomania to his paranoia.

In his first speech as President, LBJ referred to the post-assassination period with the phrase "the tragedy and torment of these terrible days."[91] "Tragedy and torment" would also describe the years of his own term as President. During the next four years he would undergo an increase of pain and a decrease of judgement.

Arthur Krock of the *New York Times* observed that LBJ's 1964 "...landslide victory seemed to have numbed his once infallible political instinct and caused him to fall into errors of policy and administration that Johnson had never made before."[92] And Mr. Krock was not even talking about the Vietnam War.

CHAPTER 13

FEAR AND LOATHING IN THE OVAL OFFICE

★ ★ ★ ★ ★ ★

Bobby Baker wasn't the only person close to LBJ who noted his emotional instability. According to Bill Moyers, who was LBJ's Press Secretary, the President's mood had wild swings from one day to the next. And LBJ's opinions about the possibility of victory in Vietnam would vary accordingly.[1] This was only one of the ways in which his illness impaired his leadership: he also governed by mood cycles. While LBJ's manias and depressions could fluctuate on a daily basis, it was more usual for them to last for weeks or months at a time. Commentators who followed his political career noticed that he would alternate periods of intense activity with periods of quiet and lassitude.[2]

LBJ's relationship with the press was complicated by his mood swings. Theodore White saw the President oscillate between rage at the press and attempts at wooing it, neither of which made a favorable impression.[3] The frequency of press conferences were also barometer's of LBJ's moods and could range from weekly ones when he was manic to months of silence when he was depressed and/or paranoid.[4]

While his mood swings attracted growing notice, the President's illness increasingly replaced his political shrewdness with delusion. The successful campaign of 1964 pushed LBJ further into the territory of grandiosity. He told Hugh Sidey that he was "the most popular President since Franklin Roosevelt."[5]

For George Reedy, there was a qualitative shift in how LBJ thought about himself after his landslide election to the Presidency. Johnson, who had been so good at reading people and understanding their motivation better than they understood it themselves, no longer noticed or seemed to care about how people responded to what he was saying and doing. This prompted him to make serious mistakes in his handling not only of individuals, but of organizations.[6]

Grandiosity continued to extend its dominion. As his presidency wore on, LBJ identified himself more and more with the country he led. He would speak of "my Supreme Court" and the "State of My Union Address."[7] The President seemed to drape the immensity and power of America over his own shoulders like a majestic cloak. He told his aide, Frank Cormier, "Look around the world. Kruschev's gone, MacMillan's gone. Adenauer's gone. ...Nehru's gone. Who's left? De Gaulle?" Cormier adds that LBJ "thumped his chest with both hands and declared, 'I am the King!'"[8]

Ambition is something that one expects to find in successful politicians. Without it, why would they risk the disappointments, sacrifice their privacy, and undertake the exhausting effort required by campaigns? LBJ may have begun with ambitions of reasonable dimensions, but he ended up with something that merged into megalomania. He had already crossed the limits of rationality into the territory of paranoia

It was evident that LBJ's ego had expanded to block everything and everyone else from view. Eric Goldman saw LBJ as a man who "...had erected the Presidency into a near-omniscient, almost unassailable institution so far as the ultimate questions of foreign policy are concerned....The President studied the situation,...arrived at a decision. He should then be supported by the people of the United States."[9]

There were occasional breaks in the dam that LBJ's mania-inflated ego erected against criticism, moments when he let his guard down. One of them occurred when he and Harry McPherson were looking over photos of LBJ. The President said: "Have you ever seen a phonier smile in your life?" McPherson was able to agree that it was a phony smile without having his head bitten off. LBJ continued: "That's the way I look when I don't want to. When I don't feel sincere, I try all the harder to look sincere and it looks all the worse every time."[10] Perhaps it was okay to agree with LBJ on that occasion because the criticism originated with him.

As his staff well knew, LBJ was likely to respond to anything negative by killing the messenger. People around the President who could have given him advance warning when things went badly were afraid to upset him, and few dared to say anything discouraging even to each other.

White House special assistant Michael Forrester was one of these: "There was tremendous nervousness that if you expressed an opinion it might somehow leak out…and the President would be furious and everyone's head would be cut off.…It inhibited an exchange of information and prevented the President himself from getting a lot of the facts that he should have had."[11]

The staff's fear had a sound basis: who could predict how he would react? A Herblock cartoon depicting LBJ as a slave driver cracking his whip over his White House staff made the President so furious that he retaliated, rather inappropriately, by canceling the 1965 Medal of Freedom awards ceremony.[12]

Shortly after his inauguration, the President gave some reporters a view of his paranoid attitudes towards South America: "I know these Latin Americans. I grew up with Mexicans. They'll come right into your yard and take over if you let them (which sounds like how the United States acquired Texas). And the next day they'll be right up on your porch, barefoot and weighing 130 pounds and they'll take that too. But if you say to them right at the start, 'hold on, just wait a minute,' they'll know they're dealing with somebody who'll stand up. And after that you can get along fine."[13] LBJ was still obsessed with proving his valor.

Cabinet members were alarmed about the changes in the President and called Moyers. He remembered calls from Secretary of State Dean Rusk to "tell me about some exchange he just had with the President that was very disturbing, and he would say that he seemed to me to be very depressed." Moyers grew even more concerned when LBJ became highly agitated. The aide decided to discuss the President's paranoia with Lady Bird. Moyers recalled: "I came away from it knowing that she herself was more concerned, because she was more routinely exposed to it."[14]

Not long after his inauguration, LBJ's paranoia convinced him that the State Department, as Senator Joe McCarthy had insisted, was riddled with fellow travelers and Communists. On February 15, he told Undersecretary of State George Ball that the State Department was under surveillance.[15] After Robert Kennedy publicly opposed the war, LBJ saw the hand of Kennedy pulling the strings, controlling both the State Department and the Department of Defense[16].

This President was convinced that the Defense Department was unreliable: "…every Defense Department official and his brother would be leakers at one time or another. And when I'd see some DOD official's picture in the paper with a nice story about him, I'd know it was the paper's bribe for the leaked story."[17]

According to Richard Harwood and Haynes Johnson, the Pentagon also fell under the shadow of LBJ's suspicions. Harwood and Johnson provide the following vignette: "At the Pentagon, he said darkly, there was a group that was out to do him in, a group that regularly 'leaked' information to the *Washington Post* and the *New York Times*. He didn't want to categorize or name them, but they came in with McNamara (his Secretary of Defense). That is to say, they were the Kennedy men.

Anyone who left LBJ's service for any reason, or who opposed the Vietnam War was ipso facto an object of suspicion. Senator

William Fulbright, who led opposition to the war, became a target for mistrust. True to form, LBJ came up with a personal and dishonorable reason for the Senator's criticisms: "Fulbright's problem is that he's never found any President who would appoint him Secretary of State.... And he takes out his frustration by making all those noises about Vietnam."[18]

Paranoia was closing over the President like a steel net. On June 23, he complained that his staff could no longer be trusted: "The other day...the *New York Times* spent four hours and twenty-five minutes...with my people. Preparing to castrate me."[19]

The following day he declared that he could no longer talk to anyone in the State Department: "So we just have to...act without it. ...Don't repeat it to anybody, but that's how dangerous our State Department thing is now."[20]

A month later, he said the military were also untrustworthy: "Some of them are awfully irresponsible. They'll just scare you. They're ready to put a million men in (Vietnam) right quick."[21] Nevertheless, in response to a request by General Westmoreland, he agreed to send forty-four combat battalions.

The President no longer trusted his national security advisor, McGeorge Bundy, said to Bill Moyers: "Bundy is going on television—on national television with five professors. I never gave him permission. That's an act of disloyalty. He didn't tell me because he knew I didn't want him to do it. Bill, I want you to go to Bundy and tell him the President would be pleased, mighty pleased, to accept his resignation. ...That's the trouble with all you fellows. You're in bed with the Kennedys." Moyers had never worked for any Kennedy.

As the tide of opposition rose against the Vietnam War, his own popularity fell and America's cities were torn by riots. While the burden of the Presidency became heavier and heavier, the President's general suspicions grew. LBJ said himself, "I don't trust anybody but Lady Bird, and sometimes I'm not sure about her."[22] McGeorge Bundy, his national security advisor, called him "the wariest man about whom to trust that I have ever encountered."[23]

Paranoia is an abhorent term to apply to a sitting President, so the American people heard only faint, unintelligible whispers of what was happening in the White House. Paranoia can become all encompassing and invade every waking moment. This happened to LBJ. He would open conversations with Cabinet members by demanding: "Why aren't you out there fighting against my enemies. Don't you realize that if they destroy me, they'll destroy you as well?"[24] He introduced his suspicions into discussions of legislation and told dinner guests about the "traitors" who opposed him. Long hours in the Oval Office were given to the President's monologues about the conspiracies against him.[25]

The people who observed LBJ at close hand were troubled. "He began to see conspiracies mounted against him," say Harwood and Johnson. "Inevitably, these strains affected his relations with the press, his staff, his old congressional colleagues, and, ultimately, the American people."[26]

While not uneducated, LBJ felt at a disadvantage socially and intellectually in the presence of people with ivy-league degrees. He was certain that they looked down on him.

Another group that aroused LBJ's suspicions both because of its affiliations with the Kennedy wing of the party and because of its criticism of his war policies was the liberals. LBJ lamented: "…there were all those liberals on the Hill squawking at me about Vietnam. Why? Because I never went to Harvard. That's why. Because I wasn't friends with all their friends. Because I was keeping the throne from Bobby Kennedy. Because the Great Society was accomplishing more than the New Frontier (Kennedy's program). You see, they had to find some issue on which to turn against me and they found it in Vietnam."[27]

This remarkable distortion of reality enabled LBJ to trivialize the opposition to the war while making it unnecessary to consider that there was any valid reason to oppose what he was doing in Vietnam. "I am not going to have anything more to do with liberals," he said. "They won't have anything to do with me. They all just follow the Communist line—liberals, intellectuals, Communists. They're all the same.... I can't trust anybody anymore. I tell you what I'm going to do. I'm going to get rid of everybody who doesn't agree with my policies....They're just out to get me, always have been."[28] He voiced all this as early as the summer of 1965.

One of the first to feel the hot breath of the President's paranoia were the people (with a few exceptions) who had worked with John Kennedy. LBJ assumed that he was being compared unfavorably to his predecessor. Unfortunately, paranoia is deaf to reassurance and impervious to correction.

Since the President clung to the delusion that his policies were always correct, he saw all opposition as personal, and not based on issues. LBJ believed Eugene McCarthy opposed the war because he wasn't chosen as Vice President in 1964. This was also the reason that LBJ gave for Robert Kennedy's opposition to the war.[29]

Robert Kennedy, while he survived and even after he died, got the blame for all that was going wrong in the country and in LBJ's life. Instead of considering that his own hostility towards the press might be having its effect, LBJ blamed Kennedy for turning the press against him.[30] Kennedy was also accused of inciting the ghetto riots through the use of Martin Luther King: "Then Bobby began to take it up (opposition to the war) as his cause and with Martin Luther King on his payroll he went around stirring up the Negroes and telling them that if they came out into the streets they'd get more."[31] LBJ saw Kennedy as the leader of a conspiracy dedicated to his political destruction.[32]

If the President's paranoia had been without consequence in the real world, it might have provided good material for a late night comedy hour. But his suspicions provided some of the motivation for keeping American forces fighting in Vietnam. He described in nightmare terms what he expected if he lost the war: "...there would be Robert Kennedy out in front leading the fight against me, telling everyone that I had betrayed John Kennedy's commitment to South Vietnam. That I had let a democracy fall into the hands of the Communists. That I was a coward. A man without a spine. Oh, I could see it coming all right."[33] The focus of his concern was that losing the war would make LBJ appear cowardly.

Paranoia augmented LBJ's already extreme obsession with secrecy, and the measures he took to control all dissemination of information from the White House eventually aroused the resentment of the press.

Press conferences were announced at the last possible minute to prevent reporters from asking well-researched questions, and were usually held on weekends for the same reason. He would begin with a long statement, allowing as little time as he could for questions. He often used national security as an excuse to withhold information.[34] When he responded to questions, he would answer only the part he wanted to, or go off on a tangent (a practice that others have mastered).[35] According to Booth Mooney, Johnson often met an unexpected question with a volley of sarcasm.[36] LBJ would have eliminated the daily press briefings given by the press secretary except that George Reedy, who then held that position, threatened to resign.[37]

Joseph Califano says that Johnson elevated even the most trivial of plans or appointments to the status of state secrets, then canceled everything if the press reported a word about it before he was ready to announce it. He would then deny that he had made the plans or appointments in the first place, this sabotaged and angered the press.[38]

Observe what LBJ did to James Farmer, the national director of the Congress of Racial Equality. The Office of Economic Opportunity was planning to launch a literacy drive with Farmer as its head. The news leaked out, and both Farmer's appointment and the literacy drive were cancelled by a furious President.[39]

To place the last straw in the back of press amity, there were the lies LBJ told. Sam, his brother, said that the President "…often hinted the opposite from what he meant; omitted important elements of some report; made outright denials of things that were obviously true...and often treated reporters as if they were the 'enemy.'"[40] In Johnson's eyes, they *were* the enemy.

LBJ had begun his Presidency benefiting from the good will the press usually accords to someone performing well in difficult circumstances. But the first sign of negative war coverage intensified his paranoia. After AP correspondent Peter Arnett had reported that U.S. forces were using gas against the enemy (it was riot control gas) and the British Foreign Secretary, Michael Stewart, repeated the story at the National Press Club, LBJ wanted the National Security Council to find out if Arnett's story had been planted by Communists. This was on March 26, 1965.[41]

Like the irresistible force that meets an immovable object, presidential paranoia collided with credibility. While LBJ was throwing accusations around, he often blamed one villain, and then another, for the same problem. Or he blamed the same villains for different problems. He claimed that the liberals were merely spouting the Communist line, following orders from the Soviet Union, and stirring up the public to oppose the war. Then he would say something that was contradictory: "Two or three intellectuals started it all, you know. They produced all the doubt, they and the columnists of the *Washington Post*, the *New York Times*, *Newsweek* and *Life*. And it spread until it appeared as if the people were against the war."[42]

When LBJ mounted his personal campaign against the press, what moved him was his conviction that the press had elected him its enemy.

LBJ particularly hated photographers, saying: "Photographers are like animals."[43] Booth Mooney remembers that in 1962, while LBJ was still Vice President, "He distrusted photographers even more than he did newspaper reporters and television cameramen. He suspected that they were in a conspiracy to picture him yawning or scratching his groin." It apparently did not occur to him that changing his own behavior would eliminate that problem. When a photographer caught him exiting a car at the White House, LBJ said: "Look how he caught me with my shoulders twisted, the way my jacket's awry. That son of a bitch did it on purpose."[44]

In a projection of his own behavior onto others, he told George Reedy that the press pool which always accompanied him on his airplane were "spies." whose only job was to find out whatever would embarrass LBJ.[45]

Since he never saw faults in himself, LBJ had to come up with some explanation for what he interpreted as persecution by the press. He decided that the Northeastern press was out to get him because he came from Texas.[46] His paranoia made him take offense where none had been intended. When a journalist innocently asked at the ranch if a live oak was a "mesquite bush," LBJ showed fury because he associated mesquite bushes with the homes of "po' white trash." This reporter had been one of his strongest supporters until LBJ turned on him and accused him of lying.[47]

On another occasion, Helen Thomas wrote a sympathetic story about LBJ's aunt. He read it as a Robert Kennedy-inspired story depicting his family as dirt-poor illiterates. George Reedy says: "The situation was grotesque. It would take a real leap of imagination to conceive of Helen Thomas as a Kennedy sycophant. ...Nevertheless, the president set out to punish her by cutting off all the special 'goodies' he reserved for the distaff side of the press. ...One or two such incidents might have been bearable. But they kept multiplying."[48]

The President took other measures against the press. During plane flights he made a practice of sitting with the press pool so that he could keep an eye on them. At first the reporters were appreciative of this opportunity to spend so much time talking to a President. Or rather, listening to one, since he did all the talking. But there was a monotony to his monologues and press enthusiasm flagged after several weeks. Finally LBJ told Reedy that there would be no more press pool."[49]

Hugh Sidey noted that the President blamed his credibility gap entirely on the press.[50] It was not just LBJ's lies, it was also his paranoia that turned the press against him and that might have done so even without the war in Vietnam.

LBJ blamed the press for his inability to make the American people believe what he told them. Katherine Graham of the *Washington Post* said LBJ's idea of a free press was one that was perfectly obedient to him, interpreting reality his way, printing only the stories that he wanted to see the light, and burying the rest. When that failed to happen, he became enraged.[51] On one occasion, an infuriated LBJ declared: "We treat those (critical) columnists as whores. Any time an editor wants to screw 'em, they'll go down on the floor and do it for $3."[52]

LBJ had the White House operators record all calls that came in to the staff, hoping to catch calls from reporters. Resourceful reporters took to using false names. At press conferences, LBJ had his stooges ask the questions he wanted to answer, consuming the time available for unwelcome questions.

The President had become a sick individual who received no treatment for his illness. Under those conditions. LBJ was alternately reckless and aggressive, or frightened and paranoid. These are not qualities that one wants in a Commander in Chief.

One of the reasons that LBJ was elected in 1964 was that many people feared Barry Goldwater had those qualities. Paranoia and aggression make a lethal combination. To these LBJ added an ego that could not face defeat.

CHAPTER 14

THE YEAR WITHOUT A TUNNEL

★ ★ ★ ★ ★ ★

Had President Johnson followed President Kennedy's plan to withdraw from Vietnam, he would have been able to fund his Great Society legislation, and he probably would have placed high in the ranks of American presidents for his accomplishments.

Instead, the stresses engendered by the war worsened his mental illness. Indeed, absent the war, LBJ would not have faced a rising tide of criticism and consequently, there would have been less to feed his paranoia. Had he been spared the daily diet of mounting casualty lists, he might have been spared some depression as well. If reality had not been so terrible, he need not have fled so often to his private world of delusion. But the reality was that Johnson continued to drive his country deeper and deeper into an unwinnable war and everything fell apart.

1965

On January 18, 1965, the President met with Congressman Wilbur Mills. He insisted that America could afford both Vietnam and the Great Society without raising taxes.[1] His State of the Union address repeated his assurance that the funds were available to pay for his domestic programs and the military action in Vietnam.[2] Reality dictated that LBJ would have to short change his Great Society to lower the cost of Vietnam.

As January drew to a close, LBJ was in the hospital with bronchitis when Winston Churchill died. Protocol was that the Vice President be sent to represent the U.S. at the funeral, since the President was unavailable. LBJ refused to send Humphrey, begrudging him the publicity.[3] The President's illness was followed by a week of depression that his wife described as "...a sort of a slough of despond.... The 'Valley of the Black Pig.'"[4]

In order to keep Congress moving on his Great Society legislation, LBJ devoted substantial effort to playing down the war. That February, his program of deceit was failing with at least one person. James Reston wrote in the *New York Times*: "It is time to call a spade a bloody shovel. This country is in an undeclared and unexplained war in Vietnam."

By February 8, 1965, LBJ and his Vietnam advisors felt that South Vietnam could not survive much longer without increased U.S. military action. The President ordered secret bombing raids on North Vietnam.[5] At the end of the month he said, privately: "I don't think anything is going to be as bad as losing, and I don't see any way of winning."[6]

The people around the President asked him to tell the truth to the American people about the increasing involvement in Vietnam. On February 15, Hubert Humphrey tried to turn LBJ away from a policy of hiding the war: "...if we find ourselves...embroiled deeper in fighting in Vietnam over the next few months, political opposition will steadily mount." National Security advisor McGeorge Bundy also pressed the President to be open about the war: "...at its very best the struggle in Vietnam will be long. It seems to us important that this fundamental fact be made clear...to our own people...."[7] LBJ paid no attention. He ignored McGeorge Bundy's advice to make his policy public even though at that time 64% of the people favored what he was doing in Vietnam.[8]

1965 was a year fissured by the President's depressions. Disappointments about the course of the war in Vietnam triggered many of them. In February, LBJ remarked to his Press Secretary, Bill Moyers: "Light at the end of the tunnel. Hell, we don't even have a tunnel; we don't even know where the tunnel is."9

This was the period during which the President crossed the threshold committing the United States to an all-out war in Asia. LBJ worried that he was putting his presidency at risk, which he was. Moyers worried that the President was becoming dangerously depressed and paranoid: "He would just go within himself, just disappear—morose, self-pitying, angry...." While lying in bed with the covers pulled over his head, the President said that he felt he was in a Louisiana swamp, getting sucked under."10

Nevertheless, LBJ was not too depressed to stick a knife into his Vice President. On February 5, he created the President's Council on Equal Opportunity, made it responsible for coordinating the administration's actions on civil rights, and appointed Hubert Humphrey to chair it. Humphrey leapt into the job with his characteristic gusto, perhaps too much gusto for LBJ.

The President had his staff write a memo taking the job away, then showed it to Humphrey saying: "I didn't want to move on it without talking to you and getting your views." LBJ had his plan dumping Humphrey typed on the Vice President's stationary, signed by Humphrey, and then insisted that Humphrey announce his own execution. "If the Vice President is so enthusiastic about this reorganization, why doesn't he come over here and announce it himself, instead of my announcing it?" said the President. "Hell, it's *his* recommendation."11

On February 15, the Vice President told LBJ the reasons he opposed escalation: it jeopardized world opinion of America and its President, it threatened to bring China and the Soviet Union into an alliance against the United States, it would certainly sour relations with the Soviet Union, impede progress on arms control, increase our own defense expenditures, require the drafting of reservists, and finally, estrange us from our European allies.12

If the Vice President had not already joined LBJ's list of suspicious characters, that certainly put him on it. Unfortunately, Humphrey's predictions were realistic and logical and came to pass.

Hubert Humphrey was high on LBJ's blacklist for another reason. The President was jealous of his Vice President and resented any publicity that Humphrey received. When the Vice President made trips outside Washington, he was not allowed by LBJ to take members of the national press along to cover him. Immediately after the inauguration, LBJ limited Humphrey's staff, saying: "What does he need all that staff for?" The Vice President could not use an official plane without asking for permission. All of his speeches were edited by LBJ's office.[13] On the other hand, Humphrey was denied any advance looks at LBJ's State of the Union speech, a slight that was reported in the press.[14]

LBJ saw Humphrey as the source of the leaks from the White House. The Vice President complained: "Sometimes I'm afraid to tell Muriel (Mrs. Humphrey) anything. I don't know anymore what he thinks is secret or not secret, important or trivial."[15] Paranoia permitted LBJ to feel good about treating Humphrey badly.

February was bleak for LBJ. On the 17th, Adlai Stevenson, the U.S. ambassador to the U.N., suggested to the President that the U.S. negotiate without setting preconditions.[16] The following month he wrote the President that negotiation was better than escalation. LBJ did not reply. Stevenson would continue to argue "that no white army will ever win another war in Asia or Africa," but his words had no effect on LBJ's policies.[17]

Also in February, Senator Mansfield told LBJ after the U.S. began repeatedly bombing North Vietnam: "I would negotiate. I would not hit back." (The Vietcong had attacked the U.S. base at Pleiku on February 7th.) The President replied: "I just don't think you can stand still and take this kind of thing. You just can't do it."[18] On February 26, he ordered units of Marines to South Vietnam, the first U.S. combat troops to be sent there. Thus began the escalation that would have more than 170,000 American troops in that beleagured land by the end of the year.[19]

The mad zigzags from mania to martyrdom and back continued. In March, LBJ said to Senator Richard Russell: "Airplanes ain't worth a *damn*, Dick!"[20] Nevertheless, on March 2[21], he initiated the massive bombing of North Vietnam referred to as "Rolling Thunder." If the peace movement had been a slumbering giant, this awakened it. It found its voice in the Congress, the press, and the universities. Any criticism pained LBJ, but he found criticism of his war particularly distressing.[22]

In March, he told the U.S. military its job was not advising the South Vietnamese military, but "killing Vietcong," signaling that it had become an American war.[23]

The March reports from Vietnam in 1965 were more discouraging than anything previous, filled with predictions of the collapse of the South Vietnam government. LBJ told Senator Russell: "A man can fight if he can see daylight down the road somewhere. But there ain't no daylight in Vietnam. There's not a bit."[24] He described himself as a man who was trying to keep from drowning by standing on a newspaper in the middle of the ocean. "If I go this way, (to the right) I'll topple over, and if I go this way, (to the left) I'll topple over, and if I stay where I am the paper will soak up and I'll sink slowly to the bottom of the sea."[25] Even more notable than his self-pity was his personalization of the war. In his mind, he *was* America.

By the middle of the month, Lady Bird was concerned about her husband's "fog of depression." The doctors who gave the President a thorough examination found him in good health, and prescribed rest and sunshine for his depression.[26]

The depression was further evident on April 3, when the President confided to Lester Pearson, the Canadian Prime Minister: "I'm beginning to feel like a martyr; misunderstood, misjudged by friends at home and abroad."[27]

On April 7, 1965, the President met with Walter Lippmann, influential political commentator, and again made it clear that negotiations for peace were out of the question: "I'm not just going to pull up my pants and run out on Vietnam.... You say to negotiate, but there's nobody over there to negotiate with. So the only thing there is to do is to hang on. And that's what I'm going to do."

On April 17, nonaligned nations met in Belgrade and called for negotiations without preconditions to end the Vietnam War. In a speech at Johns Hopkins University , LBJ explained where he stood with a phrase like the favorite saying of the Borg, a terrifying species in the "Star Trek Next Generation" TV science fiction series. Just as the Borg were about to attack and assimilate a new species, they would announce: "Resistance is futile." LBJ said: "Armed hostility is futile. Our resources are equal to any challenge. Because we fight for values and we fight for principles, rather than territory or colonies, our patience and our determination are unending."[28]

Meanwhile, the Hill was hit by a tsunami of legislation. Instead of the usual one or two requests for legislative action per month, LBJ swamped the Congress with 63 that year.[29] The President's demands depleted whatever goodwill LBJ had left among the congressmen, and his ego used up the rest. A senator complained: "There were a lot of us who broke our backs on some of these bills, but Lyndon claimed he did it all himself. And you don't make friends that way."[30]

This was a year notable for manic foreign policy with many flexings of military muscle. LBJ proved to be as aggressive in the White House as he had been in the Senate, but now he had the Army, Navy, Marines, and Air Force to play with. He began bombing North Vietnam, then sent the Marines into South Vietnam, followed closely by the Army. He also dispatched the Marines to invade the Dominican Republic and save it from a Communist revolution.[31]

What happened in the Dominican Republic was this: on April 24th, supporters of the previously ousted president, Juan Bosch, seized the country from the current president, Donald Reid Cabral. On April 28, American Ambassador W. Tapley Bennett requested American troops. An initial 400 marines were followed by 22,000.[32]

LBJ was hitting a flea with a hammer. Eventually, troops of the Organization of American States replaced American troops and free elections took place in June, 1966.[33]

The President turned this commonplace event in Latin American history into a manic circus. He sent three times the troops needed to maintain peace.[34] He also extorted Congress to provide the millions of dollars needed to support the troops. Any refusal would have looked like the abandonment of American boys.[35]

So far, none of this was unusual for American presidents. LBJ put his unique stamp on the event when he related to the American people the following fantasy: "Some 1,500 innocent people were murdered and shot, and their heads cut off. And…as we talked to our Ambassador to confirm the horror and tragedy and the unbelievable fact that they were firing at Americans and the American embassy, he was talking to us from under a desk while bullets were going through his windows, and he had a thousand American men, women and children assembled at the hotel who were pleading with their President to help preserve their lives."[36]

LBJ insisted that the Ambassador predicted "American blood will run in the streets" if troops were not sent.[37] The President added that in four days six Latin American embassies were attacked.[38] LBJ said that he had consulted with President Romulo Betancourt of Venezuela.[39] He also claimed that an internationally run Communist revolution was underway.[40] The only truth in all of this was that there were some fatalities. However only two Americans were shot and these were a reporter and a photographer who were shot by our own marines.[41]

The CIA concluded that only three Communists participated in the revolt.[42] Everything else originated in LBJ's manic imagination.

LBJ constantly blurred the boundary between truth and falsehood. He often believed his own lies. It is difficult to determine at what point he was convinced that his country was losing the war in Vietnam. Probably he believed, when he became President, that victory was a certainty. Few could anticipate that the most powerful nation in the world would be defeated by small, backward North Vietnam and a bunch of pajama-clad guerrillas in the South.

From the start of his presidency, he mislead the American people about the kind of allies they had in South Vietnam and the kind of growing enemy force they had taken on.[43] In the spring of 1965, South Vietnamese forces, which had far better weapons and outnumbered the Vietcong by three to one, were losing at a fearful rate. In addition, South Vietnamese desertions were increasing.[44]

Another well-kept secret was the fact that the people of South Vietnam were turning against the Americans and the government sponsored by the U.S. This wasn't told to the American public and the President kept piling one deception on top of another.

At last, on July 28, the President admitted publicly not to waging a war in Vietnam, but to sending "...forces which will raise our fighting strength from 75,000 to 125,000 men almost immediately. Additional forces will be needed later, and they will be sent as requested...."[45]

In the summer of 1965, Defense Secretary McNamara told LBJ that additional taxes would be needed to pay for the war if inflation were to be avoided. The President told him to get a vote count. Having done so, McNamara reported that a bill for higher taxes would not pass.

LBJ was not willing to reign in the cost of the war. Instead, he gave orders for the Defense Department to inform Congress that no more money for the war would be needed until the following year.[46] In July the President, while insisting that U.S. forces were not involved in aggressive actions, also lied to Congress about the number of troops requested by General Westmoreland and about the money needed for what American forces were planning and already doing.[47]

Another cost not yet reckoned was the delay in reducing nuclear arms that the war caused. At a meeting on July 15, 1965, between Averell Harriman and the Soviet Premier, Alexei Kosygin, the latter said that he wanted to make progress in six areas: an end to all nuclear tests, a reduction in all nuclear weapons, the nonproliferation of nuclear weapons, reductions in military spending, increased trade between his country and the U.S., and more contacts between citizens of both countries. He added that Dean Rusk and Andrei Gromyko had already agreed to reductions of military expenditures.

The Soviets had made cuts of $500 million but the U.S., disregarding the agreement, had raised expenditures by $700 million to pay for the Vietnam War. On July 21, in response to LBJ's encouraging reaction to Kosygin's words, the Premier said that only the Vietnam War stood in the way of a summit and agreements on nonproliferation and nuclear arms reduction.[48] One might assume that this was merely a cynical way to pressure the American President to pull out of Vietnam. However, the Soviet Union could ill afford the size of its military spending, the summits were eventually held and progress in all six areas specified by Kosygin eventually took place.

In August, 1965, a riot exploded in Watts, a Los Angeles ghetto. Joseph Califano was witness to another side of LBJ, the inability to cope. This often comes with depression. As we saw, LBJ could not face bad news when he was losing the Democratic nomination for President to Kennedy. The riot brought the same response. Califano says: "He just wouldn't accept it. He refused to look at the cable from Los Angeles describing the situation. He refused to take calls from the generals who were requesting government planes to fly in the National Guard."

This kind of freezing into immobility is one of the drawbacks of having an untreated manic depressive in the White House. And more trouble lay ahead. While LBJ was in office, 100 more riots would ignite America's cities, killing 225 people, wounding 4,000 and leaving in their wakes $112 billion in property damage.[49]

According to LBJ, he knew how to solve people's problems and did so with dispatch, and said so too, prompting Hugh Sidey to speak of LBJ's "feelings of omnipotence."[50] The President expected his fellow citizens to be completely satisfied with everything he had done, and to be grateful to him for his efforts. Clearly, this did not happen in the ghettos of America, where the riots were breaking out. "How is it possible after all we've accomplished?" LBJ asked, ignoring the fact that life was still grim and frightening in America's inner cities.

His paranoia explained black rage by blaming it on black leaders: "It simply wasn't fair for a few irresponsible agitators to spoil it for me and for all the rest of the Negroes. A few hoodlums sparked by outside agitators who moved round from city to city making trouble. Spoiling all the progress I've made in these last few years."[51] His sympathy was only for himself and there was none left for those who were killed or injured or lost homes and businesses as the riots burned on.

The ranch was LBJ's refuge, but by the autumn, his depression inspired him to call it "lonely acres."[52] His gall bladder operation in October was followed by another depression during which he fretted about the slowness of his recovery and the ridicule he received from the press for showing off his new scar.[53] He still expected to be exempt from criticism and demanded: "What do they want— what *really* do they want? I'm giving them boom times and more good legislation than anybody else did, and what do they do— attack and sneer! Could FDR do better? Could anybody do better?"[54] At such moments he managed to blind himself to the reality that he had plunged his country into a war no one wanted.

Hubert Humphrey became a target of suspicion again in November of 1965, when LBJ talked about sending the Vice President to Asia. Word of the plan was leaked by the Secretary of Agriculture, Orville Freeman, but the President blamed the Vice President and cancelled the trip.[55]

A simple conversation became for LBJ an opportunity for one-sided unarmed combat. Frank Cormier found out that the boss not only grabbed people, he drove a rigid finger into their chests and banged their knees hard enough to leave them black and blue.[56]

When Senator Greuning went to LBJ to discuss Vietnam, he

recalled, "I asked the President not to interrupt me for ten minutes. I didn't want him punching my chest or slapping my knee or doing those things he likes to do to keep you rattled and off balance."[57]

John Connally's wife Nellie, who worked in the office for a while, reports that she was not fast enough for LBJ when he asked her to get a phone number for him. The next moment, she was the bullseye when he threw a book. She did not feel safe with him after that.[58] Connally, who was also a witness to Johnson's violence, recalled: "...he would be just wild, *wild!,* raging, ranting, screaming, totally out of control."[59]

Johnson's attacks of rage were not confined to the privacy of his office. He spent time in the phone booths of the Senate cloakroom trying to get the obediance of fellow senators. When he failed, he exploded in rage, throwing the receivers onto the floor and assaulting the phone booth doors with his feet.[60] This is the kind of behavior that usually gets manics into hospitals.

Belligerence and arrogance combined in LBJ's version of diplomacy. After meeting Germany's Chancellor, Ludwig Erhard, the President said: "He was ready to go in the barn and milk my cows, if he could find the teats. There's only one way to deal with Germans. You keep patting them on the head and then every once in a while you kick them in the balls."[61]

By 1965, it had become obvious that every olive branch offered by LBJ contained a dagger. In April, May, July, and December, his offers to negotiate were followed by the arrival of more American soldiers arriving in South Vietnam and more bombs being dropped on North Vietnam.[62]

Mansfield tried again in June, 1965, to prevent the bombing of Haiphong Harbor in North Vietnam, insisting that it "...would not be effective, it would thwart discussions; push allies away from us, keep China involved, freeze-in Russia as an arms supplier, enlarge the war...."

John Kennedy had feared that escalation would bring China and the U.S.S.R into the war, and it happened. 300,000 Chinese soldiers were by then active in North Vietnam, freeing North Vietnamese to go south. China also supplied some 37,000 artillery pieces with almost 20 million shells for them, 2 million guns, 270 million rounds of ammunition, plus large numbers of planes and naval vessels. Soviet and Warsaw pact ships delivered munitions to North Vietnam throughout the war.[63] Chinese and Soviet aid exceeded a billion dollars a year annually.[64] Nevertheless, the bombing of Haiphong Harbor would begin that November.

Robert McNamara recalled that he lost the faith that summer, "My sense of the war gradually shifted from concern to scepticism to frustration to anguish....more and more people were being killed and we simply were not accomplishing our goals."[65]

He told the President in December: "Ultimately we must find a diplomatic solution." LBJ replied: "Then, no matter what we do in the military field, there is no sure victory?" (This was a strange question, considering his earlier pessimism, but his view changed with his mood.)

McNamara: "That's right. We have been too optimistic."[66]

It is hard to believe that LBJ was told all of this in the first year after he was elected president, yet continued for three more years, dragging his country down this hopeless road until he left office.

In the beginning, it was Robert McNamara's war almost as much as it was LBJ's and the former did not turn against the war overnight. But when he did, his days as Secretary of Defense were numbered. At a party on December 3, 1965, McNamara burst into tears while talking about the war, a spectacle that many of the Washington elite would observe from time to time for two more years.[67]

LBJ's personality was not only hurting those around him but was destroying the man himself. Mania is a cruel illness. It gave him fancy dreams and then drove him to failure. It gave him an extraordinary career. Then sabotaged it so completely that, at the end, his manic paranoia rendered him unfit for office.

CHAPTER 15

"DOWNRIGHT FRIGHTENING"

★ ★ ★ ★ ★ ★

1966

In January of 1966, Senator Vance Hartke wrote a letter cosigned by 14 senators asking that bombing not be resumed and that negotiations be pursued. The President called him a "prick" and ordered several Hartke people fired from federal jobs.[1] By February, almost half of the sixty-seven Democrats in the Senate were against the war. Speaking for many of them, Senator Albert Gore described the President as "...a desperate man who was likely to get us into war with China, and we have got to prevent it."[2]

LBJ had not abandoned deception about the American involvement in Vietnam in favor of candor, even though he resembled more and more a man trying to hide an elephant in a suitcase. 1966 saw a monthly increase in the shipping of American troops to Vietnam, but the President never revealed that he expected the American presence to be, at the end of the year, double what it was twelve months earlier.[3] Throughout that year the Joint Chiefs of Staff requested a call-up of the reserves to deal with America's problems elsewhere in the world. LBJ refused to do anything that would confirm that the country was at war.[4]

In 1966, leading economists again told the President that to control inflation taxes must be raised and spending cut. Neither policy was enacted.[5]

LBJ seemed to be coming apart at the seams. On February 4, he decided to gather people in Honolulu to discuss Vietnam. The heads of mission in Saigon, officials of the South Vietnamese government, American diplomats and their technical advisors, members of the Cabinet, and the Chairman of the Joint Chiefs of Staff were given two days notice. With no research, no planning, no time to design a workable agenda, nothing useful could result and nothing did. The meeting was merely another tribute to the President's impulsivity.

LBJ even used his impulsivity as a form of harassment. The victim, this time, was his Vice President. At 11:30 PM one night in Chicago, Humphrey was told he was leaving the following day for a two-and-a-half week trip to Asia. He recalled: "The next morning was chaos. Members of my staff...were suddenly required to get passports and a half-dozen medical shots. They went home to pack, ...say goodbye to husbands, wives and children for several weeks, unable to tell them where they were going." Humphrey concludes: "So, after a year, more of isolation than participation, I was about to embark on a major trip in a delicate area, with no time for specific preparation, no briefing papers reviewed ahead of time, no time for study in depth."[6] It looks as if the President was setting Humphrey up to fail.

The Vice President was dispatched to visit nine countries, including South Vietnam. After his return, as Humphrey's aides were getting a report ready, Jack Valenti instructed them that the President wanted to hear nothing but good news. A complaisant Humphrey made an about face and became a spokesman for LBJ's war. The Vice President wrote "...I am thoroughly in agreement with the President (about Vietnam)." A week later he was invited to join the next Tuesday Lunch Group meeting, which LBJ reserved for people he thought most trustworthy.[7]

Both Frank Cormier and Jack Valenti assert that, despite his heavy drinking, LBJ would have periods in the White House when he restricted or eliminated his consumption of alcohol.[8] Joseph Califano describes LBJ, in August of 1965, downing several glasses of scotch and soda after dinner.[9] But, says Califano, the President had a dry period in 1966 because he was worried he might be too drunk to function when a crisis in the war required clear thinking.[10]

Towards the end of February, Senator Robert Kennedy stated publicly for the first time that he thought the United States should negotiate with Ho Chi Minh and agree to a South Vietnamese coalition government. LBJ was so depressed on hearing this that he remained alone and immobile in the Oval Office for hours afterwards.[11]

The Vietnam War did not turn LBJ paranoid, for he showed symptoms of that condition even as a Senator. However, his paranoia grew more intense and found more targets as opposition to the war widened. He was losing the country and he believed the Communists were taking it away from him.

On March 12, 1966, he declared at a meeting of governors: "…our country is constantly under threat every day—Communists working every day to divide us, to destroy us. Make no mistake about the Communists….Don't kid yourself for a moment. It is in the highest councils of government—in our society. McCarthy's methods were wrong—but the threat is greater now than in his day."[12]

On April 3, 1966, senior aide Jack Valenti became a dove and wrote to LBJ: "All that you strive for and believe in, and are accomplishing is in danger, as long as this war goes on." He was too useful to let go, but LBJ never replied.[13] Others who had turned against the war did not wait to be shoved, but walked away from the inner circle on their own. McGeorge Bundy resigned on February 28, Bill Moyers left a few months later, and George Ball was gone that fall.[14]

No matter how much he had boasted to others about these wonderful people who worked for him, he now disparaged them mercilessly after their departure.[15]

In April, 1966, a warning came from CIA chief John McCone. He told the President that Rolling Thunder, with its napalm and carpet bombing, was not getting anywhere. He added that the North Vietnamese continued to support the Vietcong in the South, supplying it with reinforcements and materiel. All the bombing had accomplished, he said, was to make the North Vietnamese more obdurate. He concluded: "We will find ourselves mired down in combat in a military effort that we cannot win, and from which we will have extreme difficulty in extricating ourselves."[16] His words had zero effect.

The President blew hot and cold during the summer where his Vice President was concerned. Bill Moyers told Humphrey that the President refused to speak to the Vice President and did not allow his staff to do so. This was followed by an equally baffling thaw.[17] The only thing that was predictable about LBJ was the persistence of his paranoia. According to aide Eric Goldman, the President was convinced that anyone who opposed the war was either unhinged or treacherous. He described his boss as "depressing" and "downright frightening."[18]

Meanwhile LBJ's war with the press went into phase two. By June of 1966, the press corps was aware of most of the President's tricks and resented them. Moyers observed: "…the White House Press Corps has come to believe that we antagonize them deliberately, keep them as uninformed as possible, make their personal lives as difficult as we can, play games with them, are unduly secretive, massage them when we need them and kick them when we don't and generally 'downgrade the profession'."[19] That was absolutely accurate. Even a LBJ ally, Washington columnist Joseph Alsop, admitted that LBJ had made "attempts at news control much more aggressive, comprehensive, and I must add, repugnant to American tradition, than any other president."[20]

Whether they defied him or supported him LBJ would scold the press. He had ruled out taking pictures of him while he had lunch, so photographers would go off for their own lunch. One day, during the lunch hour, he suddenly decided to have some photographs taken. He expected the photographers to be instantly available, like water from a faucet. He got more and more angry until the photographers returned, then barked: "Where in the hell have you-all been?"[21]

Reporters were really in for it when LBJ began treating them the way he treated his wife and employees. He yelled at an overweight reporter: "C'mon Cheavers. Won't those fat little legs of yours carry you any faster than that?"[22] At a news conference he shouted at one of the participants: "You sonofabitch! Why do you come and ask me, the leader of the Western world, a chickenshit question like that?"[23] At a dance, LBJ literally threw a photographer out the door and swore at the other photographers in the room. When he saw photographers outside church the following day he became angry again and called them "little piss-ants."[24]

True to form, LBJ refused to admit any responsibility for his loss of popularity. "I really must be uninspiring if the papers and the TV said so," he remarked. "They began to think that I might be wrong about the war. And gradually they stopped coming to my speeches. And then the press gleefully reported a small crowd and an uninspiring speech."[25] In his own view, LBJ was just an innocent victim of malicious reporters.

One of the amazing aspects of this tale is how the press protected LBJ from himself. One day he offered to compare the length of his penis with that of any of the male reporters at the ranch. "I'll match mine against any of yours," he said.[26] Today that quote would appear on page one of every newspaper in the country, but the press kept silent then. On another occasion, he instructed reporters: "If I have one too many scotches under my belt, and you see it, I don't expect to read about it in the papers."[27] And he didn't. He also told them: "I may go into a strange bedroom every now and then that I don't want you to write about."[28] They protected his secrets but they couldn't protect him from himself.

Moyers became a suspect in LBJ's lineup. The day Moyers resigned, Robert Kennedy took him out to lunch, which was enough to convince the President that his suspicions were justified. LBJ complained: "When Moyers became my Press Secretary, my popularity was at an all-time high and nobody ever heard of Bill Moyers. When he left, I was at an all-time low and Bill Moyers was a world hero."[29]

At times, LBJ looked around his office and saw himself surrounded by enemies. He claimed to have heard his aides plotting to divide his power amongst them.[30] Consider how cowed his staff was. This sounds as though either he misheard or misinterpreted some real conversation. He actually said to an aide: "I can't trust anybody. What are you trying to do to me? Everybody is trying to cut me down, destroy me."[31] Hugh Sidey remarked that Lyndon Johnson's administration had become a solo performance as the President walled himself off from even his closest advisors. Paranoia is painful, frightening, and isolating for the person afflicted with it.

The United States was being led by a man who already was or rapidly was becoming psychotic. The principle signs of psychosis are delusions and hallucinations. Hallucinations are the easiest to identify. The person who experiences them sees and hears things that no one else can see or hear. Delusions can be more controversial in the early stages of psychosis, and can masquerade as fringe opinions. However, LBJ's grandiosity, megalomania and paranoia reached dimensions that could no longer pass for normalcy.

Signs of grandiosity and paranoia were present before LBJ became President, but assuming responsibility for the war in Vietnam appears to have been more stress than he could bear as 1966 wore on.

On June 29, after giving the order for what he felt was a particularly dangerous escalation of the war, the distraught President told his daughter Luci, "Your Daddy may go down in history as having started World War III. You may not wake up tomorrow." Imagine how it must feel to tell your child that you have just put her life in jeopardy. Putting all of mankind at risk is stress beyond imagining.

LBJ told Dr. Ernst Lemberger, the Austrian Ambassador, about visits from the Holy Ghost. It is not clear whether the President was merely expressing a delusion or describing an hallucination, but this is what he said to the Ambassador: "He comes and speaks to me about two o'clock in the morning—when I have to give the word to the boys, and I get the word from God whether to bomb or not."[32] It must have been very comforting to surrender responsibility for all those lives and let God make the decisions. Religious people often, in difficult times, seek guidance in prayer. Psychotics go beyond that: they see and hear what is not there.

In June, 1966, at State Department behest, Ambassador Chester Ronning of Canada went to Hanoi and returned with news that the North Vietnamese were still ready to negotiate. Within a week, LBJ ordered the first bombing of Hanoi.[33]

Besides LBJ's internal unstable weather, the summer brought a new vexation: pickets who shouted obscenities at LBJ and Lady Bird when they attended the opera in San Francisco. Rowdy and abusive pickets also met the President and First Lady when they traveled to New Zealand and Australia. Only on American air bases were they safe from chants of "Hey, hey, LBJ, how many boys have you killed today?"[34]

By September 4, the President was exhausted. He told Jack Valenti: "If I could figure some way to get out of this job I would do it now. They would say I was playing politics if I resigned and gave the job to Humphrey. But it is impossible to do the right job under these circumstances. My own party has turned against me, and the Republicans have chimed in. As it is, now I have even lost Congress."[35] He had indeed.

By September, the CIA convinced Congressman Tip O'Neill that the war could not be won. He sent the voters in his district a letter explaining his change of mind. When LBJ met with the Congressman, LBJ was hurt and angry. He said: "Tip, what kind of a son-of-a-bitch are you? I expect something like this from those assholes like (Congressman) Bill Ryan....But you? You're one of my own!"[36]

LBJ had lost several senators too. A book by Senator William Fulbright's, *The Arrogance of Power,* contained the following attack: "...the administration has converted the Vietnamese conflict from a civil war in which some American advisors were involved to a major international war in which the principal fighting unit is an American army of hundreds of thousands of men. Each time Senators have raised questions about successive escalations of the war, we have the blank check of August 7, 1964 (the Tonkin Gulf Resolution) waved in our faces as supposed evidence of the overwhelming support of Congress for a policy in Southeast Asia which in fact has been radically changed since the summer of 1964."[37]

Senator Albert Gore claimed that the Tonkin Gulf Resolution was itself based on deception and poor judgement: "...I feel that I was mislead that this was an entirely unprovoked attack, that our ships were entirely on routine patrol. The fact stands from today that they were intelligence ships; that they were under instructions to agitate North Vietnam radar, that they were plying close to shore....

"...the administration was hasty, acted precipitately, inadvisably, unwisely, out of proportion to the provocation in launching sixty-four bombing attacks on North Vietnam out of a confused, uncertain situation on a murky night,...and particularly, five hours after the task force commander had cabled that he doubted that there were any attacks, and recommended that no further action be taken until it was thoroughly canvassed and reviewed."[38]

McGeorge Bundy noted that Lyndon Johnson judged anything less than total, sincere support for his war to be disloyalty.[39] As members of the Senate joined the ranks of the doves, LBJ saw treason everywhere. "Ambassador Dobrynin (of the Soviet Union) seems to have more votes in the Senate than the President of the United States," said the President.[40] He insisted to Eric Goldman that antiwar senators were constantly getting their orders from the Soviet Union. "It's the Russians who are behind the whole thing." "The Russians," he explained, "think up things for the senators to say."[41] LBJ informed Goldman that the CIA and the FBI saw senators eating lunch and going to parties at the Soviet Embassy, that children of these senators' staffs had been observed going out with Russians. With all the intelligence he was receiving from reports on the senators, LBJ insisted: "I often know before they do what their speeches are going to say."

Goldman recalled that this new version of LBJ was both saddening and unnerving.[42] When the President wanted to be especially intimidating, he told people that his bedside reading at night included secret FBI reports in which senators and writers were seen talking to Russians.[43]

Unfortunately, another election, this one for congressmen, was in the offing. Two years of Vietnam had changed everything. the President was no longer surfing on a huge wave of mass approval, and now LBJ's reliance on impulse as a campaign strategy backfired. He crossed the country more like an absolute monarch visiting his realm than like a campaigning politician. His sudden trips allowed for no local preparation, his speeches were not relevant to the interests of the localities he visited, and he ignored the candidates he was supposedly helping.[44]

Mania revisited LBJ for a while in October, as it usually did when he traveled. He cheerfully loaded his aide Joseph Califano with gold trinkets stamped with the Presidential Seal, and then took off for the South Pacific and points west. The huge, enthusiastic crowds in Seoul, South Korea, restored the President's good mood to the point where he was lying again to the audience about his great-great grandfather having died at the Alamo.[45]

Some grandiosity was also in evidence. LBJ's luggage contained 200 busts of himself to pass out to people. As Congressman James Symington remarked, "It is, I think, unusual for a man to want to give a bust of himself in his lifetime, although it is difficult for him to give it any other time. But to make a mass production gesture really boggles the mind."[46]

Except for his Pacific travels, October was a month of uncharacteristic inactivity for the President. Showing signs of depression, he rarely left the White House.

By October of 1966, he was swearing to Joseph Califano that the Communists were the main influence on the networks...and were pulling the strings of several columnist puppets. Califano reports that within a year, Johnson would see the Communists as all powerful, successfully destroying the government's credibility as well as that of himself, Humphrey, Rusk, McNamara, and the new national security advisor, Walt Rostow. According to Johnson, the only reliable paper left in the country was the *Christian Science Monitor*.[47]

In November, LBJ was scheduled to make a "triumphal" whirlwind campaign tour during which, in local statehouses, he would sign some of the Great Society bills that had been passed. Congressional candidates had changed their schedules in preparation for his visit, halls were made ready for large rallies, and publicity was released. At the last minute, LBJ had a change of heart and cancelled the trip. Then he had the gall to deny that any trip had been planned: "First, we don't have any plans....The people of this country ought to know that all those cancelled plans primarily involve the imagination of people who...write columns." That statement made LBJ's credibility a bigger issue than the cancellation.[48]

Johnson continued to provide lies and more lies for the benefit of the public. He continued his penny-pinching act at the White House, insisting that lights be turned out and ordering Defense Secretary McNamara to "see that military contractors reduce their costs." None of this parsimony applied to his friends at Brown and Root who, according to the Government Accounting Office were charging hundreds of millions of dollars beyond what was legitimate for their construction work in Vietnam.[49]

He claimed that his great- great-grandfather had died in the Alamo, then said it was a slip of the tongue, he meant the battle of San Jacinto, then denied he had made the Alamo statement although it was recorded on tape, and LBJ was still telling the story in 1966. The ancestor had never been near either battle, but had dealt in real estate and died in bed.[50]

When LBJ told ranch guests that he had been born in a shack, his mother corrected him: "Now Lyndon, you know we had a nice house over on the other side of town."[51] He also lied about his college grades, laying claim to 35 "A"s out of the forty courses he took, whereas the reality was that, he earned only a "B" average.[52]

Perhaps the hypocrisy that eventually got LBJ into the most trouble was the two faces that he showed to the press. He declared: "We want honest, forthright discussion in this country, and that will be discussion with differences of views, and we welcome what our friends have to say, whether they agree with us or not. I would not want to label people who agree with me or disagree with me." But Frank Cormier had heard LBJ calling everyone who criticized his war policy contemporary Chamberlain's ready to surrender the free world to the forces of evil. George Reedy notes: "His public pronouncements supporting a free press were ludicrous—what he actually wanted was freedom to buy up journalists."[53]

Hugh Sidey, again speaking for the press, declared, "It is a singular experience to be told by the President of the United States... that something you know to be true is not so. Yet that is what happened repeatedly....The press, of course, was the first group to become aware of this habit of the President's." He added: "Reporters were baffled from the start as to why the President did not simply refuse to talk...rather than stage elaborate dramas to present impressions which inevitably were exposed as false."[54]

Booth Mooney offers an explanation that fits well with the grandiose delusions LBJ was developing. He says that LBJ was convinced that, no matter how fantastic his pronouncements, people would believe them.[55]

Although politicians are rarely completely candid with the public, few of them twist the truth the way that LBJ did. When they realized what LBJ was up to, reporters were unforgiving. Richard Rovere, of *The New Yorker*, wrote: "It seems...to be a fact beyond dispute that no other President has ever had to live in an atmosphere so heavy with distrust and disbelief as Lyndon Johnson.... What may well be a majority of the American people are persuaded that the President is a dishonest and dishonorable man."[56] How did they learn this? The press told them. Hugh Sidey concluded that the most difficult thing Lyndon Johnson had to do during his years as President was getting people to believe what he said. His lying encroached every aspect of his upon Presidency.[57] It left a leaden legacy of cynicism about politics and politicians that every succeeding President has inherited.[58]

The President's manic optimism not withstanding, the election on November 8 was a rout for the Democrats. Republicans gained 47 seats in the House and 3 in the Senate, as well as 8 governors and 677 state legislators.[59]

Six months earlier, Januscz Lewandowski, a Polish diplomat, had told Ambassador Lodge that Hanoi was willing to begin negotiations in Warsaw. Throughout the summer, Lodge and Lewandowski met in secret to arrange the details. A meeting was scheduled for December 5, but before the North Vietnamese representative reached Warsaw, Hanoi was bombed. Another meeting was set for December 13, but the Americans hit Hanoi again, with double the number of bombs. Lodge and others had begged LBJ to postpone the raids, but he insisted that to do so would signal weakness. On December 15, the U.S. was informed that the bombings had made the talks impossible.[60]

1966 saw the establishment of the "peace shop" and that oxymoron, the "peace offensive." LBJ made senior diplomats Averell Harriman and Chester Cooper the proprietors of the "peace shop," with the responsibility of overseeing all peace initiatives. However, McNamara observes, "...he did not give them the authority they needed to do a job he wanted to control himself."[61]

The "peace offensive" was a much more elaborate production. At the end of the year, LBJ sent Humphrey to Tokyo, New Delhi and Manila, Harriman was delegated to Warsaw, and U.N.

Ambassador Arthur Goldberg covered Paris, London and the Vatican, carrying LBJ's assurance that he really wanted peace. One hundred and fifteen countries in all got the message.

Meanwhile, at home he told George Ball to assure Senators Mansfield and Fulbright that the "peace offensive" was what they had been demanding. At the same time, Ball was instructed to assure the hawk, Senator Hickenlooper, that the bombing pause during Holy Week meant nothing—the weather was not good then for bombing anyway.[62]

CHAPTER 16

BURNING THE OLIVE BRANCH

1967

By 1967, LBJ's grandiose delusions contrasted to his growing condemnation by the press and the increasing numbers of Americans who opposed his war. He saw himself as an embattled martyr. He compared himself to Lincoln, who had been plagued by the Civil War draft riots and by dump Lincoln movements.[1]

LBJ repeated in his 1967 budget message that "…the struggle in Vietnam must be supported. The advance towards a Great Society at home must continue unabated."[2] He refused to reduce spending, and asked for a 6% surcharge on the income tax in his January 20 State of the Union address.[3]

Harrison Salisbury, a Pulitzer Prize winning war correspondent, met with Premier Pham Van Dong of North Vietnam in early January. Salisbury returned to Washington with the message that the North Vietnamese were willing to start talks at once, and without any preconditions. LBJ refused even to talk to Salisbury.[4]

The bombing of North Vietnam resumed on January 31, 1967.[5]

LBJ made sure that J. Edgar Hoover kept sending him reports as peace marches took place. Harwood and Johnson noted: "It sounded as though anyone opposed to his policies was suspect and dossiers on them were being built up, as indeed it turned out there were."[6]

There were times, despite the bravado, when the President was depressed and filled with fear: "...we're really up for grabs," he said. "We're the richest nation in the world. And the minute we look soft, the would-be aggressors will go wild. We'll lose all of Asia and then Europe and we'll be an island by ourselves."[7] Obviously, none of that has happened. The future would show that the alleged aggressors wanted green cards.

On February 6, 1967, Alexei Kosygin visited Prime Minister Harold Wilson in London. The U.S. had allowed a short bombing pause. Kosygin was willing to go to Hanoi to get peace negotiations underway, so Wilson asked LBJ to extend the bombing pause for two days to permit a safe visit. LBJ agreed to only six hours. An angry Kosygin nevertheless agreed to do what he could. The American ambassador to England, David Bruce, phoned Rusk to say that the time allotted for Kosygin to contact Hanoi and return with a reply made the mission impossible, and asked for the bombing halt to be extended by several days. Before further communications could take place, bombing resumed.[8]

That same month, LBJ's paranoia scuttled another opportunity to end the war. Robert Kennedy had met representatives of North Vietnam and returned to the U.S. with what appeared to be an opening towards negotiations. Because word of this leaked out in *Newsweek*, LBJ concluded that it was nothing but a political maneuver to make Kennedy look good. The two men had a meeting on February 6. LBJ refused to respond to the North Vietnamese rapprochement. He shouted: "The war will be over this year, and when it is, I'll destroy you and every one of your dove friends. You'll be dead politically in six months."[9]

When Kennedy asked the President to stop the bombing, LBJ said: "There isn't a chance in hell that I will do that, not the slightest chance!" He accused Kennedy and the other doves of prolonging the war. Kennedy later told a friend: "I kept thinking that if he exploded like that with me, how could he ever negotiate with Hanoi?" Later Kennedy joked to the press: "We had a long serious talk about the possibilities of a cease-fire, the dangers of escalation and the prospects for negotiation. And he promised me the next time we are going to talk about Vietnam."[10]

In May of 1967, the Prime Minister of Afghanistan, Mohammed Hashim Maiwandwal, criticized the bombing before meeting with the President in Washington. U Thant later related what happened. LBJ did not allow Maiwandwal to speak and "...started out immediately by jabbing the Prime Minister's forearm steadily with a finger like a pecking bird while he kept repeating 'We've been awfully easy on Vietnam so far.' Then after a time he stopped this, and thrust his big fist like a piston that stopped only an inch from the Prime Minister's eyes, and he yelled: 'We could really pound them if we wanted to!'"[11]

The spring and summer, as often occurred with the President, brought rising spirits although none of the President's problems diminished, or seemed likely to do so.[12]

On July 25, the day after riots in Detroit, Senator Fulbright addressed LBJ: "Mr. President, what you really need to do is stop the war. That will solve all your problems.... The Vietnam War is a hopeless venture.... I will not support it any longer. I suspect that for the first time in 20 years I may vote against foreign assistance and may try to bottle the whole bill up in the committee."

LBJ replied: "If you want me to get out of Vietnam, then you have the prerogative of taking the (Tonkin Gulf) resolution under which we are out there now. You can repeal it tomorrow. You can tell the troops to come home. You can tell General Westmoreland that he doesn't know what he is doing."[13]

August brought terrible polls. A majority of Americans disapproved of the way LBJ was conducting the war and only 39% thought he was doing a good job overall. David Lilienthal,

Chairman of the Atomic Energy Commission, attended a White House dinner that month and saw a President who showed his depression in every line of his body. The most gregarious of heads of state could only bring himself to greet a few friends before he retreated to his private quarters.[14]

Throughout 1967, the President became even more defensive about his war and less tolerant of dissenters. Leonard Marks, Director of the U.S. Information Agency, gives the following account: "One morning I was with the President in his family quarters and he was getting dressed....(Marks said to the President:) "Senator Aiken made a suggestion I think is pretty good. The Vietnamese have just held a national election.... Democracy seems to be thriving there. Why don't we say we've achieved that objective, provide equipment and take our troops out?...What do you think?"

LBJ yelled "Get out of here!" which Marks did. He was banished from NSC meetings for some time.[15]

When LBJ got bad news from Vietnam, his paranoia prevented him from assessing the information to acquire a more accurate view of what was happening there. In August of 1967, *New York Times* Saigon Bureau chief R.W. Apple learned from American officers that despite undergoing many months of heavy bombing, the Vietcong were better armed than ever before. Apple was also informed that the combined South Vietnamese and American army of 1.2 million controlled only a small part of South Vietnam, and without American aid and troops, the government of that country could not long survive. When Apple published this, the President demanded that he be replaced by journalists who were "on the Team," and insisted that Apple was a Communist.[16]

That autumn, 1967, CIA Director Richard Helms sent LBJ a secret memo saying that national security did not require the U.S. to stay in Vietnam.[17] It was evident by now that LBJ was no longer paying attention to his advisors and that he listened to them only when they told him what he wanted to hear.

The war continued to go badly and depression set in again. LBJ was certain that the Communists were financing as well as directing the peace movement. He ordered Richard Helms, director of the CIA to look into it. Helms turned in a negative report. Shaking a finger in Helms' face, LBJ declared: "I simply don't understand why it is that you can't find out about that foreign money."[18]

He gave Helms another task: to find the links between the antiwar, antidraft college students and an international Communist conspiracy. A government study of student unrest found the "Student New Left" to be "essentially anticommunist," but that did not change LBJ's opinion.[19] Two weeks after the peace march of October 21, 1967, the President declared: "I'm not going to let the Communists take this government, and they're doing it right now."

Richard Helms said: "We could find no evidence of any contact between the most prominent peace movement leaders and foreign embassies, either in the U.S. or abroad....On the basis of what we know; we see no significant evidence that would prove Communist control or direction of the U.S. peace movement or its leaders." This was read to the Cabinet, after which LBJ and Dean Rusk argued against the report. In December, a second report, came to the same conclusion. Nevertheless, LBJ insisted to Minority Leader Gerald Ford and other Republican Congressmen that the October peace march was "basically organized by international Communists."[20]

After the Kennedys, LBJ's jealousy landed most heavily on his Vice President, Hubert Humphrey, whom he would scold for getting too much attention in the news media.[21] The following story illustrates the President's jealousy of Humphrey as well as the methods he used to tear the man down. It was 1967, and there was rising opposition to the war everywhere when the Johnsons went to the Humphreys' for dinner. LBJ said: "Hubert, I hear you make the best speeches in explaining our country's effort in Vietnam. ...Here we have riots in our cities, demonstrators raising their clamor, and the President himself cannot move through the streets. Yet you can go out and make these addresses to the people. I don't know what we'd do without you. Now Hubert, I'd like to hear one of your speeches."

As LBJ said this, he was lying on a sofa in the living room, scratching himself. LBJ would not let up. Finally, the Vice President stood up to give the speech. At once LBJ got off the sofa and walked to the bathroom, saying "Keep talkin', Hubert. I'm listenin'."[22]

The Gallup poll of September 9 was dispiriting for the President. Republican George Romney led LBJ 49% to 41%.[23] That month the President decided not to run again. He considered announcing his decision the following month at a Democratic dinner, or perhaps, if not then, at another Democratic event in December. At the same time, he let his closest political aides and advisors believe he would be a candidate. He agreed to dedicate time to planning the campaign. Although in October, for the first time, a plurality of Americans thought the Vietnam War was a mistake, no announcement was made that LBJ was leaving politics.[24]

In November, the President asked General Westmoreland, the Commander of the American forces in South Vietnam, "What would my men in Vietnam think if I failed to run for reelection in 1968? Would they consider that their Commander in Chief had let them down?" LBJ mentioned that his family was against another term because of his history of heart problems.[25]

By the end of the year, McNamara recalled, his relationship with LBJ had reached the breaking point. Now the President's paranoia came into play. He became convinced that McNamara, originally a Kennedy appointee, had defected and was urging Bobby Kennedy to run.[26] Years later, LBJ still insisted that McNamara had been brainwashed by RFK.[27] During the presidential campaign of 1968, LBJ would instruct Humphrey: "You can't trust him (McNamara). Stay away from him as far as possible!"[28]

LBJ deliberately replaced the dissenters who departed from his administration with staunch hawks. McGeorge Bundy had recommended as his replacement Bill Moyers and a couple of other doves. He was amazed when the President chose a fervent hawk, Walt Rostow.[29] The choice, as LBJ revealed, was no accident: "I'm getting Walt Rostow as my intellectual. He's not your intellectual. He's not Bundy's intellectual. He's not Galbraith's intellectual. He's going to be *my* goddamn intellectual and I'm going to have him by the short hairs. (That was LBJ's favorite grip.) We're not going to have another Bundy around here."[30]

A Harris poll reported that LBJ had squandered all the goodwill that had brought him his landslide victory and had become one of America's least popular presidents. Only 23% of the people approved of the job he was doing.[31]

That was not the only news at home that darkened LBJ's mood. Opposition to the war in the Senate was no longer a position held by just a few. On December 1, the Senate passed a resolution requesting the help of the United Nations to end the Vietnam War. The vote was unanimous.[32]

Later in the month, the *U.S. News and World Report* predicted that LBJ would win a mere 12 states. This prompted him to tell Horace Busby to draft a withdrawal statement, and John Connally suggested that the January State of the Union message would be a good time to inform the nation. However, as the year drew to a close, it appeared briefly that a settlement in Vietnam might be near, and LBJ's poll numbers improved. So again, he backed away from the exit door of politics.[33]

He also left Washington. Perhaps he was running away from his political troubles. Whatever the case, the President made another trip just before Christmas. In addition to attending the funeral of Australia's Prime Minister, LBJ saw 14 leaders in 12 hours, visiting Thailand, South Vietnam, Pakistan and Italy in one frantic day.[34] When the President stopped at Vatican City, the Pope gave him a 14th century painting as a Christmas gift. Grandiose as ever, the President gave what he obviously considered to be a gift of comparable value: a plastic bust of Lyndon Johnson.[35]

By the end of 1967, half a million American troops were in

Vietnam and General Westmoreland was asking for more. LBJ set a limit of 525,000 because he thought a higher number would require a call-up of the reserves, which he still refused to permit.[36]

CHAPTER 17

"I DON'T NEED THE JOB"

★ ★ ★ ★ ★ ★

1968

Except for his manic travels, the President was depressed for most of the six months preceding his withdrawal announcement. While he was still in office, LBJ took advantage of the time remaining to him. The President misappropriated government monies for the benefit of his ranch in 1968.[1] His power and influence and skill at hiding what he was doing always protected him from the consequences of his many violations of law.[2]

LBJ kept saying: "I'm not going to take anymore of this. A man doesn't have to take this kind of thing." Many of the people around him did not take him seriously because he'd cried "wolf" so many times previously.[3] But this time the tide was clearly running against him.

His brother Sam observed: "His eyes were always bloodshot now, his face drawn and haggard. Nothing seemed to be going his way."[4] LBJ, the man who loved crowds, now hardly set foot outside of the White House because he would be besieged by angry protesters. He confined his travels on American soil to such secure areas as military bases. Hugh Sidey noted the President's visible physical and emotional exhaustion.[5]

On January 22, the North Koreans seized an American intelligence ship, the Pueblo. LBJ saw it as part of a Communist encirclement of the U.S. and expected the Soviets to strike at Berlin at any moment. However, the North Koreans had acted on their own and the Russians did nothing.[6]

The President prepared two angry speeches in response to the seizure, but decided not to give them. His manic aggressiveness was gone, and he was afraid to risk another land war in Asia. (The ship's personnel were not released until eleven months later.)[7]

He commanded a nuclear armed military force of unprecedented power, and still there was nothing he could do. LBJ was beginning to look like Gulliver tied to the ground by the many tiny ropes of the Lilliputians.

On January 30, 1968, the Communists launched a major offensive to coincide with the Vietnamese New Year holiday, Tet. A force of 84,000 men assaulted 36 of South Vietnam's provincial capitals, 64 district capitals and all but 1 of its 6 largest cities. In Saigon, the U.S. Embassy and the presidential palace were both attacked. American planes at nearby Tan San Nhut Airbase were blown up.

The American airbase at Da Nang, from which most air attacks were launched, was forced to close down, with the loss of many planes. American bases at Chu Lai and Phu Bai, and the Korean headquarters were also attacked. The Communist forces seized the center of the city of Hue, its university, provincial headquarters, the imperial citadel and the central marketplace.[8]

While the Communists held Hue, the provincial chief hid in the hospital and sent his friends to steal rice intended for refugee camps. Other South Vietnamese soldiers hid in the refugee center for 3 weeks.[9]

The Tet Offensive failed to drive out the Americans and incurred heavy losses for North Vietnam. But what it failed to do militarily, it accomplished psychologically. It was a total shock to those Americans who believed that U.S. forces were on a path to victory. The light at the end of the tunnel had just blinked out. The

Tet offensive blew away LBJ's smokescreen of deceit. LBJ's polls were sour again. On March 16, he still insisted: "...we...are going to win...make no mistake about it."[10]

Few now believed him.

The President was disintegrating in plain view. He could no longer follow what was being said at meetings. He was plagued by nightmares. He developed a compulsion to get out of bed in the middle of the night and touch Woodrow Wilson's portrait. Extreme states of depression often bring delusions about physical disease. LBJ's version was that he was going to suffer a paralyzing stroke as Wilson had.

By March 4, 1968, the President was almost alone in his refusal to recognize reality in Vietnam. He attests: "...I detected among a few advisors a sense of pessimism far deeper than I myself felt. I had much greater confidence in Westmoreland and his staff in Vietnam than many people in Washington, especially Pentagon civilians. I also had more confidence in the ability and determination of the South Vietnamese people to defend themselves."[11]

In early March, LBJ appeared to have aged drastically. The President looked battered.[12] Nevertheless, the thought of giving up politics, which had been his entire life and his identity, must have been intolerable. He kept his options open.

On March 8 he told his aides to start working on his campaign. But new blows were about to fall. Four days later, Senator Eugene McCarthy won an unexpected 42% of the votes in the New Hampshire Democratic Primary.[13]

LBJ's poor showing in the New Hampshire Primary merely demonstrated to him that: "There are a lot of people in this country working full time around the clock to lose this war for us in this country. There are a good many people who are powerful and influential who would like to see us pull out and quit."[14] He then softened his accusation a bit: "Well-intentioned, patriotic people sometimes are involved." He added a note of self-pity: "It doesn't make any difference who causes you to jump out the window after you jump."[15] Still, LBJ could not make the decision to end his political career.

Four days after that, Robert Kennedy announced his candidacy.[16] LBJ later recalled: "The thing I had feared from the first day of my Presidency was actually coming true. Robert Kennedy announced his intention to reclaim the throne in the memory of his brother. And the American people, swayed by the magic of that name, were dancing in the streets. The whole situation was unbearable for me."[17]

Finally, he admitted: "We cannot do everything we would wish to do."[18] On March 21, 1968, LBJ told Congressional leaders that he was ready to cut domestic spending and that taxes had to be raised.[19] He had waited too long. The country was now in the grip of an inflation that would last for years.[20] As he later wrote, "Throughout the fall and spring of 1968 we were struggling with the most serious financial crisis of recent years." Secretary of State Rusk warned that inflation in America could cause a financial panic in Europe and a collapse of the monetary system.[21]

It was obvious to many people that the President could not be reelected. Towards the end of March, the polls indicated a majority of Americans disapproved of what LBJ was doing in office.[22] For the previous fourteen months, protesters had kept him from appearing in public, so campaigning appeared to be impossible.[23] Predictions were made that he would lose the Wisconsin Primary and then the nomination.[24] As the final days of March arrived, all of the major newspapers, news magazines, and networks had publicly turned against the war.[25]

During the two weeks after the Kennedy announcement, LBJ worked like a Presidential candidate, giving orders to organize youth groups in his support, and lining up Democratic leaders to back his nomination. He kept a running count of delegates who would vote for him at the convention. But the polls were saying that among Democratic voters, RFK was favored 54% to 41% over the President.[26]

On March 31, LBJ was scheduled to deliver a speech on national television. That morning he still had not arrived at a firm decision about his future and spoke to his Vice President, saying: "Hubert maybe the people just don't like my face." Humphrey recalled: "Then I thought he'd break down; he was almost crying."[27]

As late as an hour before airtime, the President was still telling the people around him that he did not know what he was going to do.[28] Finally, he delivered his speech and said quietly at the end of it that he would not be a candidate for reelection. Having concluded, he told the press pool: "You fellows won't have me to pick on anymore. You can find someone else to flog and insult. The press can bring a man to his knees in a moment, but you can't bring me to my knees because I don't depend on you anymore."[29] On Air Force One, he told the reporters: "I don't need the job...the salary. I don't need your approval. I'm going to lead a full, happy life. I don't give a particular damn what you think."[30]

In his withdrawal speech LBJ lied about a reduction of bombing that was supposed to begin immediately. He said it would spare most of North Vietnam, but bombing continued 350 miles above the demilitarized zone and doubled in intensity. The 13,500 additional support troops that he said would go to Vietnam turned into nearly 50,000.[31] He was closer to the truth when he said, in the same speech: "...we were going after the enemy with our right hand by offensive action on the battlefront, but with our left hand we had to offer a peace proposal."[32] That aggressiveness and reluctance to talk peace continued during the remainder of LBJ's presidency.

After announcing, on March 31, 1968, that he would not run for President, even as peace talks were finally getting underway in Paris, LBJ insisted that only military might would get results. Instead of focussing on the negotiations, his objective, he said was to leave the next President "the best possible military posture in Vietnam."[33]

The day after his announcement, LBJ acted like a man released from prison. On April 1, he spoke enthusiastically about his retirement: he had plans for an LBJ library and an LBJ school of public affairs.[34]

On April 3, 1968, Radio Hanoi announced that North Vietnam was ready to negotiate.[35] On April 4, a strong antiwar leader, Martin Luther King, was assassinated.

In the three days that followed, rioting mobs burned cities from coast to coast. Washington D.C. was in flames and soldiers were brought in to guard the White House. LBJ was told, during the rioting that followed King's assassination Stokely Carmichael another black leader was organizing a march on Georgetown, where many columnists, editors, and television reporters lived.

The President, smiling, said: "Goddam! I've waited 35 years for this day!"[36]

The war news continued to worsen.

Later that month, Hanoi agreed to negotiate in Warsaw, but LBJ refused to accept the location. He broke his own promise to "send a trusted representative of America to any spot on this earth to talk in public or private with a spokesman of Hanoi." Although in 1967 he had offered to have peace talks in Moscow, he now complained Warsaw was not a neutral capital. What really bothered him was that Hanoi leaked its acceptance of Warsaw before the President was notified, and he considered this a deliberate insult.[37]

The President looked dreadful and had difficulty getting words out.[38] But spring brought a brightening of his spirits and a trip to visit former President Truman also helped.[39]

At the end of May, the *Chicago Daily News* reported: "A topsecret directive has gone to all U.S. field commanders in South Vietnam telling them to win the war within the next 3 months."[40]

Later in May, LBJ attended the annual White House correspondent's dinner. The President joked that after his withdrawal speech, he couldn't get into the White House without a pass.[41]

On June 4: Robert Kennedy died at the hands of an assassin.[42] He had just won the California Democratic Primary. The death of his rival did not immediately cheer LBJ, who said: "The only difference between the Kennedy assassination and mine is that I am alive and it has been more tortuous."[43] Depression engulfed LBJ during part of the summer, making him inaccessible and inactive as he cancelled plans for further domestic legislation.[44] He was plagued by regrets that he had withdrawn from the race, with his most formidable competition, Governor Rockefeller and Kennedy both gone.[45]

LBJ received a memo from his Science Advisory Committee on June 21 that should have encouraged him to stop bombing if his reasons for continuing to bomb had been rational. The report stated the by now obvious fact that bombing "...can only temporarily disrupt North Vietnam's and its Communist suppliers' ability to maintain the flow of combat materiel necessary to support the war in South Vietnam."

In July of 1968, another of LBJ's "advisors" was thoroughly trampled underfoot by the President. Assistant Secretary of State for Far Eastern Affairs, William Bundy flew to Paris to discuss Vietnam with State Department members and other LBJ senior advisors. They agreed that the bombing should be stopped and cabled LBJ to that effect.

Bundy was delegated to talk to the President. At the White House, LBJ told him: "I'm just not having any part of this. I want you to know it and not to have the slightest doubt that I'm not having any part of it. I don't want you talking about this, and I don't ever want to hear about this again." Bundy recalls: "I think I just said 'Yes, sir!'"[46]

That same month the President made the last of his international journeys, dashing through five countries of Central America in a single day.[47] He began to act like a candidate again, ordering his press office to issue "two good news stories daily."[48] The lifting of his dark mood also manifest itself as he increased his involvement with military planning for Vietnam.[49]

July drew to a close. Assistant Secretary of Defense Paul

Warnke said that bombing was not effective, and the President was informed that infiltration from the North had doubled. LBJ's advisors, Cyrus Vance, Averell Harriman, and Clark Clifford, suggested that he try a bombing halt that could be ended if the North Vietnamese took advantage of it.

The President called the suggestion "mush" and said: "...the enemy is using my own people as dupes." This is the voice of paranoia speaking. Instead of trying a bombing halt, LBJ called for an investigation of what he suspected was an international Communist conspiracy to persuade him to stop bombing.

By August, LBJ had just about reversed his decision to leave politics.[50] He told John Connally to recruit Southern Governors for a "draft LBJ" movement. Other LBJ regulars were dispatched to woo delegates. But by the opening of the National Democratic Convention, it was clear that the Paris peace talks to end the Vietnam War were going nowhere. LBJ's approval rating sank to a devastating 35%. The massing of protesters in Chicago finally convinced the President's security advisors that he could not safely set foot in that city.[51] On the evening of August 27, he sent word to the Convention that he should not be considered a candidate.[52]

Chicago was an armed camp even before the opening speech was made. Six thousand regular troops equipped with rifles, bazookas and flamethrowers, had been airlifted into the city. Another six thousand National Guard troops were at hand, armed with jeeps fronted by steel frames covered with barbed wire. These vehicles were to be used to sweep protesters off the streets. Twelve thousand police were also on hand, tear gas and clubs at the ready.[53]

LBJ was not present, but he was in firm control of the Convention nonetheless. He had chosen the date, the city, he had selected the program, and named who would run the show. Humphrey was so thoroughly excluded from power that members of his family had to stand in line for tickets each day.[54]

There was a larger problem for the Vice President, however. His only chance to win election was to emerge from the convention as a peace candidate, or at the very least, as something more than LBJ's double. The first step was to get his own Vietnam plank into the party campaign platform. He took great pains to write something that LBJ could live with, and got approval for it from the hawks, Secretary of State Dean Rusk and National Security Advisor Walt Rostow.

All to no avail. The President shouted over the phone: "This plank just undercuts our whole policy and, by God, the Democratic Party ought not to be doing that to me and you ought not to be doing it...!"[55] LBJ gave a clear demonstration of what mattered most to him: his ego. He insisted: "Hubert, don't try to pull the rug out from under my policy. The Vietnam plank will be mine—not yours." The Vice President later commented: "He didn't give a damn about pulling my rug out."[56]

Humphrey prepared a speech saying that he'd immediately stop bombing North Vietnam if the North Vietnamese reduced the rate at which they sent soldiers into the South. LBJ's response was that the speech would put his sons-in-law in danger in Vietnam and would reduce the chances for peace. For good measure, the President added that if the speech were delivered, he'd destroy the Vice President's chance of winning the election.[57]

As the days of campaigning passed, LBJ used threats to control what Humphrey said and did. Humphrey never forgot them: "Do you know what he had the nerve to say to me, after all the insults I've taken from him in the last four years? He said that if I didn't watch my p's and q's, he'd see to it personally that I lost Texas. And he intimated that he could hurt me even in some of my liberal states and that Daly (Mayor of Chicago) still listened to him. He said he'd dry up every Democratic dollar from Maine to California— as if he hasn't already!...With the trouble I've had in this campaign all because of him, you'd think he'd at least respect my loyalty."[58]

LBJ had shown himself to be ruthless in the past, and the Vice President knew it: "...Johnson is a vindictive man....You have to be practical and examine what we'd lose if he isn't handled with kid gloves. Texas could do it, and Nixon would be president."[59]

The President seemed to take a malicious joy in undermining Humphrey's confidence. On hearing that the Vice President was too sick to campaign in California, LBJ said: "Don't go to California, they're just a bunch of kooks out there. Somebody'll kill you just to even up the situation with Kennedy." Hubert replied: "You shouldn't be saying that, Mr. President." LBJ answered "I mean it."[60]

Granted, there was a growing ideological chasm between the two men. LBJ's often-stated view was: "We cannot fail those anxious and expectant millions in Asia. We must not break our commitments to freedom and the future of the world. We have set our course and will pursue it just as long as aggression threatens us. Make no mistake about it. America will prevail."[61]

Humphrey did not share LBJ's delusions and said privately: "Vietnam is a mess. I'm sure, pretty sure, that we were right going there, but we've got to get out. Fast. It's ripping the country apart. We've got to start withdrawing troops. I'd do that quickly."[62]

The President cared only about what increased or diminished his own glory. He was not motivated to help in Humphrey's campaign.

Sabotage is the word that best describes LBJ's contribution to Humphrey's campaign. For starters, the President denied the Vice President access to military and diplomatic messages and also kept from him information about the ongoing negotiations in Paris with the North Vietnamese.[63]

LBJ controlled a $600,000 fund from the President's Club for which Humphrey had raised a lot of money. But the money was withheld. The candidate asked Arthur Krim, LBJ's moneyman, "What the hell's happened now? It couldn't be the platform, he's talked to me since, and I've done nothing out of the way." Krim's reply was: "Well, it's the little things."

Humphrey's press aide had caused offense by joking, when

asked about LBJ after the convention "Lyndon who?" Humphrey had also irritated LBJ by choosing a friend to be treasurer of the campaign instead of the man LBJ wanted. The President was further incensed when Humphrey selected Larry O'Brien as campaign manager and National Committee Chairman because O'Brien had resigned from his Cabinet post in April to run Bobby Kennedy's campaign. No part of the $600,000 was ever released to the Vice President.[64]

Despite LBJ's pressure on Humphrey to stick to the party line, the Vice President knew that obedience would cost him the election. The President held the Vice President on a leash for three crucial weeks of the campaign by claiming that Humphrey's cooperation would help get the North Vietnamese to negotiate. LBJ said: "I've given up the presidency, given up politics, to search for peace....I think I can get these people at the conference table if you will help."[65]

LBJ's paranoia created another roadblock to peace on September 15. In Paris, the North Vietnamese representatives again agreed to start peace talks after a bombing halt. Ambassador to India, Chester Bowles, Clark Clifford, McGeorge Bundy, Averell Harriman, and George Ball all urged LBJ to halt the bombing. LBJ refused.

Humphrey's campaign manager Larry O'Brien was told that Greece's military dictatorship had contributed more than half a million dollars to the Nixon-Agnew campaign and it had been accepted. This was illegal. O'Brien brought this news to LBJ and added that CIA Director Richard Helms could confirm it. The President did nothing, refusing even to ask for confirmation from Helms. Thus he suppressed information which might have damaged the Nixon campaign.[66]

In October, Jim Rowe asked the President to campaign for the Vice President in Texas, New Jersey, and a few other crucial states. LBJ refused, explaining: "You know that Nixon is following my policies more closely than Humphrey." As soon as the Vice

President heard this, he asked for a meeting to affect a reconciliation. Coming straight from a Maryland campaign rally, the Vice President arrived a few minutes late. The President was no longer available to see him.[67]

LBJ gave the campaign some limited assistance on the two Sundays before Election Day, when he spoke over television and radio. He campaigned for one day, on October 26.[68]

Three days later, the President learned that Nixon had sabotaged the peace talks. The plotting began in July when Bui Diem, a friend of South Vietnam's President Nguyen Van Thieu, and Anna Chennault met with Nixon and his campaign manager, John Mitchell, to discuss the war. Chennault and Bui Diem became conduits through which President Thieu was urged by Nixon to abort the peace talks by refusing to take part in them.

On October 29, LBJ found out what had been going on from U.S. intelligence reports on South Vietnamese embassy cables. The President called Nixon to ask if the story was true. Nixon denied everything, and burst out laughing on hanging up the phone. In 1997, Mrs. Chennault said the story was indeed accurate: "I was constantly in touch with Mitchell and Nixon."[69]

Perhaps LBJ was angry at Nixon for wrecking the peace talks, perhaps the President decided that a Republican victory would look like a voters' repudiation of his administration. Whatever his motivation, LBJ appeared with Humphrey at a rally on November 3 and gave a television speech.[70] It was too little, too late.

LBJ's mental condition worsened again by the end of November. Richard Harwood and Haynes Johnson's report shows an alarmingly unstable man. The President was talking to some women reporters when: "...he became highly agitated and, waving his hand in the ladies' faces said: 'Whatever power I've had, I've used it. I've used it for good.' ...Moments later, he became quite emotional again while talking about the way he would conduct himself as President right up to the end. 'I'm going to be in charge right up 'till the last minute,' he said, almost shouting the words."[71]

Late in December, the President was back in the hospital, immobilized by depression. His wife described him as: "Not talking, not reaching, just lying still.

During LBJ's last month in office, the North Vietnamese made a partial withdrawal of their troops. Harriman, who was in contact with them, urged LBJ to reciprocate as a way to move the talks ahead. The President refused.[72] He was a prisoner of his delusions and his actions flowed logically from what he believed.

The President did not leave office with fond memories. He said: "I recall vividly the frustration and genuine anguish I experienced so often during the final year of my administration. I sometimes felt that I was living in a continuous nightmare."[73]

As LBJ had feared, the Vietnam War did destroy his presidency, made it impossible for him to run for reelection and denied him credit for those things he actually accomplished. Nevertheless, he remained its staunch advocate for the balance of his life.

CHAPTER 18

BACK AT THE RANCH

★ ★ ★ ★ ★ ★

Granted, LBJ's assumption of a presidency through the door of assassination, his landslide election, then four years marked by more assassinations, riots, protest movements and war, were enough to make a normal person swing from elation to despair many times. But he did not need these heights and depths of experience to put him on an emotional roller coaster. The symptoms of manic depression in its childhood form were manifest during his boyhood, and passing years brought him the adult version.

When he retired to his Texas ranch, he was safe from the problems which Richard Nixon found in the Oval Office. With his enormous wealth, adoring wife, commendable daughters, a home that he loved, and pleasant ways to pass the time, he was much more fortunate than almost all of his fellow Americans. But his illness had its own dynamics. Endogenous manias and depressions were part of it. Jewell Malechek, the wife of LBJ's ranch manager, recalled: "He was probably the most moody person I've ever known....That was one of the hardest things to adjust to. Some days you had to be quiet, and some days you could talk."[1]

Another witness, speechwriter Bob Hardesty, depicts the ex-

President, for the most part, enjoying his retirement, making trips to New York, seeing old friends and going to parties, and having a good time except for the occasional fit of depression. Hardesty comments that LBJ was his "normal manic depressive self."[2]

In 1969, LBJ wanted to visit Acapulco. He took the Hardestys with him, and Mary Hardesty describes the ex-President, constantly surrounded by people, at the top of his form, reminiscing, telling jokes, and doing imitations of people from his past. LBJ was the classic manic host, hospitable, entertaining and impulsive. His invitations were always spur of the moment, which annoyed some of the recipients, but these people came anyway. He was also, in true manic style, inconsiderate and domineering. A guest recalled that whatever LBJ wanted to do, that was what everyone else had to do. The host never imagined, or did not care, that his guests might have their own preferences.[3]

Indifference to the truth persisted. Biographer Doris Kearns mentions that when he told his anecdotes, his visitors would be treated to invented details or entire narrations that were untrue.[4]

And then there were the dark days. Perhaps LBJ was not more depressed in his final years than he was previously, but there were more reports of his depressions. He called his multimillion-dollar ranch on the Pedernales the place "Where no one can hurt me." But severe depression found him there anyway. In the spring of 1969, he experienced chest pains bad enough to frighten him. They may have triggered the long and painful depression that he suffered then. Lady Bird invited guests she thought might bring him out of it. One of these recorded: "Bird was obviously frantic about his state of mind."[5]

There were other guests at the ranch who were disturbed by LBJ's behavior. Senator Fred Harris found the ex-President unresponsive and distant, in short, "odd." When Henry Kissinger, Nixon's National Security Advisor, visited LBJ on official business, Kissinger was convinced that his host mistook him for the Prime Minister of Germany. Later, Kissinger said LBJ was "crazy."[6] In

August of 1969, LBJ visited President Nixon at San Clemente. The ex-President's conversation was so inappropriate that H.R. Haldeman, Nixon's domestic affairs chief later recorded "He's really psychopathic."[7]

Another familiar behavior pattern recurred during his retirement: he continued to be unfaithful to his long-suffering wife. George Reedy took note of a continuing affair.[8] There was more than one. And now that he was out of the public eye, LBJ made no effort to be discreet about the old flames who visited him at the ranch. His wife admitted that he was a "holy terror." He was also a careless one. He sent a gift for one of his women to the ranch by mistake. When Lady Bird opened the box and discovered a lavender bikini inside, she said "I don't think this is for me. It must be for one of your lady friends."[9]

Although unappreciated by her husband, Lady Bird continued to be essential to his mental health, such as it was. When she was away, he oscillated between depression and rage, giving way occasionally to paranoid rants against East Coast liberals and Robert Kennedy. As alcoholic as ever, LBJ had his car and golf cart equipped with portable bars. His already heavy drinking increased in his wife's absence. Some of the nights when she was gone, he was overwhelmed by depression and loneliness. He would cry himself to sleep. George Christian, his former press secretary, attested: "She held him together. She held all of us together."[10]

Minus the trappings of presidential power, LBJ's personality was on naked display at the ranch. Now he could really pull up the drawbridge and limit his companions, as he never could in Washington. Now he allowed passage only to people who always said "yes" and told him that reality was what he wanted it to be. He became a hermit king, rarely venturing into the public world, where he no longer had power.[11]

He played Napoleon at St. Helena, driving around his ranch empire, attending to myriad details in manic fashion. His brother, Sam noted that LBJ was giving the same meddling attention to the ranch that he had given to the presidency.[12]

Biographer Doris Kearns, who saw him at the ranch, observed: "At...morning meetings, Johnson delivered his instructions to his field hands with the same tone of voice and with the same urgency I had heard at early-morning staff meetings in the White House." LBJ would say: "Now I want each of you to make a solemn pledge that you will not go to bed tonight until you are sure that every steer has everything he needs. We've got a chance of producing some of the finest beef in this country if we work at it, if we dedicate ourselves to the job. And if we treat those hens with loving care, we should be able to produce the finest eggs in the country.... But it'll mean working every minute of the day."[13]

It may seem amusing to hear a man talking like a general addressing his troops before a major battle when it's a matter of steers and chickens, but with LBJ, livestock was never the issue: his ego was always paramount.

Retirement changed only the objects of LBJ's extravagance. Principal among these was the LBJ Presidential Library that, with its eight stories and rooftop helicopter pad, was the most expensive ever built. Its collection of manuscripts was larger than that of the Library of Congress.[14] The Pharaohs of Egypt had their pyramids, LBJ had his Library and he didn't have to wait until he was dead to enjoy it.

He devoted much effort and money to a group of monuments and shrines to himself: his birthplace, his boyhood home, the Johnson Library, and the fort, barn and house built by his grandfather. Frank Cormier noted, "The inherent immodesty of his projects sometimes amused us...."[15]

The ex-President now set out to compete with former presidents. He wanted more adulation and more people visiting his birthplace than were going to any other president's shrine. He would check the cars on its parking lot to see how many states were represented by the license plates.

He was the only hero at his personal Alamo. Everyone who opposed the war was wrong. Hubert Humphrey he called "gutless" for trying to campaign as a war moderate. Senators Fulbright, McCarthy, McGovern were cowards because they wanted peace talks to begin.[16] LBJ remained as aggressive and vengeful as ever. He was still unforgiving towards Bill Moyers, whom he believed had joined the enemy camp—not the North Vietnamese's but Robert Kennedy's.

LBJ's Texas former chief of staff, Tom Johnson, arranged a book party for Moyers and made the mistake of inviting the ex-President. LBJ asserted that Johnson was a traitor for doing anything for Moyers, hung up on him, and would not talk to him for weeks.[17]

Paranoia continued to rule his thoughts and was increasing the territory that it controlled. When writing his memoirs, LBJ predicted: "They'll get me anyhow, no matter how hard I try…. The reviews are in the hands of my enemies, the *New York Times* and the Eastern magazines. I don't have a chance." He expected that, on the publication of his memoirs, the public mind would be poisoned against him anew by the vast conspiracy ranged against him. "There's nothing I can do about it anymore. So I might as well give up and put my energies into the one thing they cannot take away from me and that is my ranch."[18]

Not only did the writing of his memoirs fan the embers of his paranoia, so did the reading of his brother's memoirs. LBJ called Sam's book, *My Brother Lyndon,* a betrayal of things told in confidence and a pack of "psychopathic lies." He said: "I don't see how Sam Houston could do it just for the money. He won't use the money anyway to pay up his bills or cover the hot checks he's given to everybody who would take them. How could he have done this to me and the family?" In actuality, the book, when not innocuous, usually gave LBJ the benefit of the doubt. But Sam never heard from his brother again and LBJ's will left him only five thousand dollars, from an estate of tens of millions, [19]

Paranoia eventually extended its reach to embrace the ranch. During one of his weirder moments of depression, LBJ declared:

"It's all been determined, you know. Once more I am going to fail. I know it. All my life I've wanted to enjoy this land. I bought it. I paid it off. I watched it improve. It's all I have left now. And then this rotten spring comes along as dry as any we've had in fifty years. Everything that could go wrong goes wrong. First the rains don't come. Then the Ford motor pump breaks down. Then the parts we order to fix it are delayed.... And if we don't get our fields watered soon, everything will be spoiled. Everything. Why, those parts were ordered weeks ago. They should have been here long before now. I can't depend on anyone anymore." The following morning he reported: "I couldn't sleep all night. Not a minute. I kept thinking about those pump parts.... And I couldn't stand it. I must have those parts before the end of the day. I simply must. If I don't, everything's going to fall apart. Everything."[20] This operatic despair is a prime example of what happens when the will of a tyrannical manic is thwarted. But paranoia is present here too, as even fate conspires against the ex-President.

Sitting alone at the ranch, LBJ turned his paranoia onto people he had formerly trusted. Bobby Baker was told during his visit to the ranch that when LBJ was President, the Communists may have influenced members of the White House staff against their Commander in Chief. LBJ was also worried that his loyalists and old friends had been reached by the Communists.[21]

The years of his retirement at the ranch were years of physical decline. He was hospitalized in March, 1970, with chest pains brought on by increasing blockages of the arteries supplying his heart. A month later, his color was a ghastly gray when he attended a press luncheon at the *Washington Post*, where he seemed withdrawn and depressed. "But," report Harwood and Johnson, "gradually his manner and mood changed....As he talked, he seemed to take on another appearance. The pallor and signs of sickness went away and all of a sudden you were sitting with a vigorous, commanding, strong man whose mind was clear, so well organized, so quick, that you instantly became aware of the power of his personality, of the ability to dominate and persuade and overwhelm."

They added: "He was overpowering. He thumped on the table, moved back and forth vigorously, grimaced,...gestured with his arms... and kept the conversation going from the moment he sat down at the dining table until hours later when Lady Bird called the *Post* and sent in a note reminding him he should come home and rest." He had talked for nearly five hours.[22]

This was a performance which would have been difficult for a man in his prime, much more so for an older one recovering from a heart attack. But such is the magic of mania. It would bring him back from beyond the edge of exhaustion to give a dynamic speech during his campaign days and it still had the power to make a sick, old man perform like a young spellbinder.

LBJ did nothing to help himself. He gained forty-five pounds, he resumed eating high cholesterol foods, he was chain-smoking, and he drank to excess. Two years later, in June of 1972, while visiting his daughter Lynda and her husband at their home in Virginia, he had a severe heart attack that required two weeks of hospitalization.[23]

LBJ's last hurrah came in November of that year, when he spoke at a symposium on civil rights. The quarreling conference participants were getting nowhere, when, says a witness, "The President bounded back up the steps...it was the LBJ of vintage times, and he put on this splendid performance that everybody remembers. Totally impromptu."[24] Mania had waved its magic wand again.

Today, there are many effective medications that bring relief from mania and depression, and people who suffer from these conditions are treated successfully all over the world. Antidepressants are widely advertised on television and in the print media. The American public has come to understand that depression and mania are physical disorders involving brain chemistry.

But politicians who are treated by psychiatrists or psychotherapists still keep it secret. In this country, so proud of its medical advances, there is still no psychiatrist on the President's medical staff: there is no one responsible for treating the mental and emotional ills of the President. There is no established procedure for helping the President through a mental health crisis, should one arise. The present occupant of the Oval Office is no better off than was Lyndon Johnson, who never received a diagnosis or treatment for his manic depression and alcoholism, or relief from his suffering.

Johnson's heart gave out on January 22, 1973.

One year later, Lithium was approved by the FDA for the treatment of manic depression.[25]

Postscript
Why Vietnam?

WHY VIETNAM?

★ ★ ★ ★ ★ ★

Many years after the last American troops had left Vietnam, Robert McNamara listed the most important issues concerning the war that the Johnson administration failed to address: (1) was it necessary to defend U.S. security in Vietnam? (2) Could South Vietnam develop a stable government and effective military? (3) How well could the U.S. fight a guerilla war? (4) How could the U.S. best negotiate a peace in Vietnam?[1] The presence in the White House of a president who was sick, suffering, and delusional, guaranteed that those issues would never be considered..

WAS THIS WAR NECESSARY?

★ ★ ★ ★ ★ ★

The United States had a small presence in South Vietnam when LBJ became President. Why did that change?

Because of the severity of his manic depression, LBJ might as well have packed time bombs in the luggage he brought to the White House. He was dangerously aggressive, paranoid, and had the grandiose delusion that he and his country had unlimited powers. Moreover, he was incapable of admitting when he was wrong, he was adverse to accepting guidance from others, and he was pathologically determined that his will would prevail. All this accepted, it is still difficult to believe that the leader of a democratic nation could, single-handedly, drag his country into a major war.

Of course, that did not happen. Many people in the government, the military, and among the citizenry believed that the U.S. had to defeat Communism in Vietnam. However, this was not a war demanded by the voters or the Congress. The opposite was true. LBJ could have kept the promises he made as a peace candidate and left the South Vietnamese to fight without us.

This war continued and expanded because LBJ insisted on it. He was not the first manic depressive leader to make his country

252

fight a huge, costly and irrational war. As long as undiagnosed, untreated manic depressives become heads of state, he will not be the last.

In 1963, LBJ wanted this war and could not permit himself to withdraw, even when he no longer wanted it. Manic depression was a major force in shaping his decisions. He manipulated his civilian advisors and misled the military, the Congress and his country. Time after time, he deliberately avoided opportunities to make peace. LBJ was the man most responsible for turning the conflict in Vietnam into an American war, a protracted and deadly war.

The war in Vietnam, when it became LBJ's war, the longest war in American history, was launched with lies. He never took the country into his confidence about what he was really doing because, he said the public had a tendency to "go off on a jag in one crazy direction or another." He told the Congress only what he wanted it to know, because he wanted no limits to his decision-making powers.[1] His paranoia was one of the sources of his obsession with secrecy.

Secretary of Defense, Robert McNamara admitted that the President kept the American people and the Congress blindfolded where the war in Vietnam was concerned, both before and after the Tonkin Gulf Resolution of August, 1964.[2]

Deceptions were made by silence, omission, and by the failure to share information that others had the need and right to know. The practice of shrouding a war in lies originated in LBJ's inordinate hunger for power, for control over everyone and everything. Disregard for truth was notable in LBJ long before he had a war to lie about. Some of the truth abut the war was dissolved in the delusions that controlled his thinking.

Over time, many rationalizations were given to explain why the United States was fighting in Vietnam. One of Johnson's favorites was that treaty obligations required it. The first of the treaties involving the U.S. with Vietnam was the Geneva Accords.

The United States did not sign, but pledged to support the

Geneva Accords, signed on July 21 and 22, 1954. of October, 1954, which divided Vietnam temporarily into two parts, North and South, at the 17th parallel. The North was left under the control of Ho Chi Minh, the South under the French. According to the terms of the accord, in two years, joint elections would be held prior to reuniting the country. The U.S. stated: "…we shall continue to seek to achieve unity through free elections, supervised by the United Nations to ensure that they are conducted fairly."

That pledge was broken. So was the next one: "The Government of the United States of America declares with regard to the aforesaid Agreements and paragraphs that…it will refrain from the threat or the use of force to disturb them…."³

An International Control commission was established by the Accords to oversee compliance in both halves of Vietnam. While there were violations in the North, the majority, it reported, were in the South. "…the Republic of Vietnam (in the South) has violated Articles 16 and 17 of the Geneva Agreement in receiving the increased military aid from the United States." The U.S. also violated the agreement by sending more than the permissable number of its soldiers to South Vietnam and setting up "a factual military alliance, which is prohibited under Article 19…," the report concluded.⁴

Ngo Dinh Diem named himself president of the Republic of Vietnam one year and three months after the Geneva Accords were signed, thus destroying the one chance Vietnam had to avoid another war, and the U.S., in supporting him, failed to support the Accords again.⁵

"If America's commitment is dishonored in South Vietnam, it is dishonored in forty other alliances or more," LBJ insisted.⁶ However, he was not referring to the Geneva Accords, which the U.S. had already violated. The treaty he had in mind was the Southeast Asia Treaty Organization pact, which took effect on February 19, 1955. LBJ: "This is the grounds for our action and policies in Vietnam. I carry this paper around with me most of the time."

Apparently, he did not bother to read it. Senator Mike Mansfield denied that the SEATO Treaty provided any such grounds: "I was a member of the three-man American delegation to Manilla…in the writing of the SEATO agreement. We agreed on an alliance of anticommunist countries there, but the American-type action in Vietnam was not included in the pact."[7]

What the treaty actually said was this: "Article IV Section I: Each party recognizes that aggression by means of armed attack in the treaty area against any of the Parties or against any State or territory which the Parties by unanimous agreement may hereafter designate, would endanger its own peace and safety, and agrees that it will in that event act to meet the common danger in accordance with its constitutional process." In other words, if North Vietnam invaded South Vietnam, the U.S. was obligated to defend South Vietnam if Congress declared war.

A second provision dealt with the possibility of a civil or guerilla war: "If, in the opinion of any of the Parties, the inviolability or the integrity of the territory or the sovereign or political independence of any Party… is threatened in any way other than by armed attack or is affected or threatened by any fact or situation which might endanger the peace of the area, the Parties (U.S., Britain, France, Australia, New Zealand, Philippines, Pakistan, Thailand) shall consult immediately in order to agree on the measures which should be taken for the common defense." "Designation of states and territory as to which provisions of Article IV and Article III are to be applicable…Cambodia and Laos and the free territory under the jurisdiction of the State of Vietnam".[8] What this meant to South Vietnam was that attacks by the local Vietcong could require the treaty members to confer about what to do and then they would act if there were agreement on what action to take.

When the SEATO treaty was originally discussed in the Senate, prior to passage, the senators wanted assurance that their country would not be dragged into war without the Congress agreeing to it. Senator Green asked Secretary of State Dulles if the appearance of a revolutionary movement in a SEATO country would obligate the U.S. to go to war against it. Dulles replied: "No. If there is a revolutionary movement in Vietnam or Thailand, we would consult together as to what to do about it...."

Senator Ferguson: "In other words, the words 'armed attack' in paragraph 1 of Article IV are the ordinary armed attack rather than a subterfuge of penetration or subversion."

Dulles answered: "Yes, sir."[9] Thus the Senate understood that the treaty obligated it to consider a declaration of war if North Vietnam invaded South Vietnam as North Korea had invaded South Korea, with a large and visible army. Subversions, penetrations by small numbers, and guerilla actions merely required consultation with treaty members.

There were two problems with LBJ's reliance on the SEATO Treaty. First was that no significant incursion of North Vietnamese troops into South Vietnam took place until after American troops arrived in large numbers and the bombing of North Vietnam had begun. Second was that Congress never declared war against North Vietnam.

According to the records of the North Vietnamese, they began to send small numbers of troops into South Vietnam at the end of 1963.[10] The President was aware of this, but kept it secret during the campaign.[11] Troops sent by North Vietnam were people native to the South until September, 1964, when the first Northerners arrived, still in small numbers.[12]

A total of 10,000 North Vietnamese troops entered South Vietnam in 1964.[13] In March, 1965, more than 30,000 Americans were on the ground and American planes were bombing both halves of the country.[14] According to Robert McNamara, the leaders of North Vietnam wanted above all to avoid inciting the U.S. to become involved in the South, and for that reason, kept most of their regular combat units out of the South until 1965.[15] Historian and North Vietnamese General Dang Vu Hup confirms this: "It was only *after* the U.S. bombed the North and brought troops into the South, in other words, *after* it was clear that the U.S. was escalating that we began to support the South with regular regiments."[16]

In summation, the SEATO Treaty required that when aggression that fell short of invasion occurred in South Vietnam, the U.S. must confer with its treaty partners. Small scale penetrations from the North to the South did take place between 1963 and 1965, but LBJ never consulted with the countries involved in the treaty, so he ignored the treaty then, and he ignored it later. Invasion from the North to the South occurred in 1965, but it was after, not before the U.S. had begun a full-scale war. The SEATO Treaty obligated LBJ to ask Congress for a declaration of war. He also failed to do that. Despite his claims to the contrary, he never complied with his SEATO Treaty obligations.

Another lie which the President often repeated was that he brought no change of policy. LBJ claimed that his war policy was merely keeping promises made by his predecessors: "We are steadfast in a policy which has been followed for ten years in three administrations. In the case of Vietnam, our commitment today is just the same as the commitment made by President Eisenhower to President Diem in 1954 a commitment to help these people help themselves."[17] He also lied when he said: "Ike has made a promise. I have to keep it."[18]

In 1965, Eisenhower told a group of Republican Congressmen that his offer of economic aid to South Vietnam's then President Diem could not be considered the basis for what LBJ was doing militarily in that country.[19] Moreover, Eisenhower had made the offer conditional on Diem's "undertaking needed reforms" which were never done.[20] As we saw, Kennedy was planning to withdraw troops from Vietnam, not to send an army of half a million, so LBJ in no way was continuing Kennedy's program either.

Another reason for fighting in Vietnam, according to LBJ, was that he was simply doing what the majority of Americans wanted him to do. But this was never a war by popular request. In actuality, the President did everything he could to convince Americans that defense of their country required them to fight in Vietnam.[21] LBJ knew that there was no support for the war when he ran as a peace candidate. He said to McGeorge Bundy, his national security advisor, on March 4, 1964: "…we haven't got any Congress that will go with us, and we haven't got any mothers that will go with us in the war…."[22]

However, he was so successful in selling the public on the war that after the reprisal attacks following the partly imaginary Tonkin Gulf incident in August of 1964, his popularity rating rose from 42% to 72%.[23] By the mid-1960s, a majority of Americans, from hard hats to academics, from journalists to congressmen, were in favor of LBJ's intervention in Vietnam.

This President did not ignore the voters entirely. He much preferred high approval ratings to low ones. That is one reason why, against the counsel of his advisors, throughout 1965 he gave the public the impression that he was not sending large numbers of men to Vietnam and that he was seeking a quick settlement of the war. He knew that Americans did not want half a million of their sons fighting and dying in Vietnam with no end in sight.[24]

By mid-1965, Johnson had convinced the public and Congress that pulling out was not acceptable. By 1967, opinion was still in favor of not giving up, but unsure that the administration was fighting the war the right way. By March, 1968, 49% of Americans thought it had been a mistake to make war in Vietnam and only 41% were willing to give the President the benefit of the doubt.[25] Thus the tide of public opinion had come in and gone out, but LBJ stood firm. Regardless of his assertion to the contrary, he did not send troops to Vietnam to fight a war that Americans demanded. He had his own reasons.

A justification he gave to the politically sophisticated was that the war was necessary to avoid a right wing backlash, although many people would agree that it was unethical to make war abroad to avoid possible political complications at home. Kennedy had had the same concern, which made him postpone complete withdrawal until after his reelection. Be that as it may, LBJ, unlike Kennedy, had been elected by a landslide, and following Goldwater's disastrous campaign, the right wing was in a much diminished state. A right wing backlash would not have been a problem.[26]

Perhaps the most egregious lie that the President told about the Vietnam War was his claim that Americans had to fight there to preserve democracy in that country. South Vietnam never was and never became a democracy. The South Vietnamese leader with whom LBJ first dealt was Ngo Dinh Diem. He had been appointed by Chief of State Bao Dai, the client-Emperor of Vietnam when it was a French colony. Bao Dai had also been titular ruler of Vietnam during the Japanese occupation and had voluntarily abdicated at the end of World War II. He was hardly in a position to lend legitimacy to Diem.[27]

In Eisenhower's opinion, an honest election would have made South Vietnam Communist: "...had elections been held as of the time of the fighting, possibly 80% of the population would have voted for the Communist Ho Chi Minh as their leader rather than Chief of State Bao Dai."[28]

On December 1, 1954, Senator Mike Mansfield declared: "In the event that the Diem government falls...the United States should consider an immediate suspension of all aid to Vietnam...."[29]

The South Vietnamese finally had a chance to vote for Diem. An election was held in October, 1955 during which all opposition papers were closed, opposing parties barred, and an opposition candidate who managed to be elected was denied his seat in the Assembly, prior to being imprisoned and tortured. Diem managed to garner 605,025 votes in Saigon, although only 450,000 voters were registered there. He was elected by 98% of the voters, a result reminiscent of elections in Hitler's Germany.[30] During his years as President, Diem violated every article of South Vietnam's Constitution.[31]

Diem turned his country into a police state. An U.S. Intelligence report stated on May 26, 1959: "The government is essentially authoritarian....members of the executive branch are little more than the personal agents of Diem whereas the legislature has no real power at all.... No organized opposition...is tolerated, and critics of the regime are often repressed."[32] Diem established concentration camps and a secret police. The camps were not merely for Communists and suspected Communists, but for anyone suspected of political opposition.[33] Ngo Dinh Diem was the man Vice President Johnson placed in the same class as Winston Churchill.

There is nothing to stand in the way of a leader's corruption in a police state. In South Vietnam, the entire Ngo family infested the country like maggots consuming a carcass. Diem's brother and right hand man, Nhu, was involved in the opium trade and with waterfront piracy. Brother Can profited from graft and extortion in the central part of the country. The two brothers were quite competitive and their agents occasionally killed each other.[34]

In 1963, brother Nhu became a real problem. On August 21, his troops surrounded a Buddhist pagoda, killed 30 of the monks and put the rest in prison. They perpetrated the same atrocities in several other cities. The following day, Nhu had the telephone lines to the American embassy cut to prevent the news from reaching the Americans.[35] By August, it was clear that Nhu, who terrified the people around him with his rages, had succumbed to paranoia. He claimed that CIA Chief John Richardson had put a price on his head and that there was an international conspiracy against his brother's administration. He hinted that he was negotiating with the North Vietnamese.[36]

Even without Nhu's and Can's contributions, Diem had managed to alienate most of the rural population, the Buddhists, the nationalists, and the Montagnards. This didn't leave many people who appreciated him.[37] By August, Ambassador Lodge had no confidence in the Diem regime and wanted McNamara and General Maxwell Taylor, who were on a fact-finding mission to Saigon, to find out what was really going on. He had the Vatican's delegate, Monsignor Asta, deliver a briefing. Asta reported that Diem was running a police state and using torture. Asta added that Diem's brother Nhu was trying to make a deal with the Communists so that he could oust the Americans. Vice President Nguyen Ngoc Tho complained that the government's police state methods were increasing support for the Vietcong.[38] These facts were not welcome news to LBJ.

South Vietnam remained a police state. Nevertheless, LBJ said on August 2, 1965: "…we insist and we will always insist that the people of South Vietnam shall have the right to shape their own destiny in free elections in the South or throughout all Vietnam under international supervision, and they shall not have any government imposed upon them by force and terror so long as we can prevent it."[39] The Government of South Vietnam that LBJ was defending with the lives of his countrymen continued to be not only autocratic, but thoroughly corrupt. This description of Vietnam's military leadership comes from a member of that group, General Nguyen Cao Ky: "Every Prime Minister or even Minister said: 'I'm here for 2 months, so money, money and if necessary I'll go abroad.'"[40]

On November 1, 1963, a group of South Vietnamese generals overthrew Diem's government. The following day Diem and his brother Nhu were killed by the military. During the next 20 months of the military merry-go-round there were ten changes of government, all military dictatorships, in LBJ's democracy.[41]

General William Westmoreland, who led the American forces in Vietnam, said in 1965 that the political turmoil reduced the effectiveness of the South Vietnamese forces because it made the division and corps commanders unwilling to risk combat until forced to do so by the enemy. If the South Vietnamese suffered no losses, their commanders would not be criticized by the South Vietnamese government, whoever it was at the time.[42]

Ky was perhaps the most colorful leader to stroll across South

Vietnam's stage. By the age of thirty-four, he had bombed the wrong targets in North Vietnam, threatened to bomb Saigon twice, and participated in one coup, two half-coups, and a counter-coup.[43] He was elected as the Prime Minister of South Vietnam by his fellow generals on June 11, 1965.

In the spring of 1966 a large popular movement led by Buddhists arose in South Vietnam's cities. This was opposed by Ky's government and the United States, joined him in his resistance to free elections and a return to civilian government.[44] Democracy was not possible in South Vietnam while the United States supplied a substantial part of the national budget and wanted to see its friends (those who opposed Communism) running the government.

LBJ insisted on continuing to provide substantial alms for autocracy. On April 2, he said that he would do whatever he could to keep General Ky in power. Two days later he said there should be "...more planning on how to pick a man before he takes over so we won't have to get out when the wrong man gets in...."[45] This does not sound very much like a man defending democracy.

General Ky was elected Vice President with Nguyen Van Thieu as President in a rigged election on September 3, 1967. Robert Kennedy reported on the election: "...one candidate, Au Trong Thanh, was barred because his advocacy of peace was considered to be evidence of communist sympathies; he had served as the Government's Finance Minister until 1966.... No candidate representing the views and interests of the militant Buddhists was allowed. No runoff between the two leading candidates...was permitted, since this would certainly have resulted in a civilian victory. ...on the eve of the election,...two Saigon newspapers were closed down and a former National Police Chief who supported another candidate was arrested."[46]

As soon as the voting for the legislature was over, President Thieu imprisoned several of the losing opposition candidates and their supporters. These people were soon joined by some twenty additional political leaders, labor leaders, and religious leaders who had been less than enthusiastic about continuing the war.[47]

Johnson tried to present the war as an act of generosity: He claimed that he was helping the Vietnamese to improve their lives. The Johnson rhetoric then focussed on the concrete needs of the Vietnamese people rather than on bloodless abstractions like defending democracy and keeping the promises of former Presidents. The result of America's activity was, in a popular phrase of the day, "saving the country by destroying it." While Diem was in power, the U.S. spent a small amount of money on industrial and agricultural development in South Vietnam, but the rest, some 90% of the total, was invested in the Vietnamese military.[48] And, one might add, invested in the Vietcong, since they captured a lot of American-made materiel.

The U.S. not only did little to help the people of Vietnam, it did much to harm them. It became U.S. policy to starve and root the Vietcong out of the jungles by destroying the jungles: an area the size of Massachusetts was stripped of crops and other vegetation of all kinds. However, the Vietcong, who were quite mobile, were hardly affected. It was the civilian population, particularly, the aged, the women, and the children, who suffered from the loss of their crops and food supply.[49] The continuing effects of poisoning a population with defoliants has yet to be reported, let alone the suffering that was caused by napalm attacks and indiscriminate bombing.

A number of different parties eventually offered their own reasons why the U.S. was fighting in Vietnam. LBJ himself gave two other explanations: 1) "We have commitments and we intend to keep them." (The problem with this was that the South Vietnamese had no continuing government to whom the U.S. had commitments and the people had no voice in whether the war was fought or not. 2) "...our national honor is at stake in Southeast Asia and we are going to protect it."[50] Presumably, "it" was the national honor, but he did not explain how national honor was protected by refusing to extricate oneself from what the world recognized as a quagmire.

The media had explanations for why the U.S. was in Vietnam. Tom Wicker of the *New York Times* explained that Americans were not fighting in Vietnam because the people of that country wanted it, nor was the U.S. defending the freedom and democratic rights of the Vietnamese people. Despite all pretense to the contrary, America was fighting on Vietnamese soil to keep the Communist Chinese in China.[51]

The American military thought they were in the country not to help the Vietnamese, but to keep the Communist forces above the 17th parallel.[52] That at least has the virtue of simplicity.

The fog of deception that enveloped the Vietnam War also affected the lowest echelons of the military. American soldiers had been sent, they were told, to fight an invading army from North Vietnam.[53] It was both disillusioning and confusing to learn that they also had to fight the people they thought they were defending.

What they were told about the Vietcong was also misleading. They thought the South Vietnamese either opposed or were indifferent to the Vietcong. Americans had to learn the hard way that local farmers often acted as spies for, and gave what help they could, to the enemy.[54] Keeping the war undeclared and hidden meant that American forces were sent to fight without a clear strategy or direction, or even an understanding of what the war was really about.[55] The impact of this misdirection on the morale of the troops was a level of cynicism, resentment, and drug use far beyond anything seen in World War II or Korea.

One of the tragic effects of waging a dishonest war was the corruption of some of the American officials and soldiers who were fighting it—and this is in addition to the drug trafficking and addictions that occurred among American troops. Americans were, whether they liked it or not, committed to supporting a venal and coercive regime.

By concealing their knowledge about what some of members the South Vietnamese government and military practiced—extortion rackets, pillage, rape, torture, and killing of innocent civilians—

Americans became accessories to these crimes. When investigators from the Department of Defense tried to find out the truth about Korean troops slaughtering large numbers of South Vietnamese civilians, Westmoreland's staff held them off for two years.[56]

Not until 1971 did members of Congress hear from dozens of honorably discharged Vietnam veterans that they had seen the South Vietnamese military throw prisoners out of helicopters and burn villages, shooting the women and children who tried to escape. Some of the veterans had seen Americans also committing atrocities, torturing prisoners, as well as raping, torturing and mutilating Vietnamese women who were unlucky enough to fall in their path.[57] The massacre by American soldiers of all the civilians in the village of My Lai took place on March 16, 1968.

LBJ not only lied about the objectives of the war, the nature of the allies and the enemy, how the war was being fought, and the fact that it was a war, he also lied about his willingness to negotiate a peace.

The Pentagon Papers show that it was LBJ's policy from early on to show two faces, one to North Vietnam and the other to everyone else. He signaled to Hanoi that Americans would not stop fighting the Vietcong and bombing the North until all Vietcong and North Vietnamese forces retreated to North Vietnam. In short, he was demanding complete surrender. Simultaneously, he followed McNamara's recommendation to make the public believe he was willing to negotiate a "political settlement" in Vietnam so as to retain the backing of the public and America's supporters.[58] It was clear that his pretense to negotiate to end the war at any moment, served to make the war more acceptable to the American people.[59]

LBJ's opinion of every bombing pause was that it "...is more a sign of weakness than anything else. All we'll get is distrust from our allies, despair from our troops, and disgruntled generals. Hanoi and Peking believe we're weak and won't do anything if we pause. If we suffer a severe reverse as a result of this, we'd never explain it."[60]

The final element in LBJ's pursuing peace sham was his denial that Hanoi was willing to negotiate. In September, 1964, and in January, 1965, U.N. Secretary General U Thant tried to get the U.S. to a meeting with North Vietnam to discuss conditions for ending the war. LBJ instructed his press secretary, George Reedy to say: "The United States has received no proposal from U Thant." The President insisted: "Candor compels me to tell you that there has not been the slightest indication that the other side is interested in negotiation."[61] LBJ wrote in his memoirs: "As I look back, I think that we perhaps tried too hard to spell out our honest desire for peace.... Never once was there a clear sign that Ho Chi Minh had a genuine interest in bargaining for peace."[62] The truth is that "meaningful" peace feelers kept coming in from Hanoi, although the President instructed his staff to insist that the opposite was true.[63]

Making a long, large, and undeclared war acceptable to the American people required not only hiding the size of the army fighting it, but also the cost of waging it. This was doubly necessary when the President wanted Congress to pass an expensive and revolutionary social program. The troop numbers were increased by what LBJ hoped was acceptable increments. The war costs underwent a similar gradual escalation. Hubert Humphrey recalled that every budget LBJ sent to Congress requested an inadequate amount of money for the war, but the President would get what he needed by hiding it in supplemental budget requests.[64]

In retrospect, LBJ observed: "...with the rising cost of the war in Vietnam on top of growing consumer demand, the economy was dangerously close to overheating in 1965....with each passing month inflation rose."[65]

This was not the way he saw it in 1965. In December of that year, Gardner Ackley, the Chairman of the Council of Economic Advisors, warned that inflation was unavoidable unless spending was controlled or taxes raised. LBJ insisted that the country could pay for both guns and butter without new taxes: "After all, our country was built by pioneers who had a rifle in one hand to kill their enemies and an ax in the other to build their homes and provide for their families."[66] Perhaps the President believed his Alamo economics.

Many people who are manic, or have developed manic personalities, have a tendency to exaggerate, to lie gratuitously, and even to deceive *themselves*.

In college, Johnson acquired a reputation for lying. He maintained it in the Senate and carried it with him to the White House. He became known for the "credibility gap." It should therefore be no surprise that truth was the first casualty of LBJ's war in Vietnam.

A WAR THAT COULD HAVE BEEN AVOIDED

★ ★ ★ ★ ★ ★

We have seen that, despite LBJ's assertions to the contrary, American involvement in the Vietnam War was not required by treaty, by popular demand in America, to preserve democracy in South Vietnam (it had never existed there), or to maintain American prestige in the rest of the world, where the folly of continuing the war was clearly seen. Nor, as it must be obvious by now, was it necessary to vanquish Communism in Vietnam in order to prevent its spread throughout Southeast Asia. Those dominos did not fall.

That which is in no sense necessary may still be unavoidable. For example, dying in the plane crash at Lockerbie, Scotland was not necessary, but it certainly was unavoidable once you boarded that plane and it took off. Of course, you could avoid dying if someone warned you that a bomb was on board and you refused to get on the plane, or if you then warned the authorities and the flight never took place The Vietnam War was neither necessary nor unavoidable. LBJ was given numerous warnings that the plane was going to crash. He ignored them.

Of course, American troops were in Vietnam before Johnson became President, and it might be useful for Americans to understand how their country got into that mess. History that is ignored is the kind most likely to take its revenge on the ignorant.

In 1945, as the war in the Pacific was clearly going against the Japanese, the French tried to regain control of their Laotian, Cambodian and Vietnamese colonies. By the end of 1947, the French had reestablished partial control over Vietnam, but they were at war with the forces of Ho Chi Minh.[1] The French army was finally defeated by the Vietnamese at the battle of Dien Bien Phu in North Vietnam in May, 1954.[2]

President Truman, citing "the loss of freedom for millions of people, the loss of vital raw materials, the loss of points of critical strategic importance to the free world," had supported the French with over a billion dollars in 1951-1952 and established a small military presence in Saigon, all to no avail.

In 1954, Eisenhower's contribution of 200 military advisors and 22 bombers did not prevent the defeated French from being driven out of the country.

There were only 685 American military advisors in South Vietnam, the number allowed by the Geneva Accords, before Eisenhower left office, and he had set limits to what the U.S. would do.[3] He refused to permit American participation in combat on the mainland of Asia because he felt the U.S. could not win a war there. The advisors were not allowed to be active outside of Saigon and they were forbidden to go into battle. It was under Kennedy that the advisors were first permitted to assist at the front.[4]

At that time, we were not yet in the pit, but on the edge. President Eisenhower was aware of the grueling ordeal France suffered in Vietnam. So did President Kennedy, although his advisors did not, according to one of them, his Secretary of Defense, Robert McNamara: "...by failing to take seriously the views of more knowledgeable and experienced allies, by acting unilaterally, we condemned ourselves to repeating the mistakes of the French. We acted as though we were omniscient." He added ruefully, "...some problems in international affairs have no solution, particularly no military solution."[5]

The policy of JFK was restrained by his caution. McNamara noted that Kennedy was less of a hawk than was Johnson.[6] Whereas LBJ worried about appearing cowardly, Kennedy looked on military action as something to do only when all else failed. His resolution of the Cuban Missile Crisis, with not a shot fired, was typical of his approach to international problems.

Since LBJ retained Kennedy's Secretaries of State and Defense, his National Security Advisor, and most of the Joint Chiefs of Staff, the two men were generally given the same kind of advice about Vietnam. (The difference was that Kennedy did not take the advice to expand the war, and Johnson did not take the advice when it eventually turned in favor of seeking peace.) Kennedy explained again and again that Congress, the American people, and America's major allies would not support America making war in Vietnam. He did not think that Indochina was a good place to fight. Moreover, while LBJ said it, JFK believed that countries threatened by Communist insurrections had, in the end, to be responsible themselves for the outcome.[7]

In April, May, July, August, and October of 1961, Kennedy opposed his advisors' recommendations for deeper involvement in Vietnam. He said Congress would never go for an intervention, and that "Troops are a last resort." He wanted to see SEATO forces involved instead. He told General Maxwell Taylor: "We are not sending combat troops." He refused to commit the U.S. to saving South Vietnam because the effort to do so could lead to war with China.[8]

During most of 1961, while agreeing that the U.S. must help South Vietnam to help itself, Kennedy resisted his advisors' push towards war, citing the lack of support from European allies, the difficulty of convincing the American people that the war was necessary.[9] He worried about the risk of China entering the conflict and had doubts about the effectiveness American bombing would have.[10] All of his concerns were justified.

Nevertheless, Kennedy found himself sucked into both escalation and secret war. Early in 1961, it was clear that the Diem regime was on the verge of being overthrown by the Vietcong. Kennedy agreed to send another 16,000 "advisors," along with airplanes and squadrons of helicopters, to assist the failing South Vietnamese army.[11]

President Kennedy initiated the policy of hiding the war from the American public. "Advisors" were not allowed to fly the American flag over their compounds, nor to receive combat decorations for service in Vietnam.[12]

His policy change did not signal a change of heart. Kennedy wanted the U.S. out of Vietnam. According to his brother Robert, "...he was determined not to send in ground troops. He would rather do anything than that." Robert added that if Saigon had fallen to the Communists, "We would have fuzzed it up, the way we did in Laos." Asked about this reluctance to fight in Vietnam, Robert responded: "...we were there! (in 1951)...We saw what happened to the French!"

In the spring of 1962, Kennedy told a staff member that he wanted a plan to get out when the opportunity presented itself.[13] He told aide Kenneth O'Donnell that complete withdrawal would have to wait until he was reelected: "In 1965, I'll become one of the most unpopular presidents in history. I'll be damned everywhere as a Communist appeaser. But I don't care. If I tried to pull out completely from Vietnam, now we would have another Joe McCarthy scare on our hands. I can do it after I'm reelected."[14]

In 1963, Kennedy reaffirmed to Senator Mansfield that he was planning a complete withdrawal of troops from Vietnam.[15] That May, Secretary of Defense McNamara informed General Harkins and others of the U.S. military leadership in Vietnam that the President wanted them to prepare a plan for withdrawal.[16]

Johnson, an aggressive cold warrior, knew about Kennedy's intentions, but was determined to defeat Communism in Vietnam.[17] He was already laying the groundwork. Kennedy had refused to send American combat troops to Vietnam. LBJ, to the contrary, signed O PLAN 34 A, which made U.S. forces available for spying and sabotage in North Vietnam.[18] The time to exit the Vietnam War was at hand, but this option was unacceptable to the new President.

LBJ could not claim that he clung to his Vietnam policy because of any shortage of prophets of doom to warn him off. The people who could have said "I told you so" about Vietnam constitute a sizeable chorus of Cassandras, and not a few of them had started out as hawks. There were warnings from credible parties in every year that LBJ was in office. As Vice President, he was getting back channel accounts of the disastrous course of the war while Kennedy was given only the official optimistic version.[19]

What follows is an account of what the President knew and when he knew it.

1963

Among the first to speak up was one of the "knowledgeable and experienced allies" that McNamara claimed were ignored. On May 15, fourteen countries signed an agreement in Geneva to keep Laos neutral. Shortly thereafter, Charles de Gaulle said to Kennedy: "You Americans wanted...to take our place in Indochina, you wanted to assume a succession to rekindle a war that we ended. I predict to you that you will, step by step, be sucked into a bottomless military and political quagmire."[20]

In August, de Gaulle urged all foreign forces to leave Indochina and allow the countries in the area to be neutralized.[21] Kennedy might have done that, had he lived, but LBJ paid no attention.

However, the new President continued to receive nothing but bad news out of South Vietnam. It was revealed to him that President Diem had been sending favorable and wildly unrealistic reports on his army's accomplishments. In reality, not only had the South Vietnamese been losing increasing numbers of weapons to their enemies, but the Vietcong had additionally been improving their armament as more materiel came down the Ho Chi Minh trail. Attacks by the guerillas continued increasing and the VC was getting better at shooting down American aircraft.[22]

1964

Senator Mansfield wrote to the President on February 2: "The people in Vietnam don't want to crusade against the Vietcong. We will find ourselves engaged in an indecisive, bloody and costly military involvement that will escalate just to preserve the status quo."[23]

General Westmoreland recorded that in May he told Defense Secretary McNamara that the situation in Vietnam was a "bottomless pit."[24]

De Gaulle tried again in June, this time with Under Secretary of State, George Ball, who passed the warning on. Ball noted that LBJ was not interested in hearing any of this.[25]

On September 25, Admiral Ulysses S. Sharp, CINCPAC, said that Saigon itself might fall to the enemy and he suggested "disengagement." So did George Ball.[26]

Even Secretary of State, Dean Rusk, was not the bloodthirsty hawk that he is often portrayed to be. LBJ recorded that "Rusk opposed air attacks and sustained reprisals in August, September, and December 1964." Rusk recalled: "I believed we should persevere with our policy of advising and assisting the South Vietnamese...rather than risk a major escalation if one could be avoided....Unless the South Vietnamese themselves could carry the major burden, I didn't see how we could succeed."[27]

In October, General Westmoreland cabled JCS Chairman General Earle G. Wheeler that without a stable government in South Vietnam, "...no amount of offensive action by the United States either in or outside South Vietnam has any chance by itself of reversing the deterioration underway."[28]

In late December, General Maxwell Taylor was sufficiently alarmed to tell the President that the Vietnamese Army was crippled by political turmoil, which made it increasingly ineffective. At the same time, South Vietnamese resentment of the American presence was growing, as were Vietcong attacks on U.S. personnel, and the whole of South Vietnam was sliding into a pit of discouragement.[29]

1965

General Taylor was not finished with his warnings. On January 6, he said he was against sending more U.S. ground troops because the United States would end up doing most of the fighting, while the civilian population became increasingly hostile. All that could be gained by sending in more troops was to buy a little time, but in the end, "like the French, we would be occupying an essentially hostile foreign country."[30]

At the beginning of March, LBJ's National Security Advisor, his Secretary of State and his Secretary of Defense told him that the chance of victory was diminishing, the Vietcong were increasing the territory they controlled, and there was no sign that the new government had the will or ability to govern the country.[31]

That same month General Westmoreland said: "...we are headed toward a VC takeover of the country."[32]

At the end of March, Senators Mansfield and McGovern warned the President that escalation would end in disaster. Mansfield insisted that Vietnam was not worth to the U.S. what it was costing in American lives and resources.[33]

One of LBJ's Vietnam advisors, Clark Clifford, told him in May: "This could be a quagmire. It could turn into an open-ended commitment on our part that would take more and more ground troops, without a realistic hope of ultimate victory." Clifford recommended negotiating a settlement.[34]

In the summer of 1965, as well as during the previous year, both of the Bundy brothers, McGeorge and William, voiced their opposition to sending large numbers of American ground troops. McGeorge told McNamara that it was "rash to the point of folly."[35]

The military leaders were equally discouraged. General Wheeler observed: "In the summer of 1965 it became amply clear that it wasn't a matter of whether the North Vietnamese were going to win the war; it was just a question of when they were going to win it."[36]

On June 16, 1965, George Ball began sending LBJ memos every few weeks, telling him that we could not, win, were clearly losing now, and that no matter how large an army we sent, victory was not possible.[37]

1966

General Westmoreland dropped a bomb at the March conference in Guam which the President attended: "...I said that if the Vietcong organization failed to disintegrate, which I saw as unlikely, and we were unable to find a way to halt North Vietnamese infiltration, the war could go on indefinitely.... On the faces of the Washington officials, who had obviously been hoping for some optimistic assessment, were looks of shock."[38] The general was addressing a flock of ostriches.

On May 8, 1966, the director of the CIA, William Raborn, told LBJ that what lay ahead was either pulling out at a very high cost or waging a much larger war than we wanted to.[39]

1967

McNamara went to South Vietnam in October, 1967, and reported to the President what he learned: "...there is no sign of an impending break in enemy morale and it appears that he can more than replace his losses by infiltration from North Vietnam and recruitment in South Vietnam.... As compared with two, or four years ago, enemy full-time regional forces and part-time guerilla forces are larger; attacks, terrorism and sabotage have increased in scope and intensity....the VC political infrastructure thrives in most of the country, continuing to give the enemy his enormous intelligence advantage; full security exists nowhere.... Nor has the Rolling Thunder program of bombing the North either significantly affected infiltration or cracked the morale of Hanoi."[40]

On November 1, the Secretary of Defense added: "Continuation of our present course of action in Southeast Asia would be dangerous, costly in lives, and unsatisfactory to the American people."[41]

1968

By the time William Bundy delivered the following message, it was news to no one except, perhaps, the majority of Americans: "South Vietnam is very weak. Our position may be truly untenable. Contingency planning should proceed toward the possibility that we will withdraw with the best possible face and defend the rest of Asia."[42]

LBJ believed that showing a willingness to negotiate was showing a yellow streak. He told George Ball to forestall those who wanted negotiations. LBJ would not even consider talking to the North Vietnamese until the bombing campaign had softened them. To avoid the Secretary General of the United Nations, the British Prime Minister, and whoever else was pressing him to negotiate, the President said he was going "to get sick and leave town." But he told the world that he would travel to *make* peace, not to avoid it. He promised to "go anywhere at anytime and meet with anyone whenever there is promise of progress toward an honorable peace."[43]

The pattern LBJ carried out throughout his Presidency was to reiterate his willingness to negotiate while intensifying the war. He always found an excuse for greater aggression.

On February 3, 1968, Senator Fulbright accurately described LBJ's methods of postponing peace: "I'm prepared to bet that you're going to…(hang) so many conditions on whatever reply you send to Ho Chi Minh you'll make sure that he'll turn you down and then you'll use that as an excuse to step up the bombing even more."[44]

The fact is that LBJ remained steadfastly unwilling to make peace without victory. George Reedy recorded that Johnson was cold if not hostile to anyone who told him that the enemy was ready to make peace. Including his own less-than-sincere initiatives, he had seventy-two opportunities to negotiate an end to the war.[45]

One of the tragedies of the twentieth century is that the Vietnam War could easily have not happened at all. A solution for the conflicts within that country was at hand well before LBJ became President. While Eisenhower was still in the White House, there was a consensus that included America's European allies, the Soviet Union, China and the North Vietnamese for reuniting Vietnam as a neutral country. South Vietnam would not have continued its opposition without assistance from the United States. Only American policy stood in the way of a settlement that would have been far more acceptable to the U.S. than the eventual Communist takeover of the South.[46] A reunited and neutral Vietnam remained a viable option throughout LBJ's Presidency.

Other lost opportunities for peace took different forms. On many occasions, the North Vietnamese and the Communist National Liberation Front in South Vietnam offered to negotiate. More than once, the government of South Vietnam wanted to start its own negotiations with North Vietnam. Frequently, the war was going so badly for the Americans that it was clearly folly to persist. But persist LBJ did.

The following chronicles the massive resistance LBJ put up against ending the war:

1963

Diem's brother, Nhu told a *Washington Post* correspondent on May 12, 1963, that in January he had asked for half of the American troops to pull out.[47] The South Vietnamese leader had his brother, Nhu, open communication with North Vietnam about reunifying and neutralizing the country.

De Gaulle got word of it. On August 29, 1963, he offered Kennedy his help in negotiating "an independent but neutral South Vietnam."[48]

Kennedy did not live to take him up on it, but the offer was repeated to LBJ on November 24, right after Kennedy was killed.[49] However, the new President had zero interest in negotiating. Instead, ignoring the negative reports coming from Vietnam, he directed his energies to winning the war.[50] He said: "The need now is not for negotiations but to get the message across to them—leave your neighbor alone and we can all have peace and go ahead with our business."[51]

On December 13, Prince Norodom Sihanouk of Cambodia was seconded by the NLF, the political arm of the Vietcong, in his requesting an international conference to create a neutral federation of the countries of Southeast Asia, including South Vietnam.

That same month, de Gaulle offered again to help in negotiating a neutral Vietnam.[52]

Vietnamese historian Luu Van Loi said that America could have had peace at the end of that year: "...the generals in charge in Saigon, following orders from Washington, rejected all overtures from the NLF, from De Gaulle, and even from some people within the U.S. government. Thus did the U.S. miss an opportunity created by the death of Diem and Nhu...for a coalition government then and there.... The NLF was ready and eager to do so at that point."[53]

1964

Autumn, 1964, was a perfect time for the U.S. to get out of Vietnam, McNamara recalled. During the Kennedy administration, American participation in the defense of South Vietnam had political stability in that country as a prerequisite. However, incoming National Intelligence Estimates predicted that political stability had no chance of developing there. In view of that, McNamara says, it was time to reassess why the U.S. was continuing to fight, but it did not happen because no one had the nerve to raise the question of pulling out."[54]

In October, LBJ's old friend, Senator Richard Russell, suggested a way to withdraw without losing face: the U.S. should see to it that the government of South Vietnam was led by a man who would demand American forces get out of the country.[55] It almost happened the following February.

December brought another offer from Ho Chi Minh to negotiate a settlement.[56] That same month, the government of Vietnam again provided a perfect justification for American withdrawal. On December 20, a group of generals, including Khanh, Ky, and Thieu, dissolved the South Vietnamese legislature and arrested some of its members for failing to obey their orders.

General Taylor wanted the status quo restored, and got into a conflict with General Khanh, whom he told to leave Vietnam. Khanh said that Vietnam could do without American aid and demanded that Taylor leave the country. The State Department authorized Taylor to reply that if he left, American support would be discontinued. Meanwhile, the American press got wind of all this and called for an American pull out.[57] This time there was no need to worry about public support for withdrawal, but LBJ was still not interested..

1965

In early February, like an answer to Senator Russell's prayer, General Khanh, who was now President, was eager to make an alliance with the Buddhists, negotiate with the NLF, and become the leader of a neutral South Vietnam which would have no need for American troops. Here was the perfect opportunity for an American withdrawal. But LBJ's people encouraged Generals Ky and Thieu to overthrow Khanh, which they did on February 19th.[58]

Later that month, U Thant tried again to arrange peace talks, this time including not only the U.S. and both Vietnams, but China, the Soviet Union, Britain and France. On February 24, a frustrated U Thant said publicly that the U.S. government was not informing the American people about opportunities for peace talks. The White House denied keeping anything secret and refused to participate in talks.[59] Two days later the *New York Times* reported that North Vietnam was ready to negotiate.[60]

In November, Giorgio La Pira, the former mayor of Florence, Italy, brought a new offer from Hanoi: an agreement to negotiate without requiring that American troops first be withdrawn. Ho Chi Minh announced: "I am prepared to go anywhere; to meet anyone." Rusk replied with an elaborate set of conditions which excluded talking to the NLF, and then Haiphong Harbor was bombed for the first time.[61]

1966

That February, LBJ again showed one face to America and another to North Vietnam. Ho Chi Minh had made another offer to begin negotiations and Senator Fulbright monitored the State Department's response, which was favorable. But a second letter was then sent secretly to Hanoi by LBJ, imposing discouraging conditions for peace talks.[62]

In the Spring, additional Buddhist uprisings against the government of South Vietnam prompted McNamara to say that it was a good time to get out: "…while the military situation is not going badly, the political situation is in 'terminal sickness,' and even the military prognosis is of an escalating stalemate."[63]

The Buddhist "Struggle Movement" appeared about to overthrow the Ky government and replace it with one willing to negotiate a coalition with the NLF. Even LBJ became discouraged enough to suggest that the U.S. might retreat to Thailand. Two days later, when 3,000 South Vietnamese soldiers joined the Buddhist protests in Hue, LBJ continued to talk about the possibility of getting out. But Ky managed to arrest the Struggle Movement leaders and defuse the crisis on March 23rd.[64]

1967

In January, 1967, the Russians conveyed the message that the North Vietnamese were ready to negotiate. There were two meetings in Moscow between John Guthrie and his North Vietnamese counterpart, Le Chang, but nothing came of them. At the end of the month, Hanoi announced that a bombing halt would have brought about immediate peace talks.[65]

By May, 1967, there had been changes in Southeast Asia which convinced McNamara that the domino effect was no longer a danger. He expressed his new point of view to LBJ: "…I pointed to the Communists' defeat in Indonesia and the Cultural Revolution then roiling China, arguing that these events showed the trend in Asia now ran in our favor, thus reducing South Vietnam's importance." He said that the U.S. should get out if "the country ceases to help itself," and advocated an end to escalation. He later realized that the U.S. had missed a good opportunity to begin withdrawing from

South Vietnam. In all likelihood, the terms accepted would have been no worse than those of nearly six years later.[66]

1968

Here is the voice of LBJ himself: "On February 21, U.N. Secretary General U Thant came to the White House. He told me that he had received an indication from unofficial sources that the North Vietnamese would be willing to begin talks with us if we stopped the bombing. If we notified Hanoi officially, the talks could begin 'immediately'....U Thant's report was interesting but hardly conclusive.... A few days later, on February 26, we received an intelligence report quoting a North Vietnamese contact as saying: 'President Ho is waiting but has insisted that the bombing be stopped first.' This was a straw in the wind....the last day of February brought still another hint of Hanoi's possible desire for talks. An Indian diplomat informed us he had information that Hanoi would enter 'prompt' and 'substantive' talks with us when all bombing ended.... these various indications of Hanoi's possible interest in negotiations played a part in my eventual decision to risk a bombing halt."[67]

What did it take to get LBJ's attention? He seemed like a man buried in a deep pit, seeing nothing and hearing only faint, indecipherable sounds from the world above. Part of his problem was his fear that North Vietnam would take advantage of bombing halts to resupply its army and the Vietcong in the South.

As early as 1964, LBJ doubted that victory was possible in Vietnam. At least he doubted it during his periods of depression. As the war expanded and the likelihood of victory diminished, LBJ saw himself trapped, unable to win and unable to end the war without victory.

He could not accept defeat for many reasons, most of them distortions of reality caused by his illness which made him extraordinarily manipulative and dominating thereby prevented the men around him from persuading him to take a less disastrous course.

WAR AND MADNESS

★ ★ ★ ★ ★ ★

Whose war was it anyway? Every President of the United States is surrounded by people who are willing or required to give him information and advice. There is no question that when LBJ became President, the advisors he inherited from Kennedy were almost unanimously gungho for the war, as he also had been before assuming that office. Senior aide Joseph Califano said that only one of Kennedy's top advisors failed to encourage LBJ to increase the speed of escalation.[1]

Johnson appeared to take their counsel seriously and to carry it out. But he was simply doing what he would have done without the advice. The President's control of his advisors was so absolute that he was able to turn the prosecution of the Vietnam War, like his government, virtually into a solo performance.

LBJ was never just a simple small-town boy who was putty in the hands of a gang of Harvard men. According to one of them, National Security Advisor McGeorge Bundy: "It is 'total baloney' that we, Rusk, McNamara, and Bundy, were running the government. We understood that we were working for a President who …insisted on making his own decisions."[2] Historian Eric Goldman confirms that Johnson's decisions were quite independent of the men and groups around him.[3] Indeed, if there was any putty in the White House, it was LBJ whose hands were shaping it.

The National Security Council, which included the President, Vice President, Secretaries of State and Defense, the Director of the Office of Emergency Planning, the Director of the CIA, and the Chairman of the Joint Chiefs of Staff, with an additional 5 to 23 people occasionally in attendance, was supposed to help the President arrive at decisions on matters such as the war.[4] However, LBJ's method of eliciting advice was to announce a decision and then ask each person in turn if he agreed with it. A former NSC staff member recalls indulging in a Walter Mitty-like fantasy in which he would have the courage to stand and actually express disagreement with Johnson. But that never happened.

The President in effect turned the NSC into a rubber stamp. By February of 1965, he was eager to punish the Vietcong. He had, says historian Eric Goldman, prepared the ground with congressional conferences and other measures to shape public opinion. The Vietcong attack on the American base at Pleiku on February 7 gave him a perfect opportunity to go on the offensive. LBJ called an emergency meeting of the NSC, waved the Pleiku casualty list in the air and exclaimed "I've had enough of this!"[5] Who could resist that grand bit of stagecraft?

Although the National Security Council was compliant, its membership was set by law, and that was not good enough for LBJ. The President preferred to create his own handpicked group of advisors, which became known as the Tuesday Lunch Group because that was when it met.

It first assembled 11 weeks after LBJ assumed the presidency. No military man was included except by occasional invitation.[6] LBJ's rationale for forming his own select group was "The National Security meetings were like sieves...."[7] Political problems and how to win the war provided most of the topics for discussion. Getting out of Vietnam was not an acceptable subject. The Director of the United States information Agency, Leonard Marks was one man who did not understand this, did suggest pulling out and he despite being an old friend of LBJ, was given a chilly response.[8]

For members of the Tuesday Lunch Group, LBJ selected people who agreed with him, or were at least unwilling to disagree with him. Humphrey commented that "Until...1968, I heard very little counsel from any of those genuinely close to the President that could in the most generous fashion be interpreted as opposition to further commitments of American power."[9]

In 1968, after Tet, the most influential advisors, McGeorge Bundy, Henry Cabot Lodge, Douglas Dillon, Dean Acheson, and Cyrus Vance, all expressed variations on the theme that the U.S. should quit Vietnam. The President told them: "Your whole group has been brainwashed."[10]

Secretary of State Dean Rusk confirms that Cabinet members did not disagree openly with LBJ: "At most cabinet meetings Lyndon Johnson asked Bob McNamara and me to comment on Vietnam, and then he would go around the table, asking each cabinet officer, 'Do you have any questions or comments?' Everyone sat silently."[11]

Rusk and McNamara could be relied on to express LBJ's point of view about Vietnam until McNamara ceased to be a true believer. Rusk had no faith in the effectiveness of bombing in general, but once the Rolling Thunder bombing campaign and massive troop increases were underway, he backed LBJ one hundred percent.[12]

The White House became more autocratic as the war dragged on, and such dissenters as there were, vanished. Bill Moyers left his job as LBJ's Press Secretary at the end of 1966. Hugh Sidey, observed that after Moyer's departure, there was no one left around to tell Johnson "No."

There was opposition in the government to LBJ's Vietnam policy, but it had to stay "in the closet," and there is very little one can do from the vantage of a closet. Harry McPherson, special counsel and speechwriter, became a clandestine dissenter because he felt that openly opposing the war would exclude him from participating in discussions of the war and having any effect on Johnson's decisions.[13] However, his playacting did not pay off.

Rusk notes that silence prevailed at the State Department: "Others at State and within the administration had doubts about the war....Several people resigned and later attributed their resignations to Vietnam, but while they were in office they didn't say a word."[14] As for the White House staff, it seems that it consisted of not hawks, but of rabbits who were convinced that they should do their jobs for LBJ and not question his Vietnam policy.

When Johnson moved into the White House, America's military leaders did not know it, but they were in for a hard time. Back in 1942, after his own limited Navy service, he announced: "We must get rid of the indecisive, stupid, selfish, and incompetent in high military positions."[15] He was talking about the men who won World War II.

The military did not appear more attractive to LBJ from his seat in the Oval Office. A former Senate colleague noted that Johnson had no regard for high-ranking officers, and considered their intelligence below his own.[16] It was not simply a matter of the President's lack of respect for military leaders. LBJ had adopted a program of gradual escalation because he thought it would win in Vietnam without revealing to the American public that a war was going on. The JCS thought this was folly and wanted either a complete pullout or, preferably, full scale war.[17] Because of the people involved, these positions were irreconcilable.

Though for the most part, he ignored them, what contact the President had with his generals did not add to their happiness. "...I made sure," he said, "that I had more control over the generals than any other civilian President in history. I insisted on that."[18] LBJ added: "By keeping a lid on all the designated targets, I knew I could keep control of the war in my own hands."[19]

General Westmoreland wanted to have some say over the choice of bombing targets, and believed that it verged on folly to try to make every military decision, including the most minute, from the Oval Office. After his headquarters selected a group of targets, a different set often was chosen in Washington. The President also insisted that the South Vietnamese, who were to participate in the bombing, not be told where it would take place.

Orders and counterorders flew back and forth while the pilots spent sleepless nights, waiting for a final decision.[20] Westmoreland adds that the President made a practice of cancelling at the last minute missions which had been months in planning and preparation. (That was the way LBJ ran his election campaigns too.) President Johnson boasted on one occasion that 'they can't even bomb an outhouse without my approval.'"[21]

At one point a distraught General Wheeler told the JCS that the President had led them "into a trap." LBJ was demanding that more VC be killed, but instead of the three new divisions the JCS wanted for Vietnam, he was only letting them send a measely 5,000 Marines. The President threatened to blame the JCS publicly for any failures and insisted "...as long as I am Commander in Chief, I am going to control (the war) from Washington!"[22]

George Reedy attributes to Lady Bird some of the responsibility for estranging her husband from reality, especially in the White House, where she permitted no one to oppose LBJ, or express doubt about anything he favored, or even tell him bad news.[23] This is understandable. Bad news could drive her husband into rages or bottomless depressions.

One way of avoiding unpleasant facts is to avoid the people who bring them up. Some of the people closest to the President lost access to him when they disagreed with him about Vietnam. Hubert Humphrey was treated harshly for his independent thinking. His first memo to LBJ telling him not to bomb North Vietnam infuriated the President. After a second one was sent, LBJ replied "we do not need all these memos."

By law, the Vice President could not be banned from NSC meetings, but LBJ shifted all the important Vietnam business to the Tuesday luncheons, which excluded Humphrey. The Vice

President's speeches now came under severe censorship, and he was not even permitted by the President to speak in praise of peace to the Pope.[24]

On January 6, 1966, at a dinner party given by historian and war critic, Arthur Schlesinger, McNamara stated that the only solution for Vietnam was "withdrawal with honor." The host later wrote that the Secretary of Defense was in despair at the prospect that an indefinite escalation lay ahead.[25]

A year later, McNamara was even more visibly despondent about the war and told a friend: "We have poured more bomb loads onto North Vietnam than in the whole of World War II, yet we have no sign that it has shaken their will to resist, none."[26] That May, he sent LBJ a memorandum stating that victory was impossible and he recommending settling even for unfavorable peace terms.[27] On October 25, the Defense Secretary got the JCS up in arms when he reported to a Senate subcommittee that bombing would not suffice to make Ho Chi Minh sue for peace. The JCS threatened to resign en masse. The President berated McNamara for three hours, even though the CIA had already told him that the bombing would not bring victory.[28]

In November of 1967, without telling McNamara what he was doing, LBJ had him appointed to the presidency of the World Bank. This appointment was not an expression of confidence in the Secretary of Defense: the President was dumping a man he considered "an emotional basket case."[29]

Before he was gone, McNamara attended a meeting at which General Westmoreland asked for 205,000 more troops to go to Vietnam. McNamara said it was "madness." Then he rose and said he was leaving, but instead he blasted "...the goddamned bombing campaign, it's been worth nothing. It's done nothing. They've dropped more bombs than in all of Europe in all of World War II and it hasn't done a fucking thing." He then addressed his successor, Clark Clifford: "We simply have to end this thing. I just hope you can get hold of it. It is out of control."[30]

The case of Undersecretary of State George Ball, who was a dove from the beginning, is a curious one, perhaps an instance of the camel that one keeps inside the tent because one would rather have him inside, pissing out, than outside, pissing in. LBJ treated Ball and his former law partner, Adlai Stevenson, with the same wary courtesy and pretense that he saw merit in their opinions, and for the same reason: the President was afraid of the damage the two could do if they made their dissent about Vietnam public.

LBJ calculated correctly that they would not talk to the press as long as they still hoped they could influence him.[31] On one occasion, LBJ had Bill Moyers lie to Ball. LBJ's message was that he would not decide to raise the troop level in Vietnam above 100,000 men. Actually, he had given the order to do so three days previously.[32]

The initial line-up among the people close to the President were as follows. The hawks were the Joint Chiefs of Staff; McNamara, the Secretary of Defense and his aides; William Bundy and John McNaughton; Secretary of State Rusk and his planning director, Walter Rostow; and National Security Advisor McGeorge Bundy. The opposing team consisted of George Ball, Averell Harriman and Roger Hillsman, and Paul Kattenberg at State; John Galbraith, Ambassador to India, Arthur Schlesinger at the White House; and Senators Mansfield, Russell and Morse, and of course, Hubert Humphrey and Bill Moyers. By the end of 1964, Hillsman and Harriman had no responsibilities, and only George Ball was left in position.[33] LBJ could not rid himself of the senators.

After the Tet Offensive in early 1968, there were hardly any hawks left except for LBJ himself. His replacement for McNamara was Clark Clifford, who recalled that "I had come to the conclusion that my overwhelming priority as Secretary of Defense was to extricate our nation from an endless war!"[34]

Dean Acheson, a cold warrior of long-standing, proclaimed in March: "We can no longer do the job we set out to do in the time we have left and we must begin to take steps to disengage."[35]

LBJ did his best to keep Congress isolated from the decision-making about the war, and he succeeded.[36] But there were senators opposing the war who were too important to disregard entirely. One of them was Majority Leader Mike Mansfield. In January of 1964, responding to a request for his opinion, Mansfield told LBJ that other nations should be brought in to settle things in Vietnam. Thereafter, the President continued to ask for Mansfield's opinion and continued to ignore it, the end result being merely a large file of memoranda from the Senator.[37]

Richard Russell had a much closer relationship with LBJ, having been one of his mentors. He remained a close friend of the family, whom he continued to visit frequently throughout LBJ's presidency. Russell talked to the President several times a week. In 1954, Senators Russell and Johnson had worked together to prevent the U.S. from joining the French in their struggle to keep Vietnam a colony. Russell also tried to stop Kennedy from further involving the U.S. in Vietnam. He said: "It would be a festering sore. We'd still be sitting there three or four years from now." In 1965, Russell said "I have never seen where Vietnam has strategic, tactical or economic value...."[38]

Lady Bird considered Russell to be the man whom her husband respected above all others.[39] Which raises the question: why didn't LBJ listen to him? Furthermore, why did LBJ change from a man who saw the folly of France in Vietnam to one who wanted to fight to the bitter end there?

Although skeptical about Vietnam, Senator Fulbright retained his access to LBJ until September 1965. Then he publicly criticized the invasion of the Dominican Republic and the escalation in Vietnam. After that, says Fulbright, LBJ "never had another private conversation with me."[40]

In 1969 two reporters known by LBJ for years, returned from talks with the North Vietnamese leadership about negotiations and tried to meet with the President. When Senator Fulbright heard that they were denied this opportunity, he confronted the President at a social function at the White House. LBJ replied: "I'd like to see them, Bill, but you know I can't talk with everybody who's been over there talking with Ho Chi Minh."[41]

When the ambassadors from Chile, Denmark and Great Britain complained about the bombing of North Vietnam, the President flew into rages and scolded them mercilessly.[42]

What drove LBJ to defy not only his critics, but his own doubts in seeking an unobtainable victory in a war that no one believed was needed? There is no simple answer to this question. The President was caught in the web of his own delusions.

DELUSION'S WEB

L BJ's manic furies and incapacitating depressions, his pathological ego, megalomania and paranoia were products of his manic depression. Unfortunate though they were for him and the people with whom he came in contact, their effects became tragic when he took over the conduct of the Vietnam War. He arrived at the White House equipped with a number of delusions acquired during the decades of his illness. They caused him to make unrealistic assumptions and faulty decisions from the very beginning.

His years as President during one of the most tumultuous periods of the 20th century subjected him to stress that a healthy man would have found hard to bear. The effect on LBJ was catastrophic. His illness worsened past the point of psychotic collapse. The consequences were fatal, if not for him, certainly for those who died in Vietnam in this needless war—LBJ's war—for he would not accept guidance from the advisors who might have imparted some degree of sanity to his decisions.

Some of the President's delusions, false beliefs, and misapprehensions were part of the political climate of the times and were widely held by his fellow citizens. Nations always have not only aspirations and dreams, but nightmares as well. Begin with the delusions that LBJ shared with his advisors, many people in the government, and a majority of the American people.

The 1950s were years of Red witch-hunts and children hiding under school desks during atomic bomb drills. Communists and atomic bombs were real enough, but the nightmares that they inspired generated solutions that were, at times, worse than useless. During the late fifties, the nation's nightmares began to feature monolithic Communist blocs and Asian dominos.

Vietnam, little known in America, became fertile ground for the growth of fantasies about its people North and South.

While Eisenhower had been reluctant to send U.S. troops to fight on Asian soil during his own administration, the night before Kennedy's inauguration, he lectured the President-elect on the importance of defending South Vietnam. If that country went completely Communist, he maintained, the red tidal wave would quickly wash over Laos, Cambodia, Burma, the rest of Southeast Asia, overrunning the Philippines, and perhaps submerging Australia and New Zealand as well.[1]

Although the Truman administration held that a Communist Indochina would threaten the security of the United States, Eisenhower was the first American President to talk about dominos falling in Asia.[2] LBJ brought the domino theory with him to the Presidency. He declared: "…I knew that if the aggression succeeded in South Vietnam, then the aggressors would simply keep on going until all of Southeast Asia fell into their hands…at least down to Singapore and almost certainly to Djakarta….and soon we'd be fighting in Berlin or elsewhere. And so would begin World War III."[3] Sometimes the geography varied. Another version was: "…if we quit in Vietnam, tomorrow we'll be fighting in Hawaii and next week we'll have to fight in San Francisco."[4]

William Bundy disputed the domino theory as early as November 19, 1964, when he told LBJ that the losses of South Vietnam and Laos would not be fatal to American security. He suggested that instead of pursuing the war, a Geneva Conference to neutralize Vietnam plus U.S. support for Thailand would stop the spread of Communism in Asia.[5] That solution was unacceptable to the President.

An aggressive, expanding China was one of the foundations of the domino theory. And China lived up to its reputation prior to 1966. In August of 1965, while India was busy fighting Pakistan over Kashmir, the Chinese positioned their troops on the border with India and demanded more territory. But India's prompt victory induced the Chinese to withdraw. Affairs also did not go well for China when Sukarno was overthrown in Indonesia and 310,000 Communists were killed. That domino definitely was not going to fall.

Complicating China's expansive ambitions was the failure of Mao's Great Leap Forward to improve the economy of China. This was followed by the anarchy of the Cultural Revolution, and China was kept too busy with internal affairs for another ten years to involve itself in foreign adventures.

A fundamental mistake made by one American administration after another was the belief that Ho Chi Minh and his people were obedient servants of China and the Soviet Union. The truth was that Vietnam had suffered under Chinese rule for the first thousand years of its history, and was repeatedly invaded by China during the second thousand years. The Vietnamese had long memories.[6] Ho Chi Minh and his people were nationalists before they were Communists.[7]

According to U.S. Intelligence sources, in 1945, the Vietnamese leader, looking for recognition and help from America, and expecting little from the U.S.S.R., was ready to abandon Communism.[8] In 1945, Ho Chi Minh began asking the United States for recognition of his country. That same year between one and two million Vietnamese died of starvation.[9] With aid to and recognition of Ho Chi Minh's government, Vietnam could have become an ally of the United States, or at worst, an independent Communist state like

Yugoslavia. There was a five year window of opportunity: The Soviet Union did not grant recognition to North Vietnam until 1950.[10]

In addition to misinterpreting the history of Vietnam, the U.S. government harbored numerous errors about the countries that North Vietnam and South Vietnam had become. First mistake: in the American view, the Vietcong were Hanoi's puppets. In reality, it was not until five years after the French defeat that the Vietcong got Hanoi to help it in its rebellion against Ngo Dinh Diem. The North Vietnamese were reluctant to do anything that would elicit more U.S. involvement.[11]

This was a time and Vietnam was a place where fantasies grew thick and fast. According to CIA Director John McCone, the South Vietnamese province and district chiefs lied to those higher up in the government about how strong South Vietnamese forces were and how weak the Vietcong were. U.S. commanders, furthermore, were not averse to indulging in wishful thinking and did a poor job monitoring the progress of the war. On the whole, what the Americans were told was what the South Vietnamese thought Americans wanted to hear.[12]

America's military, government, and people, along with the President, were told repeatedly that the war was going well and victory would take just a while longer. But it was never true.

LBJ and many in his administration also had false beliefs about what the North Vietnamese wanted in South Vietnam. McNamara says one of these faulty judgements was that South Vietnam could never have a neutralist government composed of Communists, anticommunists and neutrals because Ho Chi Minh was determined to conquer and rule South Vietnam.

Long after the war, McNamara became convinced that, while the North Vietnamese wanted to overthrow Diem, they had intended to replace him with a neutral coalition consisting of people from the South. They were hoping for a settlement similar to the one made in Laos.[13] But LBJ's view on January 11, 1964, was, and remained: "Neutralization of South Vietnam would only be another name for a Communist take over."[14] This false conviction did much to prolong the war.

Another of LBJ's and his administration's failures to understand the enemy became the justification for the bombing campaign. McNamara states that they believed bombing would totally demoralize the government of North Vietnam and prompt it to abandon its NLF allies in the South. It was also believed that bombing would, in effect, disarm North Vietnam by crippling its production of essential war materiels and, consequently, Hanoi would have to surrender.[15] It took the administration quite a while to realize that Hanoi did not need to make its own war materiel. It was kept well supplied by China and the Soviet Union. As for the expectation of breaking Hanoi's will, that was based on a common error that arises during wars: the delusion that the enemy does not possess one's own virtues of courage and persistence.

Overreliance on bombing brought the President and his advisors together in another denial of reality. McNamara notes: "Data and analysis showed that air attacks would not work, but there was such determination to do something, anything to stop the Communists that discouraging reports were often ignored."[16] Although LBJ stopped the bombing eight times in three years, nonetheless, he always did so grudgingly.[17]

When McNamara and Rusk finally suggested that bombing be limited to areas south of the 20th parallel, sparing large population centers while concentrating on areas of maximum military activity, Johnson was completely opposed, insisting that continuing the massive air bombardment would bring victory to America before the next election.[18]

The President, his administration, and the military also succumbed to the delusion that American forces, because of their general superiority, would prevail regardless whether they used appropriate methods or not. McNamara confesses: "...the President, I, and others among his civilian advisors must share the burden of responsibility for consenting to fight a guerilla war with conventional military tactics.... It could not be done, and it was not done."[19]

To the misinterpretations, falsifications, and wishful thinking that blinded the government to the realities of Vietnam, LBJ added some that were peculiarly his own. Vice President Johnson, on returning to Washington, advised Kennedy to make "a major commitment" to South Vietnam. "Hell, Vietnam is just like the Alamo," he said.[20] His comment shows that his thinking about that Asian country was deeply dyed with fantasies in which he played the part of Heroic Texan, while American forces were the fearless pioneers of Texas who subdued the land and killed Indians to make the country safe and peaceful.[21]

LBJ entered the presidency with a delusional sense of mission: "I had to take the dead man's program and turn it into a martyr's cause. That way Kennedy would live on forever and so would I."[22] He was determined, not to continue Kennedy's work, but to surpass it, not only domestically, but militarily.

Two days after Kennedy's death, Ambassador Lodge reported, as LBJ already well knew, that "...the army won't fight" and the people had no alliegiance to the South Vietnamese government.[23] LBJ was sure he could get better results. He told the Cabinet:"I am not going to be the President who saw Southeast Asia go the way that China went." He instructed Lodge to "...tell those generals in Saigon that Lyndon Johnson intends to stand by our word."[24]

In a sense, LBJ's megalomania was responsible for much of what went wrong in the American intervention. Robert McNamara observed, years later, "We created the entity called South Vietnam in order to halt the advance of Communism. We created a President, Ngo Dinh Diem, to lead this entity and to participate with us in nation-building. These were all attempts to solve what we took to be the problem of an advancing Communist-surge in Southeast Asia....our 'solutions' became the problem."[25]

Another delusion of LBJ was that there was no limit, if he was clever enough, to what he could make the American people accept and do. According to George Reedy, LBJ believed that American political leaders and voters alike would for years be willing to continue a war without victories or territory gained and held in a far distant country that most Americans had never heard of.[26] Here is a prime example of the delusion of political omnipotence and a lesson of history that may apply to a war against terrorism.

At a seven nation conference held in Manila in late October of 1966, LBJ pledged the U.S. to be the peace officer (Texan parlance for a sheriff) of Southeast Asia. Commentator Walter Lippmann called this "Manilla madness" and "messianic megalomania." Alliteration aside, he hit the nail on the head. In Manila, LBJ proclaimed: "What we ask for we are going to get, we are going to keep, we are going to hold."[27]

Grandiosity blended with paranoia in the President's apocalyptic vision of the war. At a press conference in 1965, he declared: "...as long as there are men who hate and destroy, we must have the courage to resist, or we will see it all, all that we have built, all that we hope to build, all of our dreams for freedom—all, all will be swept away on the flood of conquest. So, too, this shall not happen. We will stand in Vietnam."[28]

As his paranoia grew, the domino theory assumed terrifying dimensions for the President. He appeared to take the theory very personally. He recalled: "...I was as sure as any man could be that once we showed how weak we were, Moscow and Peking would move in a flash to exploit our weakness. They might move independently or they might move together. But move they would.... And so would begin World War III." He added: "...it was the thought of World War III that kept me going every day."[29]

LBJ berated the Joint Chiefs of Staff because he feared their war plans would push him into starting World War III. And he was afraid that not fighting in Vietnam would start World War III. His fears placed him in a bind: he believed that no matter what he did, he might cause the end of the world. This is the double whammy of paranoid terror combined with the pessimistic delusions of depression.

Through the lens of the President's paranoia, the Communists became as influential and ubiquitous as the devil of the Puritans in Salem. Even after he left the Presidency, LBJ insisted that the Communists "...control the three networks, you know, and the forty major outlets of communication. It's all in the FBI reports. They prove everything. Not just about the reporters but about the professors too....you see the way it worked: the opponents of the war went on jags which pretty much originated in the Communist world and eventually found their way to the American critics....

"Senator Morse came in and told me the Soviet Ambassador said that such and such would happen if we stopped the bombing. They were telling the same thing to Fulbright, Clark, Mansfield, Church and others. Then McGeorge Bundy had lunch with Dobrynin and suddenly he became an ardent advocate for peace.... I thought it (a bombing pause) was wrong, that it would make us look like a weak sister. But I hated to see history record that I stood in the way of peace. So again I ordered a pause and again nothing happened. Isn't it funny that I always received a piece of advice from my top advisors right after each of them had been in contact with someone in the Communist world? Isn't it funny that you could always find Dobrynin's car in front of Reston's house the night before Reston (of the *New York Times*) delivered a blast on Vietnam?"[30]

Here we have two mutually reinforcing fantasies. First there is the classic paranoid delusion that the enemy is all around and all powerful, trying unceasingly to defeat LBJ. Second, his paranoia helps him to construct an elaborate defense of his ego. Since he is infallible, the people who disagree with him about Vietnam must be wrong, and have turned against him because they have fallen under the influence of his enemies. As is the case with paranoid worldviews, everything that happens is incorporated into LBJ's delusional system. Each event is interpreted as confirming evidence that his suspicions are accurate.

While his illness intensified under the strain of his presidential responsibilities, manic depression not only made LBJ a prisoner of his delusions, it interfered with his thinking processes. Many of the decisions about the conduct of the Vietnam War were made during the meetings of the Tuesday Lunch Group, albeit by LBJ, and what was accomplished depended entirely on the President's mood.

Because LBJ ruled and was ruled by impulse, the meetings had no agenda, nor did the group adopt the discipline of making reports on its decisions. When he was manic, he could not stick to a topic, and wasted hours in rambling, pointless monologues. Things went especially poorly when he was depressed. He spent the time complaining about his critics and indulging in self-pity. Attempts to return him to more pressing matters would enrage him.[31]

The manic optimism of the President was often reinforced by megalomania. In 1964, despite Ho Chi Minh's record of successfully fighting France for almost a decade, LBJ was certain that the war in Vietnam would end in a year to a year and a half, too short a time, he felt, to have much impact on America.[32] Manic optimism can be beneficial when it encourages people to undertake what is worthwhile and possible. But it can also lead to great folly because it replaces reality with enthusiasm. And, as we have seen, it can be contagious. As Dean Rusk said, "We thought we could win."[33] LBJ made another manic prediction to the historian Eric Goldman when the Rolling Thunder bombing campaign began. The President declared that it would drive North Vietnam to start peace talks on LBJ's terms in a year to a year and a half.[34]

The President made war the same way he campaigned: by impulse. When it was the War Against Poverty, he announced it without any sort of plan or analysis in hand. The Great Society was another slogan that had to acquire bricks and mortar without benefit of a blueprint. Similarly LBJ's 1964 decision to escalate the war in Vietnam was made without a full consideration not only of the pros and cons, but of the hows and whys.[35]

In addition to being impulsive, the manic often lacks any sense of limits. Just as he drowned the Congress and the American people in a flood of legislation without allowing them time to understand his programs or develop means of implementation, LBJ did the same thing to South Vietnam. There were soon more programs and advisors than the South Vietnamese could possibly absorb.[36]

The worst and most dangerous excess in which LBJ indulged was the amount of explosive dropped on Vietnam. In just five years, 1965-1969, U.S. planes dropped five hundred pounds of bombs for every human being in Vietnam.[37] Let us not forget that neighboring countries were also bombed.

Mania causes its victims to take risks that no normal person would consider. We have seen the manic LBJ drinking and driving at ninety miles an hour on the wrong side of the road in Texas. In an impressive example of international recklessness, LBJ insisted that Hanoi be bombed even when the Soviet head of state, Anatoly Kosygin was in the city. Humphrey remarked: "It could only excite the Russians and make their commitment to North Vietnam firmer than ever."[38] That was true. But beyond that, did the President consider how the Russians would have reacted if one of those bombs had killed Kosygin?

Like many manic depressives whose behavior varies radically with their moods, the President was a paradox. His oscillations between mania and depression lead to inconsistent and confusing behavior. At times he was terrified of igniting World War III and based his decisions on that fear. At other times he recklessly did things that could start a global atomic war. He disregarded both the Department of Defense and the Department of State when they furnished him, in July, 1965, with a study indicating that escalation risked not only bringing China and the Soviet Union into the war, but could lead to the use of atomic weapons.[39]

Manics are competitive people. Competitiveness on a personal level encouraged LBJ to wage a very big war. He saw himself surpassing Franklin Roosevelt, who had launched a domestic revolution with his New Deal and then gone on to fight a world war. But unlike LBJ, FDR did not try to do both at the same time.[40] Megalomania convinced LBJ that he could do both simultaneously: "I was determined to be a leader of war *and* a leader of peace. I refused to let my critics push me into choosing one or the other. I wanted both, I believed in both...."[41] When he was manic, he thought that for him to want something was enough to make it possible.

He also saw himself in competition with every American President who had preceded him, and he was determined not to lose that contest either. He said repeatedly: "I'm not going down in history as the first American President who lost a war."[42] He even felt competitive with Ho Chi Minh. After Senator McCarthy almost won the New Hampshire Democratic Presidential Primary in March of 1968, and the nation had shown that it was longing for peace, LBJ still saw victory in Vietnam hinging on whether he or Ho could take punishment the longest.[43]

It is the manic's practice to deliver criticism with hammer blows and to cry out from pin pricks. We have seen that LBJ had a remarkable intolerance for criticism. One of reasons he refused to call up the reserves was his desire to avoid criticism from Congress and the public. He complained that such opposition would make him a "lonely man."[44]

In addition, he could not permit the U.S. to withdraw from Vietnam because of the criticism he would receive from his fellow Americans: "I knew that if we let Communist aggression succeed in taking over South Vietnam, there would follow in this country an endless national debate... that would shatter my Presidency, kill my administration, and damage our democracy."[45] Kennedy was determined to withdraw from a hopeless war in Vietnam although he expected the act to blacken his name. Johnson refused to take that risk, even though he eventually also realized that the war could not be won. It is part of his and the nation's tragedy that his refusal to give up the war actually produced all of the outcomes that he feared. But he never recognized that. The mere thought of pulling out made him "shudder to think what all of 'em would say."[46]

LBJ, ignorant as he was of the long history of Vietnam, viewed that country in terms of Texan traditions and myths. He claimed early on that Vietnam was just like the Alamo. He clung to this fantasy even during his last days in office, referring to the spirit of the Alamo many times. What he meant by that was the willingness of the Texans to hold on unto death in the face of overwhelming odds.[47] He failed to notice that it was the Vietcong and North Vietnamese who now exhibited the spirit of the Alamo.

In April of 1964, he declared: "We are in this battle as long as South Vietnam wants our support and needs our assistance to protect its freedom." He never asked his country if it was willing to keep that open-ended promise. He never asked the people of South Vietnam what *they* wanted. His pledge was made to "South Vietnam" when its government was a police state with a revolving door of military coups, as he knew. But his ego was in the saddle, riding him hard. LBJ insisted: "When the going gets tough, the tough get going."[48] He told his wife: "...we can't turn and run."[49]

Commentator Hugh Sidey observed: "Johnson's feeling about individual men was often reduced to simple terms of courage and endurance." Sidey adds that "...there was a lot of simple respect for the old-fashioned hero left in Lyndon Johnson, and it profoundly affected his decisions about Vietnam."[50]

He was delighted when his sons-in-law both requested service in Vietnam. Patrick Nugent had 400 combat missions. Charles Robb, although wounded in action, was ready to fight again. LBJ gloated: "Goddamn, isn't that a son for you. Wounded, not even out of the hospital, and he wants to go back."[51] His sons-in-law enabled him to be a hero by proxy, but it was the war, as he saw it, that gave him the chance to be a hero in his own right.

Furthermore, in 1968, drastically misjudging the national mood, LBJ thought that showing himself as the heroic wartime President pursuing victory despite all opposition, would get him reelected.[52] LBJ also was inhibited from seriously considering withdrawal from Vietnam because, as he said to Senator Russell: "They'd impeach a President who'd run out, wouldn't they?"[53]

According to LBJ: "...everything I knew about history told me that if I got out of Vietnam and let Ho Chi Minh run through the streets of Saigon, then I'd be doing exactly what Chamberlain did in World War II."[54] He was referring to the accommodation that England's Prime Minister Neville Chamberlain had made with Hitler, hoping to achieve "peace on our time." It was a faulty analogy. The fate of the world was not at stake. Ho Chi Minh merely wanted *eventually* to unify Vietnam under a Communist government independent of both China and the Soviet Union. He was not a madman bent on world empire, as Hitler had been. And LBJ failed to calculate the damage that the fear of seeming cowardly would make him do to Vietnam.

The strength of the President's obsession with cowardice is revealed by a nightmare that he had repeatedly. He was tied to the ground while a crowd of thousands ran up to him, stoning him and yelling "Coward! Traitor! Weakling!"[55]

History was a mirror for the ego of LBJ. Hugh Sidey observed: "...he is deeply concerned that his courage might be questioned or that his resolve might be found wanting in the pages of history. ...On the other hand he anguishes over the billions of dollars that are going for bombs instead of being used to build this country— and his own legend."[56] One can see why LBJ thought he had nowhere to turn. He believed that history would condemn him if he withdrew from Vietnam. But fighting in Southeast Asia took the money he needed to win the War on Poverty at home and to build the Great Society.

The egotism of mania grew to monstrous proportions when LBJ was President. His biggest concern in 1964 was to be elected in his own right. It would have been unbearable for him to be rejected by his fellow Americans.

As long as the country was at war, he believed, the voters would keep him in the White House: "I don't seem to remember many Presidents that the American people turned their backs on in time of crisis or in time of war. No President has ever been turned upon when he was trying to protect his country against a foreign foe."[57] Here was a president implying that a war was worth fighting if it would keep him in office. LBJ's egotism was so all-enveloping that he no longer saw it's abnormal dimensions and hence made no effort to disguise it.

What motivated LBJ most strongly was the identification of his ego with the U.S. Often one could not say where he left off and America began. He would point to McNamara and say: "That's the fellow who has got to keep me in Vietnam." Then he would indicate Dean Rusk and add: "And there's the fellow who has got to get me out."[58] When he spoke of America he often used the pronouns I, me, and my. It was really his ego that he was defending in Vietnam, not Vietnamese "democracy," not even American geopolitical interests or the profits of Brown and Root.

Because LBJ's ego would not allow him to settle for less than victory, and he had prolonged the fighting to the end of his term, he looked back on his prosecution of the Vietnam War with some satisfaction: "Now my service was over, and it had ended without my having had to haul down the flag...."[59] That is all he cared about.

Appendix

AN INTRODUCTION TO MANIC DEPRESSION

★ ★ ★ ★ ★ ★

An Overview of the Illness as an Entity

Emotions Out of Whack

Manic depression is an illness that affects people's emotions, manner of thinking, beliefs, behavior, bodily functions such as sleep and appetite, and even appearance. Often the most obvious sign is that something is wrong with the person's emotions. They seem to be excessive, or inappropriate, or they drag on too long, or change too quickly.[1] People fly into rages over nothing, the news that they have cancer makes them cheerful, sadness over a quarrel goes on for months and months.

An attack of mania or depression can range in duration from a few hours to a year or more, as well as anything in between.[2] The change from one state to the opposite can be sudden or so slow as to be imperceptible.[3] This seems to be a totally unpredictable illness, but not even that generalization holds for everyone. Some people cycle from mania to depression every day, for months at a time.[4]

The behavior of a manic is so different from the same person in a depressed state that it is as if two separate personalities are involved. A woman who is quiet and staid when depressed can turn into a stranger who is talkative, energetic and sexually provocative.[5]

Each personality has its own set of opinions. On a manic day the world is a marvelous place, on a depressed day everything is going to hell in a handbasket. It becomes impossible to determine what the manic depressive really believes, or who he is. Inconsistency seems to be the only thing you can count on. (For simplicity's sake, masculine pronouns will be used here rather than the awkward "he or she," "his or her," etc.) Some manic depressives develop personalities that are predominantly manic or depressive. They will persist in manic or depressive behaviors and views of reality even when they are not experiencing manic or depressive episodes.

Triggers

Except, perhaps, for the people who have clearly defined cycles of twenty-four or forty-eight hours, it is impossible to predict when mania or depression will begin. Some physical conditions may trigger or worsen manias or depressions. Premenstrual periods can do it, as can pregnancies and childbirth. Time zone changes or other changes in one's sleep schedule may precipitate or intensify manias and depressions.[6] That is something to keep in mind when a manic depressive is choosing a profession.

Major events in one's life can also lift one into mania or drop one into depression, but what will happen is not predictable. Loss, such as the death of someone dear, a suicide, or a murder in the family, can bring on either depression or mania. A crisis, or something threatening, such as surgery, can sometimes rouse a person to a manic response.[7] Illness can lead to both mania and depression.[8] Good news can make one manic. On the other hand, getting a promotion or a better job can precipitate a depression.[9] So can failure to get that job or promotion, or losing a job.[10] In short, any major stress can bring on an attack of depression or mania. But these also can arrive on their own, out of the blue.[11] About the only generalization one can make is that most manic-depressives will have more than one attack.[12] Episodes of mania and depression are like cock-roaches: if you see one, you know that you will see more of them.

Seasonal Affective Disorder, or "SAD," is slightly more predictable. Those who have it never know what day or hour a mania or depression will arrive, but they can expect that spring and summer are the seasons when mania to some degree and in some form will be present, while the part of the year when daylight is shortest—fall and winter—will be a period heavy with depression. They also find cloudy weather more depressing than most people do. Moving to sunnier climates brings relief to some people, as does treatment with full spectrum artificial light. Like other forms of manic depression, this is an inheritable disorder.[13]

Varieties Of Manic Depression

There are two major varieties of manic depression that are recognized at present: Bipolar I Disorder and Bipolar II Disorder. The difference between them is that people with Bipolar II have the depressions, but not the full-blown manic attacks. But they do have at least one hypomanic episode, or else they would not be classified as manic-depressives at all.[14] Someone who has four or more major depressions, manias, hypomanias or mixed states (which combine manic and depressive symptoms) in a year is considered to be a rapid cycler. The significance of this is that the outlook is not good.[15]

Back to Bipolar I, the classic manic depressive. Most of these people have normal intervals between attacks, but up to a third of these manic depressives are a bit peculiar all of the time. And some become very peculiar. They can become psychotic during mania, depression, or even weeks after what was a non-psychotic episode.[16]

Another form of manic depression is Cyclothymic Disorder. The person who fits this category goes through many cycles of hypomania and hypodepression, and rarely has more than two months in a row that are symptom free. However, the depressions and manias do not develop into full-blown attacks. Cyclothymes don't end up in hospitals.[17]

Even those who do not hallucinate or have delusions can give their families a bad time when they are having severe attacks. They may beat their spouses and children, break things, wreck the house and create havoc. Manic depressive children may become truants or flunk out of school, while their manic depressive parents may have failed careers, be unable to hold a job, keep the marriage together, or stay out of jail. If that is not trouble enough, there are other mental disorders that often occur in tandem with manic depression: Anorexia Nervosa, Bulimia Nervosa, and drug and alcohol abuse. As many as 15% of the people with Bipolar I manic depression kill themselves.[18]

Mania

Mania, like depression, can range in intensity from a condition that is barely noticeable to one that is terrifying. According to DSM IV, the diagnostic criteria for hypomania are at least four consecutive days of elevated mood, plus three out of the following list of symptoms, or four days of irritability plus four of the following symptoms. The symptom list includes grandiosity, the ability to feel well with very little sleep, pressure of speech (non-stop talking), racing and disorganized thoughts, inability to pay attention to anything for long, hyperactivity, and risky behavior, financial, sexual or otherwise.

While the hypomanic keeps functioning, does not need hospitalization and does not become psychotic, this is not necessarily true for the manic.[19] Mania is more intense than hypomania, may last longer, and it has a greater impact on one's work, relationships and social activities.[20]

A Brain In Overdrive

Insomnia

Manics seem to have brains that need to keep busy and, that work much faster than normal brains. One of the first noticeable signs of the approach of mania is that one gets along quite well with much less sleep than usual.[21] Some people feel fine with three hours sleep, night after night, and can miss a night's sleep without any fatigue.[22]

Flight Of Ideas

One of the things that keep manics awake at night is the ceaseless flow of thoughts racing through their heads, which also goes on in the daytime. When they are talking, other people can see that their ideas are chaotic, constantly branching off into unrelated subjects. The manics themselves cannot follow anything that is systematic but complicated. Manics may complain that they cannot organize their thoughts, or even complete them.[23]

Distractibility

The manic who tries to concentrate on anything may be distracted not only by his unruly thoughts, but also by whatever is going on around him.[24] He can't shut anything out. It is the rare manic who can overcome this and complete what he is doing before leaping off to do something else that seems pressing at the moment, something that may also be abandoned, after being barely begun, for the next task.

High Energy And Restlessness

By now you must have a picture in your mind of someone—the manic—who is jumping around doing a lot of things, though not necessarily doing them very well. If you do, that picture is accurate for many manics. They are strangers to fatigue and seem to have more energy than they know how to use.[25]

Sometimes they pace, or sit in a chair jiggling a foot.[26] They may have moments of rest and quiet, but it doesn't take much to set them off again. They go off on walks, run errands, rearrange the furniture: they do find things to do, not only their own projects, but the affairs of others.[27] This energy is available for all kinds of projects, often artistic ones. It is the fortunate or unusually disciplined manic, however, who can complete a work before the mania (which he thinks of as inspiration) runs out.

Impulsivity

With a brain that is breaking the speed limits, the manic can not spend a long time ruminating about what to do next. He reacts quickly and follows his impulses. Indeed, he cannot resist them. Decisions that others take some time to consider, he makes in an instant—long trips, major projects, career changes—all may come from a sudden inspiration.[28] Many a manic's business has failed because it was started on impulse, or served no real purpose, or was not needed, the manic knew nothing about the business, or he lost interest in it.

Impatience And The Pursuit Of Novelty

To the manic, the rest of the world is thinking, talking and moving in slow motion. It is therefor difficult to wait for others to finish what they are saying, or to wait until they finish what they are doing, or are ready to go somewhere.[29] Manics become bored easily and have a preference for new things, new people, and new experiences.[30] This may make them iconoclasts in the arts and sciences, and innovators or revolutionaries in public affairs.

Pressure Of Speech

Manics talk too fast, too much, too loud, and too long for the people who have to listen to them.[31] Forget discretion. Manics have to say whatever they think when the flood is in full spate.[32] They have a need to communicate, whether face to face, by telephone, or by the written word. They will keep talking even when their voice is entirely gone or no one is present to hear them.[33]

Let It All Hang Out

Speech isn't the only thing a manic has trouble controlling. Everything begins to come loose. One manic confessed: "In a rational state, I realize the disadvantage of yielding extensively if at all to...impulse; in an irrational state, I show signs of losing entirely the concern."[34] Manners can go out the window, foul language often emerges, and farts may punctuate conversations without the manic feeling that he has done anything amiss.[35] In this regard, mania is like being drunk.

Euphoric Mania

The first thing to remember about euphoric mania is that it can vanish in the blink of an eye and be replaced by the other kind—irritable mania.[36]

Heaven On Earth

The second thing is that euphoric mania is the kind of state that people get drugged or drunk to achieve. Everything is beautiful, wonderful. The manic feels fine physically: pain hardly exists for him. He has a tranquil temper, appreciates everything, and enjoys everything and everyone.[37]

Manic Humor

The euphoric manic knows how to enjoy life. He finds time for games and brightens his conversation with humor, even making jokes about himself.[38] These people are very entertaining, so long as you are willing to be just an audience and don't try to steal the spotlight.

Social Butterflies

Manics love to be with people, to meet new people and make friends. They love to invite people over and to arrange outings. They are the life of the party, whether they give it or someone else does.[39] They can also be quite charming.

Appearance

Butterfly is a term that fits the euphoric manic in more ways than one. Manics tend to favor colorful, attention-getting clothing, hairstyles and, for the women, makeup. Their wardrobes are full of picturesque and exotic outfits.[40] Moreover, they have a physical glow, a spring to their step, an aura of vigor. They look younger than they do when depressed. They are at their most attractive as long as the euphoria lasts.

An Emphasis On Sex

Sex and mania often go together. Both men and women become flirtatious, dress and talk and behave provocatively.[41] They fall in love often and often with people they normally would not look at. Love affairs, pregnancies, divorces, all kinds of complications can result from a heightened libido in someone who is impulse-driven.[42]

Generosity, Altruism, And Public Affairs

Sexual affairs are not the only kind that occupy euphoric manics. Some of them get involved in politics or with politicians.[43] One manic initiated a campaign to clean up the avenues of Boston. Manics may evolve into odd-ball reformers, sponsoring a wide variety of causes.[44] Extravagant generosity often appears in manic behavior. Luxurious gifts, large tips, and treating their friends to meals at expensive restaurants, are not unusual for euphoric manics.[45] Often the giving is done whether a manic can pay for it or not. In one instance, a man donated money to prostitutes until his bank account was empty.[46]

Lability

Delightful though euphoric mania is, it resembles cotton candy, vanishing almost before you can enjoy it. Mania that begins with euphoria often deteriorates into irritability, hostility, and even on to paranoia.[47] Depression and rage can alternate rapidly with euphoria without apparent causes.[48] The smiling manic can bewilder his family with sudden bouts of crying that are just as quickly replaced by cheerfulness.[49]

Irritable Mania

While the euphoric manic is enjoying life, the irritable manic is making it hell for everyone else. Unfortunately many manics spend more time in the irritable state than in the euphoric.[50] The lack of inhibition operates here too—irritable manics make no effort to conceal their displeasure with everything and everyone.[51] They are faultfinding, intolerant, and often insulting. They argue about everything and with everyone. Many of them get into fights or become entangled in needless lawsuits.[52] It is difficult to be around them. They are complainers, critical, sarcastic, verbally abusive, and they often make scenes without real provocation.[53] They are like people without a skin. There is no pleasure in this state. Even physical discomforts are intensified.

Intolerance Of Criticism And Opposition

Nobody likes criticism or opposition, but irritable manics

explode when they encounter them. Any contradiction, any sign of disagreement with their desires or judgement can ignite fury.[54] Just questioning them can set them off if they think it implies criticism.[55] Failure to immediately satisfy their demands can enrage them.[56] Any frustration of their desires or opposition to their will is a cause for anger and sometimes violence.[57] This kind of manic is like a bellicose drunk.

Hostility, Aggressiveness, And Rage

Manics can be the most hostile patients that a psychiatrist encounters.[58] Rage is quite common, and very little is needed to set it off. Irritable manics will, over trivia, scream abuse, and threaten and attack their families and others. They will make these attacks with their bare hands, or by throwing things, or by going at their victims with knives and guns.[59] Unipolar patients, that is, those who only experience depressions, have a divorce rate of 8%. The manic depressives, by contrast have a divorce rate of 57%. No doubt their rages contribute to that. When spouses stay in the marriage, they often have to act as peacemakers with the people their spouses have offended or hurt.[60]

Intense Egotism

Me, My, And Mine

The fixation on oneself is found in both the euphoric and irritable mania, although in euphoric mania it can be somewhat mitigated by generosity and the ability to appreciate others. Both types of manics are their own favorite topic of conversation. Sometimes they even talk about themselves in the third person as though they were celebrities with whom they have the good fortune to be acquainted.[61] They look at the good points of others through the wrong end of a telescope, while magnifying their own. They have no interest in the needs or feelings of others except as means to manipulate those people.

Anything in the external world is only of interest insofar as it is useful to them or identified with them in some way. Even their philanthropy is merely another means of self-advertisement.[62] No

315

one else really matters and all they care about is what they want.[63] While some manics are not like this and genuinely care about others, these are exceptional people.

Arrogance, Boasting And Lies

Arrogance is the style of the irritable manic.[64] The euphoric is less abrasive, but no less given to boasting. For both kinds of manic, the territory between truth, exaggeration and downright falsehood has no divisions. Always demanding special recognition, the manic may behave conspicuously, to the point of embarrassing the people who are with him. He not only overestimates the things he is proud of about himself, on top of that, he inflates his accounts of his abilities, the things he has done, his wealth and position, sexual conquests, etc.[65] He also minimizes the features that he considers drawbacks.[66] Some of these manics seem to prefer lying to telling the truth.[67]

Greed And Extravagance

More than two thirds of manics spend too much money, and on things they do not need.[68] Everything becomes irresistible to them—clothing, cars, houses—and they order lots of whatever they are buying. They go on buying sprees, whether they can afford it or not.[69] Psychologist Kay Jamison, who wrote about her own experience with manic depression, said that when she was manic, "...I couldn't worry about money if I tried. So I don't. The money will come from somewhere; I am entitled; God will provide."[70] When God is a little slow, manics may simply, without a tremor of shame, help themselves to the possessions of others.

Monstrous Will

Meddling in Everything

Even when failing to meet their own obligations, many manics cannot resist trying to manage other people's affairs, or tell them how to behave, or, indeed, how to run their lives.[71] Manics believe that they always know best. Even though they undertake far more than they or anyone can accomplish, they cannot resist interfering in what others are planning or doing. Nor do they have any respect for the rights or privacy of others.[72]

Devious And Manipulative

The manic is an expert at salami slicing; taking one thin slice of privilege after another until he has everything he wants. And he can do this with such an air of innocence that anyone who tries to stop him at any point is made to feel unreasonable and arbitrary.[73] While the manic is eager to take credit for the achievements of others as well as for his own, he always attributes his failures to somebody else. And the manic usually believes sincerely that the other fellow messed up.[74] What is most painful to people who are being manipulated is the manic's ability to find their vulnerabilities and attack them precisely there. The manic knows how to raise and lower his victim's self-esteem as a means of exerting leverage, and he can generate or use the conflicts within groups for his own purposes.[75] He knows how to push everyone's "hot button."

Dominance

Not only does the manic display dominating behavior and dominating body language, in any group it is the manics who will become dominant.[76] They feel it is their place to control whatever is going on.[77] They assert their dominance with haughty behavior and by teasing and deriding those they consider their inferiors, which is almost everyone.[78]

The Will Without Limits

Manics are willing to take risks of all kinds—whether it is driving too fast, investing in unlikely enterprises, going into places of danger, or taking up sports like skydiving.[79] Some of their daring behavior comes from thinking their abilities are greater than they are, some comes from a misplaced sense of invulnerability, and some comes from simply refusing to recognize limits to their will, even those limits imposed by laws of nature. It is not that they are courageous, but simply that they have no fear.[80]

Manics who have no respect for the laws of nature also despise traditions, regulations, and the laws of man. Some of these manics are frauds, swindlers, and thieves with a sense of entitlement. No matter how nefarious their actions, they are self-righteous about what they do. Because it benefits them, it is alright.[81]

The Delusions Of Mania

Unfounded Optimism

The euphoric manic believes not only that the present is marvelous, but that the future will be even better, and will deliver everything he wants. Every project will be a roaring success, every work of art a masterpiece, every business a gold mine. The manic can imagine nothing but happiness in the future.[82]

Delusions About Oneself

The manic already thinks too well of himself. When he crosses the threshold of delusion, his self-regard may have not the slightest basis in fact. He may believe that people who hardly notice him are in love with him.[83] He may believe that he is wealthy, supremely talented, attractive, incomparably intelligent, that he can solve all problems.[84] As he moves deeper into the kingdom of delusion, he comes to believe that he is incapable of being mistaken about anything, and that he can do anything: his powers are unlimited.[85] Not only is he infallible, he is incapable of doing anything wrong and is therefore permanently guiltless.[86] One manic admits: "I have never actually thought I was God, but a prophet, yes...."[87] Manics may feel that they are getting messages directly from God, and that they have been singled out by God for some divine purpose.

Paranoia And Hallucinations

By the time a manic is paranoid, he has passed out of euphoria and into the irritable phase. Along with the belief in one's supreme importance can come the delusion that one is being persecuted, and that there are conspiracies designed for one's humiliation or destruction.[88] Some paranoid manics believe that others are trying to control them, but it is not necessarily clear to them who are doing it.[89]

Hallucinations may accompany paranoia. Sounds as well as images can appear in hallucinations, and these may be vaguely threatening or downright terrifying. Kay Jamison, when manic and paranoid, saw a vision of herself in an evening gown, pouring blood into a centrifuge which exploded, spattering blood everywhere.[90]

Depression brings a different set of delusions, which will be discussed below.

Depression

Mania in its early stages can be mistaken for normal high spirits or a cheerful personality. Depression, in its early stages can be mistaken for sadness, disappointment, discouragement, and even physical illness. However, like mania, depression is much more complicated than the emotions associated with it. The DSM IV criteria for depression require either a feeling of sadness or a loss of interest in everything and four of the following for at least two weeks: unintentional weight loss or gain, changes from one's customary amount of sleep, agitation or a physical slowing down, lack of energy, harsh self-criticism, indecisiveness and difficulty thinking, and finally, having death or suicide on one's mind.[91]

Severe depression is distinct from sadness in its duration, intensity, and its interference with day-to-day living.[92]

Signs Of Physical Illness

Sometimes one can see depression in a person's face: the muscles go slack, the complexion loses its fresh color. The posture is that of fatigue.[93] Clothing, hair, makeup and even hygiene may be neglected. Garments get no attention and may be spotted, wrinkled, or ragged.[94]

Often the depressed person feels physically ill. The digestive system becomes disordered, with nausea, vomiting, indigestion, flatulence, diarrhea or constipation as possibilities. Some people experience headaches, blurred vision, neck and back pain and other muscle cramps.[95] Others complain of chest pains and palpitations, shortness of breath, and numbness.[96] The weight loss or gain may be caused by

319

loss of appetite or by nervous eating. Hormonal changes associated with depression are probably responsible for the loss of sexual appetite so commonly reported.[97] Depressives may suffer from insomnia or constantly sleep more than is normal for them.[98] Difficulties in getting up in the morning and constant fatigue are problems for some, while others are tormented by an inability to relax. It is apparent that at least two kinds of depression exist.

Anxious Depression

Enveloped In Gloom

Most depressives inhabit a world of mild, but unrelenting dread. They are afraid of any change, of anything new. Pessimism clouds their view of the world, and they fear that disaster lurks behind every corner.[99] They worry a lot about things that are unlikely to happen.[100] Expecting the worst, everything they attempt to do, whether cooking a meal or performing a task in the office, seems too difficult. They see only problems to be overcome and never rewards to be enjoyed. The casual round of life becomes a heavy burden.[101] They feel unhappy, anxious, and despairing much of the time and are given to tears.[102] Theirs is an economics based on fear. They are afraid that they will lose their job, be unable to find work, their business will fail, the stock market will collapse. Consequently, they stop spending money even when they are financially well off.[103]

Their Own Harshest Critic

Depressives remember their failures rather than their triumphs. Work gives them little satisfaction because they focus on their mistakes. They have no confidence in their strength or abilities. Consequently, they avoid responsibility for fear of failure and try to stay within routine. They may be ambitious but caution keeps them from moving ahead.[104] They are critical of what they see as their own personal inadequacies and character flaws.[105] They may understand that they underestimate themselves, but they think that is better than doing the opposite. But they also blame themselves for their consequent lack of daring and enterprise.[106] Nothing about themselves is right: they see themselves as ugly, awkward, too fat, too thin, too tall, or too short. They think they are foolish, boorish, socially clumsy, ugly, and not wanted anywhere.[107]

Except during irritable depressions, depressives are submissive and dependent.[108] That can be the result of their low self-esteem, or of their reduced mental capacity, of which more below.[109] If they are caught in conflicts, depressives give way or run away, except when in an irritable depression.[110] They may have authority figures that they no longer respect, or have come to despise, but they cannot break free of them because they are also dependent upon them.[111]

Because they are so prone to feeling guilty, depressives are overly conscientious and will go to great extremes of effort to avoid even the possibility of criticism.[112] They are motivated by a sense of duty rather than by seeking personal gain or pleasure. They tend to work incessantly, but without the joy and spontaneity of the manic.[113] Some depressives work exceedingly long and hard not just because they are hard task masters to themselves, but because the work distracts them from the pain of depression.

A Monastic Existence

Perhaps monastic is the wrong term, because monks usually live with large numbers of other monks. Depressives limit their contacts with others. They feel that they do not know how to talk to people, or how to behave. They are anxious and uncomfortable, not only with strangers, but also with friends.[114] They find it hard to perform casual social activities, like saying hello to the mailman.[115] It is difficult for them to fill their social roles in school, at work, and at home.[116] They stop answering their telephone, and do not respond to letters or invitations.[117] They are most comfortable alone in their rooms and like to retreat to bed.[118] Needless to say, these are not public-spirited citizens: they, like monks, but for different reasons, have retired from the world. The depressive becomes humorless, has forgotten how to play or won't allow himself to, and tends to brood. He may become agoraphobic and try to stay within the shell of his room, like a hermit crab.[119]

Agitated, Irritable And Agonizing Depression

Agitated Depression

Agitation is one of the symptoms of depression that also occurs in mania. Like the manic, the depressive may find it impossible to stay still in a chair without moving some part of his body, and he may be given to endless pacing.[120] What makes this different from the manic's hyperactivity is the emotional tone. The agitated depressive seems anxious, pessimistic, has doubts about himself. In short, he has the dark view of reality that one would expect from a depressive. He may have racing thoughts, but they are racing down dark highways towards scenes of destruction and death.[121]

Irritable Depression

Agitation may combine with irritability in depression, or the irritability may arrive alone. In the beginning stages, one hardly realizes what is happening. One just notices that life has somehow become an endless series of small annoyances. The depressive becomes touchy and gets into trivial arguments. He remembers old slights and enmities.[122] The annoyances grow. Everything seems to be going wrong. Other people notice that the depressive seems to become excessively critical, complaining, demanding, and intolerant of any kind of frustration. Depressives are often discontented with everything.[123] However, unlike the manic's, the depressive's anger emerges suddenly from a mood of melancholy.[124] And the depressive's rage may be coupled with fear, not only of the world, but of himself.[125]

The most unendurable part of the kind of depression we have examined so far is the mental agony that can accompany it. Many patients have said that it is the worse thing they have ever experienced.[126] It can reach a point where even death is preferred.

Reductive Depression

Loss Of Feeling

What gets reduced is just about everything: activity, talking, thinking, even emotion. This type of depression can come as a relief from the anxious, irritable, agitated and agonizing variety. Some degree of it can actually accompany the other kinds of depression. People who are feeling sad or irritated may also notice that they have no pleasure in what they used to enjoy, that everything seems boring, tedious. They may become aware that nothing seems interesting any longer, nothing seems worth doing.[127] They may consider dropping out of school, canceling a visit or a trip, even abandoning career plans or the project they are working on.[128] They may feel that they have lost their aim in life, and that everything is pointless.[129]

As this reductive depression progresses, people lose the capacity both for worry and for hope. They can no longer respond to events and they become indifferent even to bad news. Not only does their irritability or anxiety disappear, so does their anguish. They become emotionally numb.[130] For many, their apathy is as welcome as an anesthetic relieving unendurable pain.

The Mind Going Dark

Not only does the emotional function of the brain seem to be shutting down, so does the intellectual function. Out of thirty-three depressed patients who were interviewed, thirty complained not only of a slowing of their thinking, but of a loss of clarity and loss of the ability to concentrate on anything.[131] Some depressives find it hard to follow an ordinary conversation. Their memory decreases and they become absentminded. They even forget how to execute tasks that they have done many times.[132] Reading a book and remembering who all the characters are becomes too difficult to attempt.

The depressive can't find the words he needs to express a thought when he has one, and he can't construct coherent sentences. He says less and less, both because talking has become so difficult and because his interest in communicating with people has vanished. Often, his mind seems to be empty. He feels quite stupid.[133] Psychologist Kay Jamison reported that when she went to class in this condition, "I understood very little of what was going on."[134]

One of the first things to go is the ability to make decisions. Not only does the depressive doubt his own judgement, his brain refuses to deliver a choice, whether it is an item on a restaurant menu or the making of travel plans. Consequently, the circle of a depressive's activity becomes smaller and smaller.[135]

Becoming Inert

By now, the depressive no longer is interested in doing much of anything. But even when he is motivated to act, whether it is a question of going out to buy groceries or simply a matter of getting dressed, he finds that he has no willpower left. For a while he remains capable of doing what is habitual or routine, but eventually that capacity diminishes. Consequently, reductive depression takes away both work and leisure activities. Tasks are left unfinished or not begun. Even the minimal care of one's body is neglected.[136] Gradually, the depressive slows down, moving less and less. His speech also slows down, and he may become unable to finish a sentence because he has forgotten what he wanted to say.[137]

This process of the brain turning off can continue until the depressive falls into a stupor. He may reach the extreme of inertia called catatonia. Then his body, like a figure made of damp clay, holds whatever position it chances to be in until someone else moves it.[138]

Delusions Of Depression

While depression can cause real symptoms of physical illness, it can also bring delusions about the body and mind. Depressives may believe that they have some incurable, fatal disease, other than manic depression, which is incurable but not always fatal. They may believe that they are becoming demented, which is true only for the period during which they have a severe, reductive depression. Less realistically, they may develop convictions that parts of their bodies have dried up or disappeared completely.[139]

The psychotic phase of depression can also bring delusions of loss: loss of loving relationships that in fact continue, loss of money that actually remains. The depressive may believe that he is poor when he is far from that.[140] Depressions can also generate phobias.[141]

The depressive's image of himself may become distorted far out of recognition. He may feel totally helpless, a complete failure.[142] He may think that everyone rejects him, that the world and his family in particular are better off without him.[143] He feels guilty for being sick. He may imagine that he has committed sins and done terrible wrongs when none of it is true.[144]

Paranoia And Hallucinations

Like the manic, the depressive paranoiac may develop ideas of reference—that is, false beliefs that people, even strangers, are talking about him, that newspaper articles and books make references to him. He may misunderstand overheard remarks, twisting them into negative comments about himself.[145] The paranoia of melancholy has a bitter flavor not unlike that of the paranoia of mania. One patient thought his brother was a spy.[146] Others think that burglars or terrorists are invading their homes. They believe that poison is pouring out of their faucets.[147]

Depression can also bring hallucinations, usually threatening ones, of hearing and sight.[148]

Suicide

It is not always obvious that someone is going to commit suicide. There may not be a note. Some suicides don't require a lot of planning. Suicide by automobile can be a result of impulse. If a person mentions having suicidal fantasies of driving into bridge abutments, that may be all the warning that is given.[149]

The reasons for killing oneself may result from delusions of being worthless and unwanted. Furthermore, in the darkness of depression, the world may appear too hopeless, too cruel to bear any longer.[150] And finally, As Kay Jamison said, "One would put an animal to death for far less suffering."[151]

Fortunately, death is not the only way to end the suffering of depression or mania, for that matter. Appropriate medication augmented by psychotherapy can do wonders to make the life of the manic depressive not only manageable, but eminently worth living and even productive.

It may take several attempts to find the therapist who can be most helpful and the medications that best fit one's individual brain chemistry, but persisting in the effort to tame one's illness is worth all the effort it takes.

BIBLIOGRAPHY

★ ★ ★ ★ ★ ★

The books listed below are those that are the sources of information or quotations in this book. All end notes refer to these books by number or letter, then by page number or numbers. For example. [3]48,213 refers to pages 48 and 213 in book 3. In the following list, where more than one book is the source, the endnote might read [3]48, 213, [A]67-8, the second entry being page 67 through 68 from tape A.

1. Acheson, Dean. *Sketches From Life: Of Men I Have Known.* New York: Harper and Brothers, 1961.
2. Anderson, Jack, with George Clifford. *The Anderson Papers.* New York: Random House, 1973.
3. Ashmore, Harry and William C. Baggs. *Mission to Hanoi: A Chronicle of Double-Dealing in High Places.* New York: G. P. Putnam's Sons, 1968.
4. Baker, Bobby, with Larry L. King. *Wheeling and Dealing: Confession of a Capital Hill Operator.* New York: W. W. Norton and Co., Inc., 1978.
5. Baker, Leonard. *The Johnson Eclipse.* New York: The Macmillan Co., 1966.
6. Barber, James David. *The Presidential Character: Predicting Performance in the White House.* Englewood Cliffs, NJ: Prentice Hall, Inc., 1972.
7. Barrett, David M. *Uncertain Warriors: Lyndon Johnson and His Vietnam Advisors.* Lawrence, Kansas: University Press of Kansas, 1993.

8. Belmaker, Robert H., M.D. and H.M. Van Praag, Ph.D. *Mania: An Evolving Concept*. New York: S.P. Medical and Scientific Books, 1980.

9. Berman, Edgar, M.D. *Hubert: The Triumph and Tragedy of the Humphrey I Knew*. New York: G. P. Putnam's Sons, 1979.

10. Bernstein, Irving. *Guns or Butter: The Presidency of Lyndon Johnson*. New York: Oxford University, 1996

11. Bird, Kai. *The Color of Truth: McGeorge Bundy and William Bundy: Brothers in Arms: A Biography*. New York: Simon and Schuster, 1998.

12. Bishop, Jim. *A Day in the Life of President Johnson*. New York: Random House, Inc., 1967.

13. Bornet, Vaughn Davis. *The Presidency of Lyndon B. Johnson*. Lawrence Kansas: University Press of Kansas, 1983.

14. Califano, Joseph A. Jr. *The Triumph and Tragedy of Lyndon Johnson*. New York: Simon and Schuster, 1991.

15. Caro, Robert A. *The Years of Lyndon Johnson: The Path to Power*. New York: Alfred A. Knopf, 1982.

16. Caro, Robert A. *The Years of Lyndon Johnson: Means of Ascent*. New York: Alfred A. Knopf, 1990.

17. Caro, Robert A. *The Years of Lyndon Johnson: Master of the Senate*. New York: Alfred A. Knopf, 2002.

18. Carpenter, Liz. *Ruffles and Flourishes*. New York: Doubleday and Co., Inc., 1970.

19. Cormier, Frank. *LBJ The Way He Was*. Garden City, NY: Doubleday and Co., Inc., 1977.

20. Dallek, Robert. *Lone Star Rising: Lyndon Johnson and His Times 1908-1960*. New York: Oxford University Press, 1991.

21. Dallek, Robert. *Flawed Giant: Lyndon Johnson and His Times 1961-1973*. New York: Oxford University Press, 1998.

22. Davies, James C. *Human Nature in Politics: The Dynamics of Political Behavior*. New York: John Wiley and Sons, Inc., 1963.

23. Dugger, Ronnie. *The Politician: The Life and Times of Lyndon Johnson*. New York: W. W. Norton and Co., 1982.

24. Evans, Rowland and Robert Novak. *Lyndon B. Johnson: The Exercise of Power*. New York: The New American Library, 1966.

25. Fieve, Dr. Ronald R. *Moodswing: The Third Revolution in Psychiatry*. New York: Bantam, 1979.

26. First, Michael B. M.D. *Diagnostic and Statistical Manual of Mental Disorders, Fourth Edition*. Washington, D.C.: American Psychiatric Association, 1994.

27. Fitzgerald, Frances. *Fire in the Lake: The Vietnamese and the Americans in Vietnam*. New York: Vintage Books, Random House, 1973.

28. Georgotas, Anastaseos and Robert Cancro. *Depression and Mania*. New York: Elsevier Science Publishing Co., Inc., 1988.

29. Gershon, Samuel and Baron Shopsin, eds. *Lithium: Its Role in Psychiatric Research and Treatment*. New York: Plenum Press, 1973.

30. Goldman, Eric F. *The Tragedy of Lyndon Johnson*. New York: Dell Publishing Co., Inc., 1969.

31. Graves. Alonzo. *The Eclipse of a Mind*. New York: The Medical Journal Press, 1942.

32. Harwood, Richard and Haynes Johnson. *Lyndon*. New York: Praeger Publishers, 1973.

33. Helge, Lundholm. *The Manic-depressive Psychosis*. Durham, NC: Duke University Press, 1931.

34. Heren, Louis. *No Hail, No Farewell*. New York: Harper and Row, Publishers, 1970.

35. Humphrey, Hubert. *The Education of a Public Man: My Life in Politics*. Garden City, New York: Doubleday, 1970.

36. Jamison, Kay Redfield. *An Unquiet Mind: A Memoir of Moods and Madness*. New York: Alfred A. Knopf, 1995.

37. Johnson, Lady Bird. *A White House Diary*. New York: Holt, Rinehart and Winston, 1970.

38. Johnson, Lyndon Baines. *The Vantage Point: Perspectives of the Presidency 1963-1969*. New York: Holt, Rinehart and Winston, 1971.

39. Johnson, Sam Houston and ed. Enrique Hank Lopez. *My Brother Lyndon*. New York: Cowles Book Co., Inc., 1970.

40. Kaiser, David. *American Tragedy: Kennedy, Johnson, and the Origins of the Vietnam War*. Cambridge, MA: The Belknap Press of Harvard University Press, 2000.

41. Kaplan, Bert, ed. *The Inner World of Mental Illness*. New York: Harper and Row, 1964.

42. Karnow, Stanley. *Vietnam: A History*. New York: Viking Press, 1983.

43. Kearns, Doris. *Lyndon Johnson and the American Dream*. New York: Harper and Row, 1976.

44. Kraepelin, Emil, trans. Mary Barclay, ed. George M. Robertson. *Manic-depressive Insanity and Paranoia*. Edinburgh, Scotland: E. and S. Livingston, 1921.

45. Krock, Arthur. *The Consent of the Governed and Other Deceits*. Boston: Little, Brown and Co., 1971.

46. Luree, Leonard. *Party Politics: Why We Have Poor Presidents*. New York: Stein and Day, 1980.

47. MacLear, Michael. *The Ten Thousand Day War: Vietnam 1945-1975*. New York: St. Martin's Press, 1981.

48. MacPherson, Myra. *The Power Lovers: An Intimate Look At Politicians and Their Marriages*. New York: G. P. Putnam's Sons, 1975.

49. McMaster, H. R. *Dereliction of Duty: Lyndon Johnson, Robert McNamara, the Joint Chiefs of Staff, and the Lies that Led to Vietnam*. New York: Harpercollins, 1997.

50. McNamara, Robert. *In Retrospect: The Tragedy and Lessons of Vietnam*. New York: *New York Times* Books, 1995.

51. McNamara, Robert, James G. Blight, and Robert K. Brigham with Thomas J. Biersteker and Col. Herbert Y. Schandler. *Argument Without End: In Search of Answers to the Vietnam Tragedy*. New York: Public Affairs, 1999.

52. McPherson, Harry. *A Political Education*. Boston: Little, Brown and Co., 1972.

53. Mendels, Joseph. *Concepts of Depression*. Boston: John Wiley and Sons, Inc., 1970.

54. Miller, Merle. *Lyndon: An Oral Biography*. New York: G.P. Putnam's Sons, 1980.

55. Miller, William "Fishbait," as told to Frances Patty Leighton. *Fishbait: The Memoirs of a Congressional Doorkeeper*. Englewood Cliffs, NJ: Prentice-Hall, Inc., 1977.

56. Mooney, Booth. *LBJ an Irreverent Chronicle*. New York: Thomas Y. Crowell Co., 1976.

57. Newlon, Clark. *LBJ the Man From Johnson City*. New York: Dodd, Mead and Co., 1966.

58. Newman, John M. *JFK and Vietnam: Deception, Intrigue, and the Struggle For Power*. New York: Warner Books, 1992.

59. Nicholl, Armand M. Jr., ed. *The New Harvard Guide to Psychiatry*. Cambridge, MA: Belknap Press of Harvard University, 1988.

60. Paplos, Demitri F., M.D., and Janice Paplos. *The Bipolar Child*. New York: Broadway Books, 1999.

61. Paykel, E.S., ed. *Handbook of Affective Disorders*. New York: The Guilford Press, 1982.

62. Pearson, Drew and Jack Anderson. *The Case Against Congress*. New York: Simon and Schuster, 1968.

63. Provence, Harry. *Lyndon B. Johnson: A Biography.* New York: Fleet Publishing Co., 1964.

64. Reedy, George. *Lyndon B. Johnson: A Memoir.* New York: Andrews and McMeel, Inc., 1982.

65. Reeves, Thomas C. *The Life and Times of Joe McCarthy: A Biography.* New York: Stein and Day, 1982.

66. Riedel, Richard Laugham. *Halls of the Mighty: My 47 Years at the Senate.* Washington, D.C.: Robert B. Luce, Inc. 1969.

67. Rusk, Dean. *As I Saw It.* New York: W. W. Norton and Co., 1990.

68. Russell, Jan Jarboe. *Lady Bird.* New York: Scribner, 1999.

69. Sheehan, Neil. *A Bright Shining Lie: John Paul Vann and America in Vietnam.* New York: Random House, 1988.

70. Shogan, Robert. *None of the Above: Why Presidents Fail and What Can Be Done About It.* New York: New American Library (Mentor Book), 1982.

71. Shopsin, Baron, M.D. *Manic Illness.* New York: Raven Press, 1979.

72. Sidey, Hugh. *A Very Personal Presidency: Lyndon Johnson in the White House.* New York: Atheneum, 1968.

73. Simon, Paul. *The Glass House: Politics and Morality in the Nation's Capital.* New York: Continuum, 1984.

74. Solberg, Carl. *Hubert Humphrey: A Biography.* New York: W. W. Norton and Co., 1984.

75. Steinberg, Alfred. *Sam Johnson's Boy: A Close-up of the President From Texas.* New York: The MacMillan Co., 1968.

76. Strout, Richard L. *TRB: Views and Perspectives on the Presidency.* New York: MacMillan Publishing Co., Inc., 1979.

77. Valenti, Jack. *A Very Human President.* New York: W. W. Norton and Co., Inc., 1975.

78. Weissman, Myrna M. *The Depressed Woman: A Study in Social Relationships.* Chicago, IL: The University of Chicage Press, 1974.

79. Westmoreland, General William C. *A Soldier Reports.* Garden City, NY: Doubleday and Co., Inc., 1976.

80. White, Theodore H. *The Making of the President 1964.* New York: The New American Library, Inc., Mentor Book, 1965.

81. Peter C. Whybrow, M. D. *Depression, Mania, and Other Afflictions of the Self.* New York: Harpercollins Publishers, Basic Books, 1997.

82. Wicker, Tom. *JFK and LBJ: The Influence of Personality Upon Politics.* New York: Penguin Books, 1976.

83. George Winoker, Paula J. Clayton, Theodore Reich. *Manic Depressive Illness.* St. Louis, MO: C. V. Mosby Co., 1969.

84. Wittkower, Rudolf and Margaret Wittkower. *Born Under Saturn*. New York: W. W. Norton and Co., Inc., The Norton Library, 1963.

85. Wolpert, Edward A., ed. *Manic-Depressive Illness: History of a Syndrome*. New York: International University Press Inc., 1977.

86. Zellnick, Bob. *Gore, A Political Life*. Washington D.C.: Regnery Publishing, Inc., 1999.

Tapes

A. Beschloss, Michael A., ed. *Taking Charge: The Johnson Whitehouse Tapes 1963-1964*. New York: Simon and Schuster, 1997.

B. Beschloss, Michael A., ed. *Reaching For Glory: Lyndon Johnson's Secret Whitehouse Tapes, 1964-1965*. New York: Simon and Schuster, 2001.

END NOTES

★ ★ ★ ★ ★ ★

Chapter One

1 [69] 685
2 [32] 97
3 op. cit. 449
4 [21] 341-2
5 [14] 47
6 [51] 347
7 op. C170
8 [3] 335, [51] 1
9 [21] 491
10 [4] 44-5
11 [21] 371
12 [68] 244-5
13 [46] 236

14 [10] 541
15 [21] 281
16 op. cit. 521
17 op. cit. 379
18 [23] 153-163
19 op. cit. 24
20 [46] 23
21 [29] 211, [53] 92
22 op. cit. [225]
23 [81] 18
24 [60] 302-3
25 ibid.

26 [44] 8, [83] 88-9
27 [8] 387-8, [25] 143
28 [28] 89
29 [81] 44
30 ibid.
31 [81] 46
32 [14] 17
33 [8] 388
34 [28] 89
35 op. cit. [64]
36 [33] 117-8
37 [14] 10

Chapter Two

1 [20] 13-14
2 op. cit. 26
3 [56] 3, [64] 33
4 [20] 36
5 [43] 24-5
6 [16] 80
7 [54] 5

8 [20] 48
9 op. cit. 167
10 op. cit. 48
11 op. cit. 21-4
12 [32] 23
13 op. cit. 31
14 [20] 56-7

15 op. cit. 46-47
16 op. cit. 38-8
17 [23] 90
18 [20] 38-9
19 [54] 21
20 [20] 47-8
21 [23] 633-5

²² [15] 90
²³ [20] 22
²⁴ [23] 633-5
²⁵ [54] 7,9
²⁶ [56] 191
²⁷ [68] 118
²⁸ [56] 205
²⁹ [17] 432-3
³⁰ [60] 7
³¹ op. cit. 22
³² [23] 66-7
³³ [20] 34
³⁴ [75] 15, [20] 34, 42
³⁵ ibid.
³⁶ [56] 4
³⁷ [20] 44-5
³⁸ [60] 18
³⁹ op. cit. 40-41

⁴⁰ [75] 23
⁴¹ [43] 244-5
⁴² [15] 100
⁴³ [43] 87
⁴⁴ [39] 184
⁴⁵ [54] 11
⁴⁶ [20] 44
⁴⁷ [54] 15
⁴⁸ [15] 71
⁴⁹ [54] 15
⁵⁰ [39] 11
⁵¹ [20] 43
⁵² ibid.
⁵³ op. cit. 41
⁵⁴ [23] 77
⁵⁵ [20] 33-4
⁵⁶ op. cit. 42
⁵⁷ op. cit. 43-4

⁵⁸ ibid.
⁵⁹ [44] 275-6
⁶⁰ op. cit. 13
⁶¹ [43] 34
⁶² [20] 50
⁶³ [20] 50
⁶⁴ ibid.
⁶⁵ op. cit. 41-2, 50
⁶⁶ op. cit. 52, [23] 94-5
⁶⁷ [23] 96
⁶⁸ ibid.
⁶⁹ ibid.
⁷⁰ [20] 56
⁷¹ op. cit. 44
⁷² [23] 96
⁷³ [20] 43, 56-7
⁷⁴ [20] 60
⁷⁵ [23] 104

Chapter Three

¹ [70] 47
² op. cit. 423
³ [75] 43
⁴ [23] 120-1
⁵ op. cit. 37
⁶ [20] 67
⁷ [23] 120-1
⁸ [20] 68
⁹ [15] 156
¹⁰ [23] 120-1
¹¹ [15] 164
¹² [75] 44
¹³ [20] 68-9
¹⁴ [75] 37
¹⁵ [15] 150-1
¹⁶ op. cit. 194
¹⁷ [20] 66
¹⁸ [15] 145-6,199
¹⁹ [23] 120-1

²⁰ [15] 190
²¹ [23] 120-1
²² [16] 8
²³ [20] 85
²⁴ [15] 146-7
²⁵ [23] 110
²⁶ [43] 65
²⁷ [15] 172
²⁸ [23] 115-8
²⁹ [75] 46
³⁰ [23] 115-8
³¹ [54] 34
³² [20] 78,80
³³ [15] 171
³⁴ [54] 33
³⁵ [75] 46
³⁶ [23] 155-8
³⁷ [54] 30-1
³⁸ [15] 207

³⁹ [13] 38
⁴⁰ [15] 213
⁴¹ [43] 70
⁴² [15] 226, 235
⁴³ op. cit. 226
⁴⁴ [23] 171
⁴⁵ [75] 67-8
⁴⁶ [23] 172
⁴⁷ op. cit. 166
⁴⁸ op. cit. 175
⁴⁹ [23] 177
⁵⁰ op. cit. 172
⁵¹ [20] 97
⁵² [16] 8, [15] 161
⁵³ [23] 175
⁵⁴ [54] 52
⁵⁵ [23] 175
⁵⁶ [68] 109
⁵⁷ [43] 82

58 [68] 115

59 op. cit. 141-2

60 op. cit. 166

61 [15] 231,271

62 [15] 229

63 [23] 170-1

64 [20] 102-4

65 [15] 278-9

66 [68] 8

67 [16] 181-3

68 [15] 228

69 op. cit. 334

70 [43] 84

71 [49] 47

72 [15] 226

73 [43] 85

74 [20] 141

75 [15] 359

76 [20] 142

77 [20] 139

78 [17] 732-4

79 [75] 99

80 [20] 101-2

81 [15] 351

82 ibid.

83 [23] 205

84 [56] 75-6

85 [20] 101

86 ibid.

87 [15] 240

88 [16] 118

89 op. cit.115-6

90 [20] 65

91 [15] 352

92 [75] 126-7

93 [16] 57

94 [54] 354

95 [75] 98

96 [16] 56

97 [54] 352

98 [68] 117

99 op. cit. 112

100 [20] 120

101 [17] 229

102 op. cit. 119-20

103 [23] 436

104 [75] 127

105 [17] 230

106 [68] 119

Chapter Four

1 [15] 425

2 [63] 54

3 [15] 425-6

4 [39] 178

5 [68] 130

6 [16] 180

7 [15] 457

8 [20] 355

9 [75] 118-9

10 [16] 194

11 [15] 454

12 op. cit. 457

13 op. cit. 668

14 [23] 215

15 [54] 74

16 [20] 163-4

17 [15] 761

18 [75] 129

19 [15] 392-3

20 op. cit. 333-4, 758

21 [57] 71

22 [23] 220

23 [75] 124

24 [15] 477

25 op. cit. 483

26 [23] 254

27 [68] 196, 212-3

28 [23] 308

29 [15] 551

30 op. cit. 657-8, 626-30

31 [54] 76

32 [16] 81-2, [75] 255

33 [75] 280

34 op. cit. 282

35 [43] 98

36 [4] 82

37 [75] 220-1

38 [23] 271

39 [23] 273

40 [75] 200

41 [16] 273

42 ibid.

43 [15] 458

44 [80] 71

45 [15] 553

46 [15] 533

47 [54] 76

48 [20] 163

49 [15] 544

50 [37] 376

51 [75] 123

52 op. cit. 228, 210

53 [54] 213

54 [70] 8

55 [20] 101-2

56 [54] 213

57 [39] 223

58 [16] 107-9
59 op. cit. 113, 133.

60 [75] 198
61 [20] 172-4

62 op. cit. 170

Chapter Five

1 [54] 84
2 [75] 170
3 [15] 695
4 [20] 213
5 ibid.
6 [68] 133
7 [15] 731
8 [23] 234
9 [15] 740
10 [43] 93-4
11 [68] 134
12 [43] 94
13 [16] 30, 45-6
14 [67] 93
15 [57] 90
16 op. cit. 50
17 op. cit. 48
18 [23] 251-2
19 [16] 511-3
20 [68] 141

21 [15] 750-2
22 [75] 209, [20] 141
23 [16] 273
24 [75] 214-5
25 [63] 73
26 [16] xxviii
27 op. cit. 139-40
28 [24] 22
29 [75] 234
30 [16] 125
31 [75] 237
32 [23] 3307
33 [43] 100
34 [75] 239
35 [54] 119
36 [75] 244
37 [43] 101
38 [16] 205-6
39 [72] 511-2
40 [16] 236-7

41 [75] 256
42 [16] 242
43 op. cit. 239
44 op. cit. 268
45 op. cit. 239-40
46 [20] 322
47 [16] 240
48 op. cit. 223-9
49 op. cit. 228-233
50 op. cit. 242-3
51 op. cit. 285-6
52 [75] 243
53 [16] 287
54 [54] 122-3
55 [16] 314-7
56 [23] 329
57 [16] 395-7
58 op. cit. 353-6
59 op. cit. 357-8
60 [54] 135

Chapter Six

1 [63] 159
2 [18] 33-5
3 [43] 121
4 [75] 276-7
5 [21] 352-3
6 [4] 40-1
7 op. cit. 174
8 [14] 55
9 [9] 55
10 [35] 245-6
11 [4] 66
12 [54] 175
13 [24] 94

14 [75] 283
15 [68] 172
16 [19] 135
17 [20] 392-3
18 [75] 723
19 [6] 88-90
20 [23] 371
21 [75] 380
22 [43] 117
23 op. cit. 381-2
24 [65] 584-5
25 [82] 154
26 [63] 94-5

27 [20] 472-3
28 [20] 472-3
29 op. cit. 87
30 [54] 149
31 [20] 476
32 [54] 147
33 [4] 42
34 op. cit. 64
35 [43] 114-6
36 op. cit. 116
37 op. cit. 381
38 [75] 111
39 [5] 50

40 [82] 214
41 [43] 131
42 [75] 412
43 [75] 719
44 [4] 45
45 [75] 406
46 [4] 72

47 [64] x
48 [20] 354
49 [24] 90-1, [75]414
50 [68] 178-9
51 [24] 72
52 ibid.

53 [75] 112
54 [23] 44-5
55 [24] 297
56 [75] 444
57 [20] 548
58 op. cit. 547

Chapter Seven

1 [72] 44, [63] 94-5
2 [54] 179-80
3 [56] 58-9
4 [75] 404
5 [24] 93-4
6 [20] 487
7 [4] 151
8 [56] 62
9 [43] 125
10 op. cit. 176-8
11 [17] 635
12 [68] 179
13 [20] 493
14 [54] 185
15 [56] 25
16 [43] 130
17 [19] 49
18 [39] 98
19 [15] 455
20 [14] 26
21 [32] 157
22 [54] 536
23 [64] x
24 [75] 277
25 [12] 81
26 [4] 41
27 [16] 133-4
28 [72] 252
29 [43] 131-2
30 [68] 170

31 [56] 74
32 [54] 213-4
33 [56] 85
34 [5] 242
35 [39] 67-7
36 [64] 48
37 [56] 27
38 [54] 352
39 [30] 424
40 ibid.
41 [20] 189
42 [64] 52, 32, 35
43 op. cit. 35-7
44 [68] 170-1
45 op. cit. 165-6
46 [4] 78
47 [64] 52
48 [68] 168-9
49 [19] 158-9
50 [15] 485
51 [68] 172-3
52 [20] 407
53 op. cit. 505
54 op. cit. 540
55 [54] 302
56 [16] xxix, 106
57 [75] 334
58 [4] 82
59 [43] 99
60 [75] 204-5

61 [4] 82
62 [75] 334, 650
63 op. cit. 240-1
64 [23] 384
65 [45] 190-1
66 [4] 76
67 [64] 34, 53
68 [17] 617
69 [68] 177
70 [13] 4
71 [80] 75-6
72 [64] 52
73 [20] 540
74 [4] 42-3
75 [17] 805
76 [54] 197
77 [17] 808
78 ibid.
79 op. cit.812
80 op. cit.816
81 [54] 197
82 [35] 268
83 [20] 532-3
84 [17] 1040
85 [64] 127-8
86 [20] 344, 546
87 [64] 127-8
88 op. Cit. 54
89 [20] 561-2
90 op. cit. 564-5

91 [4] 119
92 [20] 565
93 [75] 508

94 [20] 562
95 [75] 511
96 ibid.

97 ibid.
98 [4] 121

Chapter Eight

1 [75] 533
2 [5] 6
3 [75] 534
4 ibid.
5 [24] 297
6 [4] 44-5
7 [75] 509
8 [72] 115
9 [64] 72, [75] 541
10 [24] 295-6
11 [75] 553-4
12 op. cit. 509
13 ibid.
14 [21] 4
15 [75] 509
16 [4] 44-5
17 [54] 273
18 [4] 132
19 op. cit. 133-4
20 [17] 1039

21 [43] 164
22 [5] 27-8
23 [4] 135
24 op. cit. 34
25 [10] 8-9
26 [68] 205
27 [75] 574
28 [21] 87
29 [75] 552
30 [21] 12
31 [43] 165
32 [56] 143, 147
33 [64] 121
34 op. cit. 127
35 [10] 10
36 [32] 57
37 [75] 565
38 [64] 57
39 [75] 566
40 [19] 11

41 ibid., [56] 11-12, [54] 441
42 [30] 458
43 [42] 214
44 [72] 164
45 [21] 13
46 [32] 51
47 [40] 288-9
48 [54] xviii
49 [75] 567
50 [54] 284
51 [54] 542-3
52 [19] 206
53 op. cit. 135
54 op. cit. 211-2
55 op. cit. 570
56 op. cit. 117
57 [64] 124-5
58 [64] 124-5
59 op. cit. 4

Chapter Nine

1 [38] 42
2 [10] 19-20
3 [43] 170
4 [21] 55
5 [10] 19-20
6 [54] 342
7 [34] 13
8 [14] 340
9 [67] 403
10 op. cit. 335
11 ibid.

12 op. cit. 292-3
13 [10] 34
14 [30] 412
15 [77] 157
16 [15] 455
17 [39] 129
18 [54] xviii
19 [30] 140
20 [80] 442
21 [15] 354-5
22 [13] 17

23 [54] 471
24 [43] 78
25 [18] 44-5
26 [54] 535
27 [64] x
28 [54] 538
29 ibid.
30 [19] 217
31 [14] 150
32 [68] 615
33 [64] x-xiv

34 op. cit. 9
35 [19] 138
36 op. cit. 142
37 [67] 237
38 [75] 282, 492
39 [64] 21
40 [43] 8-9
41 ibid.
42 [19] 139-40
43 op. cit. 144
44 [72] 48
45 [80] 293
46 [72] 117
47 [56] 13
48 [4] 134
49 [75] 491
50 [54] 536
51 [40] 287
52 [43]7, [72] 97-8
53 [75] 491

54 [A] 476
55 [68] 94
56 [10] 540
57 [15] 485
58 [45] 186
59 [77] 301-2
60 [21] 96
61 [43] 244
62 [52] 44
63 [14] 96
64 [21] 40
65 op. cit. 407-8
66 [67] 338
67 [14] 9
68 [49] 522-3
69 op. cit. 88-9
70 [40] 248
71 [50] 29,34
72 [69] 375
73 [A] 88

74 [3] 261-2
75 [75] 595
76 [56] 153-4
77 [5] 242
78 [75] 595
79 [54] 296
80 [56] 153-4
81 [54] 29
82 [64] 124-5
83 [43] 178
84 [19] 49
85 [30] 116
86 [12] 129, [30] 116
87 [18] 33
88 op. cit. 32
89 [14] 22-3
90 [34] 36-7
91 op. cit. 18-9
92 [80] 72
93 [32] 31

Chapter Ten

1 [64] 139
2 [19] 54
3 [12] 57
4 [7] 95
5 [75] 280
6 [43] 102
7 [14] 25
8 [54] 535
9 op. cit. 535-6
10 [19] 49
11 [14] 26
12 [21] 97-8
13 [20] 357
14 [35] 306
15 [72] 48
16 [24] 407-9

17 [43] 6
18 [64] xiii-xiv
19 [56] 88-9
20 [54] 534
21 [7] 186
22 [80] 74
23 op. cit. 78
24 [56] 172
25 [19] 158-9
26 [9] 44
27 [68] 272
28 [64] 32
29 [20] 189
30 [45] 185
31 [21] 187
32 [54] 541

33 [56] 231
34 [14] 58-9
35 [13] 38
36 [64] 4
37 [21] 186, [54] 542-3
38 [64] 157
39 [54] 540
40 [14] 21-2, 9
41 [21] 14
42 [19] 39
43 [56] 186
44 [54] 539-40
45 [68] 172-3
46 [19] 132
47 [54] 539-40
48 [19] 135

49 [24] 407-9

50 [75] 673

51 [72] 156

52 [24] 410

53 [21] 173

54 [20] 476

55 [19] 4,5

56 op. cit. 52

57 [75] 652

58 [32] 62-3

59 [64] 61

60 [19] 199

61 [75] 771

62 [32] 75

Chapter Eleven

1 op. cit. 105-6

2 op. cit. 97

3 [A] 214

4 [40] 421

5 [75] 762

6 [27] 352

7 [75] 730-1

8 [21] 91

9 [19] 86-7

10 [49] 70

11 [32] 51-2

12 op. cit. 68-9

13 [49] 96-7

14 [50] 148

15 [54] 376-7

16 [A] 370

17 op. cit. 372

18 [30] 114-5

19 [19] 83

20 [10] 132

21 [21] 141

22 op. cit. 105

23 op. cit. 146

24 [13] 105-6

25 [77] 153

26 op. cit. 74

27 [32] 68

28 [43] 203

29 [10] 135

30 [32] 73-5

31 [51] 404

32 [75] 763

33 [42] 372

34 op. cit. 757

35 op. cit. 409

36 [11] 289

37 [80] 337-40

38 [A] 529

39 op. cit. 531

40 [19] 98

41 [80] 337

42 [10] 13

43 [80] 344-6

44 [35] 305

45 [74] 265-6

46 [3] 255

47 [80] 442-3, [43] 207

48 [24] 477

49 [21] 172

50 [24] 475, [56] 159-60

51 ibid., [32] 16

52 [80] 421

53 [72] 115-6

54 [39] 179

55 [19] 120

56 [19] 45

57 [56] 10

58 [20] 6

59 [80] 420

60 [72] 122

61 [75] 690

62 op. cit. 769

63 [19] 129

64 [30] 300

65 [13] 290

66 [16] 139-40

67 [13] 290

68 [54] 116

69 [20] 46

70 [64] 53

71 [40] 353

72 [43] 209

73 op. cit. 375-6

74 [47] 82

75 op. cit. 74

Chapter Twelve

1 [72] 154

2 [24] 4

3 [32] 104

4 [72] 254

5 [56] 70

6 [72] 252

7 [30] 328

8 [56] 182

9 [75] 626

10 op. cit. 574, 820-1

11 [19] 143, [34] 19

12 [4] 270

13 [75] 572

14 [39] 2

15 [75] 576

16 [54] 375-6
17 [64] 145
18 [43] 398
19 [21] 64-5
20 ibid.
21 [10] 139
22 [21] 160
23 [43] 227
24 [75] 711
25 op. cit. 5
26 ibid.
27 [20] 245
28 op. cit. 715
29 [10] 380
30 [75] 596-7
31 [77] 11
32 [21] 185-6
33 [18] 175
34 [30] 24
35 [43] 240
36 [14] 143
37 [72] 248
38 [54] 69
39 [38] 566
40 [43] 90-1
41 [13] 46

42 op. cit. 103
43 [43] 213
44 [7] 18
45 [12] 220
46 [43] 11,22-3
47 [72] 101-2
48 [10] 457
49 [67] 404
50 [13] 164
51 [7] 158-9
52 [21] 232
53 op. cit. 105
54 [64] 46
55 [43] 287-94
56 ibid.
57 [75] 722-3
58 [13] 221
59 [21] 592
60 [38] 549
61 [23] 84
62 [75] 247
63 [23] 310
64 [52] 137
65 [19] 164-5
66 [64] 158
67 [43] 191

68 [7] 185
69 [13] 134
70 [14] 55
71 [10] 62-3
72 [75] 707-8
73 [34] 31
74 [13] 229-30
75 op. cit. 98
76 [17] 1009
77 op. cit. 35
78 [21] 228
79 [35] 286-7
80 [74] 266-7
81 [32] 117
82 [21] x
83 [14] 338
84 [80] 54
85 [38] 566
86 [43] 194
87 ibid
88 [75] 789
89 [13] 109
90 [43] 141
91 [54] 339
92 [45] 71-2

Chapter Thirteen

1 [21] 283-4
2 [72] viii, [24]116
3 [80] 73
4 [43] 248
5 [72] 100
6 [64] 140, 142
7 [19] 133
8 op. cit. 134
9 [30] 489
10 [19] 356-7

11 [49] 88-9
12 [75] 718
13 op. cit. 91
14 op. cit. 282-3
15 [49] 240
16 [32] 129
17 [43] 319-21
18 [43] 313
19 [B] 368-9
20 op. cit. 370

21 op. cit. 408
22 [46] 236
23 [49] 50
24 ibid.
25 ibid.
26 [32] 125
27 [43] 312
28 [11] 322
29 [9] 158
30 [64] 63-4

31 [43] 314-7
32 op. cit. 200-1
33 op. cit. 253
34 [21] 288
35 [43] 284
36 [56] 162-3
37 [64] 135
38 [14] 173

39 [75] 717
40 [13] 149
41 [40] 422
42 [43] 314-7
43 [72] 163
44 [56] 168
45 [64] 64

46 [30] 100
47 [64] 76
48 op. cit. 66
49 op. cit. 64
50 [72] 195-6
51 op. cit. 185-6
52 [21] 288

Chapter Fourteen

1 [13] 242
2 [43] 106
3 [34] 69
4 [B] 170
5 [10] 345
6 [21] 247-8
7 [B] 1194
8 [21] 252-3
9 [50] 173
10 [21] 255
11 op. cit. 282
12 [14] 64-5
13 [35] 322
14 [74] 278-9
15 op. cit. 303
16 [9] 92
17 [40] 407
18 [3] 176
19 [7] 18
20 [3] 287
21 [B] 212
22 [21] 257-8
23 [49] 324-5

24 [B] 213
25 [7] 24
26 [B] 227
27 [21] 259
28 [40] 423-4
29 [43] 217
30 [75] 706
31 [32] 96
32 [54] 427
33 op. cit. 428
34 [72] 23
35 [49] 282-3
36 [72] 178
37 [16] xxiv-v
38 [30] 468
39 [75] 741-2
40 [16] xxiv-v
41 [19] 188
42 [30] 468
43 [49] 194-5
44 op. cit. 347
45 [38] 153

46 [49] 312-3
47 op. cit. 330
48 [40] 470
49 [43] 305
50 [72] 191
51 [43] 305
52 [30] 397-8
53 [14] 98
54 [30] 399
55 op. cit. 106
56 [19] 50
57 [75] 774
58 [68] 135
59 [17] 645
60 [17] 5589
61 [21] 87
62 [3] 307-8
63 [13] 82-3, 85
64 [47] 187
65 [50] 207
66 [51] 316-7
67 [11] 345

Chapter Fifteen

1 [42] 485
2 [75] 787
3 [21] 345
4 [51] 357-9

5 [45] 283
6 [35] 329-30
7 [74] 285
8 [19] 111-2, [77] 172

9 [14] 92
10 op. cit. 121
11 [75] 787-8
12 [21] 359

13 op. cit. 361
14 [10] 407-8
15 [32] 127-8
16 [10] 346
17 [74] 296
18 [30] 591
19 [21] 368
20 [3] 187
21 [19] 198
22 [16] 241
23 [75] 714
24 op. cit. 70-1
25 [43] 314-7
26 [56] 173
27 [75] 653
28 [19] 4
29 [72] 251-2

30 [32] 130
31 [72] 269
32 [23] 160, 161, 429
33 [3] 78-9
34 [10] 412
35 [77] 155
36 [21] 485-6
37 [3] 275
38 op. cit. 276
39 [11] 329
40 [32] 129
41 [30] 592
42 [21] 366-7
43 [32] 129
44 [72] 115-6
45 [14] 150
46 [54] 455-6

47 [14] 173-4
48 op. cit. 151
49 op. cit 669
50 [43] 15, [56] 221, [72] 23
51 [56] 166
52 [23] 120-1
53 [64] 38
54 [72] 159-60
55 [56] 153-4
56 [16] 387-8
57 [72] 195-6
58 [16] 387-8
59 [10] 410-1
60 [50] 248-9
61 [51] 241-2
62 [21] 346-7

Chapter Sixteen

1 [34] 172
2 [13] 241
3 [38] 426
4 [10] 412-3
5 [21] 346-7
6 [32] 129
7 [43] 313
8 [50] 250-1
9 op. cit. 259-60
10 op. cit. 447-8
11 [75] 813
12 [19] 242-3

13 [7] 2-3
14 op. cit. 105]
15 [7] 98-9
16 [21] 474-5
17 op.cit. 297-8
18 [54] 488
19 [10] 399
20 op. cit. 488-90
21 [74] 278
22 op. cit. 302-3
23 [76] 310
24 [21] 523-7

25 [79] 233
26 op. cit. 495
27 [20] 319-21
28 [74] 346
29 [11] 348
30 op. cit. 348-9
31 [82] 271
32 [3] 350
33 [7] 105, [21] 523-7
34 [19] 54-5, [77] 281
35 [54] 494
36 [27] 456

Chapter Sixteen

1 [13] 38
2 [21] 38-9
3 op. cit. 497
4 [39] 227

5 [72] 290
6 [10] 473
7 [13] 209

8 [21] 503-4, [27] 519-20
9 [27] 530
10 [34] 201

11 [38] 398	32 [38] 410	53 [34] 217
12 [21] 528-9	33 [34] 225	54 [74] 354
13 op. cit. 523-7	34 [43] 349	55 [13] 313
14 [32] 131-2	35 [69] 277	56 [9] 180-1
15 op. cit. 131-3	36 [14] 279	57 [74] 348
16 [10] 372	37 op.cit. 168-70	58 [9] 210-1
17 [43] 335-43	38 [32] 137	59 op. cit. 217
18 [13] 241	39 [43] 349	60 [74] 347
19 [38] 409	40 [3] 194	61 [34] 196
20 [34] 139	41 [21] 530-1	62 [35] 8
21 op. cit. 406-7	42 [10] 372	63 op. cit. 347-8
22 [7] 113-4	43 [32] 137	64 [74] 373-4
23 [32] 260, 262	44 [43] 349	65 [13] 316
24 [21] 528-9	45 [34] 216	66 [21] 579-80
25 [43] 335	46 [11] 370	67 op. cit.) 580
26 [21] 573-4	47 [19] 254-5	68 op. cit.) 588-9
27 [9] 157	48 [21] 530-1, 527-9	69 op. cit.) 586-7
28 [72] 277	49 [43] 349	70 op. cit. 558
29 [56] 187-8	50 ibid.	71 [32] 138-9
30 [19] 262-3	51 [34] 217	72 [34] 228-9
31 op.cit. 113-5, [3] 128	52 [21] 573-4	73 [38] 533

Chapter Eighteen

1 [21] 605	10 op. cit. 306-7	18 [43] 357
2 op. cit. 604	11 [43] 358-9	19 [56] 207-8
3 [54] 548	12 [54] 545	20 [43] 361
4 [43] 88-9	13 op. cit. 358-90	21 [4] 270
5 op. cit. 544	14 [32] 150	22 [32] 160-3
6 [21] 605	15 [19] 140-1	23 [13] 295-6, [21] 619-20
7 op. cit. 606	16 [4] 270	24 [54] 562
8 [64] 153	17 [21] 606	25 [60] 79
9 [68] 307		

Postscript: Why Vietnam

1 [51] 388

Postscript: Was This War Necessary?

1 [43] 280	23 [51] 331	45 [21] 360
2 [51] 394	24 [40] 491	46 [3] 333-4
3 [3] 218-9	25 [7] 161, 164, 165	47 [27] 451
4 op. cit. 233, 235	26 [40] 555-6	48 op. cit. 460
5 op.cit. 238	27 [47] 14	49 ibid.
6 [23] 146	28 [3] 221	50 [72] 224
7 [75] 775	29 op. cit. 231	51 [3] 111
8 [3] 266-7	30 [47] 53	52 [27] 161-2
9 ibid.	31 [27] 117-9	53 op. cit. 498
10 [51] 92	32 [51] 203	54 op. cit. 499
11 [79] 105	33 [3] 240-1	55 [49] 275
12 [51] 185	34 [27] 169	56 [27] 490
13 [42] 334	35 op. cit. 181	57 op. cit. 497
14 [27] 347	36 ibid.	58 [69] 554
15 [51] 404	37 [3] 240	59 [40] 5
16 op. cit. 210	38 [40] 259	60 op. cit. 257-8
17 [3] 251	39 [3] 307	61 [75] 782-3
18 [23] 147	40 op. cit. 260	62 [38] 250
19 [75] 775	41 [47] 82	63 [30] 488
20 [23] 147	42 [79] 99	64 [35] 340
21 [13] 334	43 [27] 365	65 [38] 439
22 [40] 305	44 op. cit. 378	66 [43] 296, 283

Postscript: A War That Could Have Been Avoided

1 [47] 19	14 [57a] 322-3	27 [67] 446-7
2 [69] 45	15 [69]. 260	28 [49] 165-7
3 [7] 13-4, [67] 431	16 [57a] 315-6	29 [79] 114
4 [45] 13	17 op.cit. 443	30 [41] 389
5 [51] 394-5	18 op. cit. 446	31 [21] 255
6 [11] 331-2	19 op. cit. 225, 227	32 [7] 23-4
7 op. cit. 3-4	20 [47] 59	33 [49] 258-9
8 op. cit. 133-4	21 [49] 164	34 [11] 332, [49] 287-8
9 op. cit. 121	22 [13] 73-4	35 ibid.
10 op. cit. 212	23 op. cit. 68-9	36 [7] 23-4
11 [27] 164	24 op. cit. 115	37 op. cit. 29
12 [69] 51	25 op.cit. 164	38 [79] 214
13 [11] 259-60	26 op. cit. 165-7	39 [49] 287

40 [50] 262-3
41 [51] 316-7
42 [7] 126
43 [49] 258-9
44 [3] 67
45 [13] 278
46 [40] 395-6
47 op. cit. 1
48 [50] 56
49 [75] 761

50 [13] 69
51 [30] 479-80
52 [51] 113
53 op. cit. 202
54 [50] 154
55 [49] 165-6
56 [3] 286
57 [40] 382-3
58 op. cit. 394

59 op. cit. 406
60 [3] 286
61 [3] 78-9, 299
62 op. cit. 7-9
63 [50] 261
64 [11] 357
65 [51] 406
66 op. cit. 269-70
67 [38] 395-6

Postscript: War and Madness

1 [14] 10
2 [21] 90
3 [30] 474
4 [38] 65
5 [30] 478
6 [49] 85
7 [43] 319
8 [7] 164
9 ibid.
10 [7] 149-152
11 [67] 473
12 op. cit. 418
13 [10] 407-8
14 [68] 281

15 [63] 71
16 [3] 175
17 op. cit. 63
18 [43] 330-1
19 op. cit. 264-5
20 [79] 117
21 op. cit. 119
22 [49] 273
23 [68] 280
24 [74] 272-9
25 ibid.
26 [7] 78
27 [69] 684
28 [21] 478

29 [69] 692-3
30 [11] 366-7
31 [41] 449
32 op. cit. 450
33 [10] 327, 341
34 [10] 478
35 [69] 722
36 [49] 243
37 [13] 68-9
38 [7] 35
39 op. cit. 36, 37
40 [21] 288
41 op. cit. 65
42 [30] 451

Postscript: Delusion's Web

1 [47] 59
2 op. cit. 31
3 [43] 330
4 [75] 776
5 [41] 352-3
6 [47] 23
7 op. cit. 6
8 op. cit. 14-6
9 op. cit. 11-2
10 op. cit. 17
11 op. cit. 40

12 [50] 48
13 [51] 403
14 [3] 257
15 [51] 407
16 op. cit. 114
17 [42] 556
18 [34] 142-3
19 [50] 212
20 [75] 753-4, 760
21 [23] 41
22 [20] 178

23 [57a] 444
24 op. cit. 442
25 [51] 395
26 [13] 264
27 [75] 796
28 [41] 482-3
29 [43] 253
30 op. cit. 314-7
31 op. cit. 322-3
32 [30] 477-8
33 [13] 279

34 [21] 257	43 [34] 195-6	52 [34] 195-6
35 [40] 380	44 [49] 316	53 [40] 320
36 [79] 132	45 [43] 252-3	54 [43] 252-3
37 [10] 352	46 [49] 297	55 [23] 150-1
38 [35] 320	47 [34] 181	56 [72] 199
39 [40] 471-2	48 [13] 77	57 [75] 829
40 [43] 285	49 [37] 158	58 [3] 177
41 op. cit. 283	50 [72] 211	59 [38] 566-7
42 [72] 211	51 [23] 32	

Appendix: An Introduction to Manic Depression

1 [53] 19	28 op. cit.56-7	54 [44] 23-4
2 op. cit. 22	29 [44] 26-7	55 [53] 19
3 [44] 150	30 op. cit. 26	56 [84] 259
4 [53] 19	31 [36] 37	57 [44] 56-7, [85] 257
5 [83] 176-7	32 [83] 68-9	58 [61] 15
6 [44] 68 [24a] 353	33 ibid.	59 [44] 56-7, 64. [83] 65-6
7 [81] 60, [83] 57-8	34 [31] 490-1	60 [8] 302
8 [28] 59	35 [44] 126, 58-9,	61 [44] 60-1
9 [81] 32	[78] 156	62 [33] 30-1
10 ibid.	36 [30] 135	63 [71] 59
11 [29] 224	37 [44] 56	64 [44] 22-3
12 [81] 249	38 op. cit. 6-7, 120	65 op. cit. 55-6,58
13 [28] 104	39 [71] 60	66 [28] 156
14 [26] 350-1,359	40 [44] 126, [71]63	67 [83] 116-7
15 op. cit. 353	41 [71] 59-60	68 op. cit. 70
16 op. cit. 353	42 [44] 59-60	69 [44] 26-7, [59] 314
17 op. cit. 363	43 op. cit. 57	70 [36] 74
18 op. cit. 352	44 [33] 30-1	71 [44] 178-9, 26-7
19 op. cit. 338	45 [44] 27	72 op. cit. 126-7
20 op. cit. 328	46 [41] 52-3	73 [8] 355
21 [83] 72-4	47 [8] 201	74 [61] 14-5
22 [41] 154	48 op. cit. 9, [83] 65-6	75 [8] 354, [29] 224
23 [44] 14	49 [44] 24	76 op. cit. 9, [44] 60
24 [83] 68	50 [61] 14	77 [28] 57
25 [41] 154	51 [83] 63	78 [44] 126
26 [83] 65-6	52 [44] 56-9	79 [81] 102, [28] 156
27 [44] 26-7,57	53 [71] 59	80 [44] 13, 57

81 op. cit. 128-9, 196
82 [28] 521-2
83 [44] 120
84 [53] 19
85 [85] 258-9
86 [71] 59
87 [81] 455-6
88 [28] 156
89 [81] 45-6
90 [36] 79
91 [26] 327
92 [71] 440
93 [44] 36
94 op. cit. 87-9
95 op. cit. 104, [59] 312
96 [83] 89-90
97 [85] 511
98 [44] 46
99 [28] 71
100 [83] 46
101 [44] 119-121
102 [53] 6
103 [44] 121-2
104 op. cit. 118-21

105 [36] 111
106 [44] 435
107 op. cit. 122-4
108 [28] 165-9
109 [31] 533
110 [28] 532
111 [44] 434-4
112 op. cit. 121
113 op. cit. 434-5
114 [44] 78
115 [29] 217
116 [59] 310-1
117 [36] 44-5
118 [44] 121-2
119 [28] 91-2
120 op. cit. 6
121 [36] 45
122 [33] 31-2
123 [85] 52-67
124 [83] 87
125 [36] 218
126 [83] 84-7
127 [85] 52, [44] 75-6
128 [36] 44-5

129 [44] 24
130 [85] 52
131 [83] 87-8
132 [31] 532-3
133 [44] 75
134 [36] 44-5
135 [44] 36, 121-2
136 op. cit. 36, 38
137 [83] 89, 90
138 [59] 310-1
139 [44] 19
140 [28] 71
141 [44] 76
142 op. cit. 34
143 [44] 75-6
144 [44] 37, 119-121
145 [44] 84-6
146 [41] 152
147 [44] 20
148 op. cit. 80-2
149 [44] 87-9
150 [83] 89-90
151 [36] 115

INDEX

Acheson, Dean, 131, 146, 147, 284, 288
Ackley, Gardner, 266
Ackley, Gordon, 169-170
Administration voting rights bill, 179
A.F.L., 76
Africa, 198
Agency for International Development, 176
Aiken, George, 90, 223
Air Force One, 147, 232
Alamo, 215, 216, 267, 296, 302
Alsop, Joseph, 210
Alsop, Stewart, 92, 148
Apple, R.W., 223
Arnett, Peter, 192
Arrogance of Power, The, 214
"Asian Bay of Pigs", the, 152
Asian Development Bank, 176
Atomic Energy Commission, 223
Australia, 213, 255, 292
   Port Moresby, 68

Baker, Bobby, 12, 15, 80-81, 85, 88-89,
   94, 100, 103-05, 114, 120-21, 133, 137-
   138, 171, 184, 246
Baker, Lynda, 138
Baker, Lyndon, 138
Baker, Russell, 103
Ball, George, 143, 187, 209, 219, 238,
   273, 274, 276, 288
Baltimore Sun, the, 149
Bean, Woodrow, 91
Bennett, W. Tapley, 200

Berlin, Dick, 108
Betancourt, Romulo, 201
Black, Hugo, 78
Blough, Roger, 169-70
Bosch, Juan, 200
Bowles, Chester, 238
Bradlee, Benjamin, 80
Brazil, 143
Brinkley, David, 146
Brown and Root Construction
   Company, 55-56, 58, 60, 66, 69-70, 72,
   76, 216, 304
Brown Building, the, 60
Brown, George, 59-60
Brown, Herman, 59
Brown, Madeline, 100
Brown, Pat, 108
Brown, Steven, 100
Bruce, David, 221
Buchanan, James P., 51
Bundy, McGeorge, 49, 153-54, 157, 188,
   196, 209, 214, 225-26, 238, 258, 274,
   282, 284, 288, 298
Bundy, William, 234, 274-75, 288, 292
Burma, 292
   Rangoon, 159
Busby, Horace, 58, 75, 118, 125-26, 134,
   143, 163, 226

Cabinet, the, 180, 208, 224, 296
Cabral, Donald Reid, 200
Califano, Joseph, 20, 126, 136, 139, 142,
   147, 172, 181, 191, 203, 209, 215-16,
   282

Cambodia, 255, 278, 292

Capitol Hill, 79, 97, 117, 163, 177, 189, 200

Carmichael, Stokely, 233

Carpenter, Liz, 139

Castro, Fidel, 151

Caucus of Democratic Senators, the, 87

Central America, 234

Chadwick, John, 89

Chamberlain, Neville, 217, 303

Chennault, Anna, 239

Chicago Daily News, the, 233

Chile, 290

China, 12, 151, 197, 205, 207, 264, 270, 277, 279-80, 293, 295-96, 300, 303
  Peking, 265, 297

Christian, George, 243

Christian Science Monitor, the, 216

Church, Frank, 171, 298

Churchill, Winston, 15-16, 196, 260

CIA, the, 58, 164, 201, 210, 213, 215, 223-24, 238, 260, 275, 287, 294

Citizens National Bank, 167

Civil Aeronautics Administration, the, 103

Civil Rights
  Act of 1964, 179, 180
  Bill, 179
  Commission, 180
  Program, 178

Clark, Ed, 133

Clark, Ramsey, 130, 131, 134, 298

Clifford, Clark, 235, 238, 274, 287-88

Colby, William, 164

Cold War, the, 137

Colorado
  Denver, 161

Communism, 10, 77, 119, 252, 262, 268, 271, 293, 296

Communist(s), 58, 72, 77, 83, 137, 164, 187, 190-92, 200-01, 209, 216, 223-24, 229, 234, 246, 260-61, 270-71, 277, 280, 292, 293-95, 298, 301, 303

Chinese, 153
  Conspiracy, 235

Community Relations Service, 180

Congress of Racial Equality, 191

Connally, John, 49, 67, 73, 140, 205, 226, 235

Connally, Nellie, 49, 205

Connor, John, 143

Consular Treaty, the, 176

Coolidge, Calvin, 133

Cooper, Charles S., 11

Cooper, Chester, 218

Corcoran, Thomas, 56, 57, 76, 105, 106

CORE, 177

Cormier, Frank, 118, 141, 149, 154, 161, 185, 204, 209, 217, 244

Corporation for Public Broadcasting, the, 174

Corpus Christi Naval Air Training Base, 60

Corrupt Practices Act, the, 70

Council of Economic Advisors, the, 266

Cuba, 10, 116

Cuban government, the, 151

Cuban missile crisis, the, 116, 270

Cutty Sark, 98, 103, 117, 149

Dai, Bao, 259

Daly, Richard, 236

Davidson, T. Whitfield, 78

Deason, Willard, 66

de Gaulle, Charles, 167, 185, 272, 273, 277, 278

Democratic National Convention, the, 12, 105-06, 108, 109-10, 136, 144, 156-57, 159, 235

Democratic Party, the, 170, 178, 236

Democratic Policy Committee, the, 87

Democratic Senate Policy Committee, the, 107

Democratic State Convention, the, 91

Dengue Fever, 68

Denmark, 290
Copenhagen, 120
Depression, the, 45, 48
Diem, Ngo Dinh, 14, 118-19, 164, 254, 257, 259, 260-61, 263, 270, 272, 278, 294, 296
Diem, Nhu, 277-78
Dillon, C. Douglas, 148, 284
Dillon, Matt, Marshal, 111
Dirksen, Everett, 138
Dodd, Thomas, 155
Dominican Republic, the, 200, 289
Dong, Pham Van, 220
Douglas, Helen Gahagan, 58
Douglas, Paul, 85-86
"Draft LBJ" movement, the, 235
Duckworth, Allen, 134
Dugger, Ronnie, 14
Durr, Virginia, 172

Eagleton, Thomas, 2
Economic Opportunity Act, the, 175
Eisenhower, Dwight D., 80, 83, 92, 131, 178, 257, 259, 269, 276, 292
Elementary and Secondary Education Act, the, 175
Emancipation Proclamation, the, 6
England, 221
London, 219, 221
Ensley, Grover, 85
Equal Pay Act, the, 180
Erhard, Ludwig, 205
Executive Order, 45
Europe, 117, 181, 221, 231, 287
European allies, 197

Fair Deal, the, 72, 168
Fair Employment Practices Commission, the, 178
Fair Packaging and Labeling Act, the, 174
Farmer, James, 191

Federal Bureau of Investigation (FBI), the, 136, 215, 298
Federal Communications Commission (FCC), the, 102
Federal Drug Administration (FDA), the, 248
Federal Housing Authority, the, 46
Federal Power Commission, the, 60
Federal Reserve Board, the, 180
Federal Trade Commission (FTC), the, 71
Fleeson, Doris, 149
Food for Freedom program, the, 176
Food for India program, the, 176
Ford, Gerald, 224
Ford II, Henry, 167
Forrester, Michael, 186
Fortas, Abe, 13, 54, 128
France, 255, 269, 279, 289, 299
Paris, 120, 219, 232, 234, 237-38
Peace talks, 235
Franklin, Benjamin, 15, 20
Freedom of Information Act, the, 175
Freeman, Orville, 204
French, the, 254, 269, 271, 274, 289, 294
Fulbright, William, 12, 85, 88, 137, 182, 188, 214, 219, 222, 245, 276, 280, 289, 298

Galbraith, John Kenneth, 129, 226, 288
Geneva Accords, the, 253-54, 269
Geneva Agreement, the, 254
Germany, 65
Berlin, 120, 121, 229, 292
Glass, Alice, 57, 58
Goldberg, Arthur, 219
Goldman, Eric, 127, 185, 210, 214-15, 282-83, 299
Goldwater, Barry, 10, 102, 153-54, 157-60, 194, 259
Goodwin, Richard, 12-13, 148
Gore, Albert, 87, 207, 214

Government Accounting Office, the, 216

Graham, Katherine, 80, 147, 159, 194

Great Britain, 255, 279, 290

Great Emancipator, the, 181

Great Manipulator, the, 81

Great Society, the, 23, 72, 148, 152, 162, 168-69, 172-73, 177-81, 189, 195-96, 216, 220, 299, 303

Greece, 238

Green, Charles, 46, 255

Greenfield, Meg, 80

Greuning, (Senator), 205

Gromyko, Andrei, 203

Guam, 275

Gulf of Tonkin, the, 157

Guthrie, John, 280

Gwyn, John, 48, 49-50

Halberstam, David, 14

Haldeman, H.R., 243

Hardesty, Bob, 241, 242

Hardesty, Mary, 242

Harkins, (General), 271

Harlow or Harlowe, Bryce, 64, 80

Harriman, Averell, 202, 218, 235, 238, 240, 288

Harris, Fred, 242

Harris Poll, 226

Hartke, Vance, 109, 207

Harwood, Richard, 20, 96, 152, 153, 187, 189, 221, 239, 246

Helms, Richard, 223, 224, 238

Herblock cartoon, 186

Hickenlooper, (Senator), 219

Hicks, John, 64, 97

Higher Education Facilities Act, the, 175

Highway Safety Act, the, 175

Hillsman, Roger, 288

Hitler, Adolf, 303

Hong Kong, 117, 171

Hoover, J. Edgar, 62, 114, 220

Hopkins, Willy, 31, 76

Housing Act, the, 174

Humphrey, Hubert, 15, 81, 86, 114, 138, 145, 152, 155, 159, 161, 196-98, 204, 208, 210, 213, 216, 218, 2240-25, 232, 235-39, 244, 266, 284, 286, 288, 300

Humphrey, Muriel, 159, 198

Hup, Dang Vu, 256

India, 176, 293
  Kashmir, 293
  New Delhi, 218

Indiana Primary, 109

Indochina, 270, 272, 292

Indonesia, 280, 293
  Djakarta, 292
  Sukarno, 293

International Control commission, the, 254

Internal Revenue Service (IRS), the, 69, 70, 170, 171

Interstate Commerce Commission, the, 60

Italy, 226
  La Pira, Giorgio, 279

Jackson, Andrew, 118

Japanese, the, 68, 269

Japanese air base, 68

Japanese fighter planes, 68, 69

Jenkins, Walter, 59, 77, 94, 100, 108, 116, 158

Johns Hopkins University, 200

Johnson, Ava, 36

Johnson, Haynes, 20, 96, 152, 153, 187, 189, 221, 239, 246

Johnson, Josefa, 26

Johnson, Lady Bird, 26, 41-42, 49, 50, 52, 55, 58-59, 62-63, 74, 90, 95, 98-99, 100, 103, 106, 111, 115, 120, 126, 132, 135, 139, 140, 149, 159, 160, 174-75, 187-88, 199, 213, 242-43, 247, 286, 289

Johnson, Lucia, 26, 139, 212

Johnson, Lynda Bird, 62, 110, 148, 247

Johnson, Rebekah (mother), 21-22, 24-25, 27, 32, 163

Johnson, Rebekah (sister), 26, 28

Johnson, Sam Houston, 22, 25-26, 28-29, 52, 63, 96, 98, 191, 228, 243, 245

Johnson, Sam, 22,-25, 30, 32-33, 55, 62, 163

Johnson, Tom, 245

Joint Chiefs of Staff, the, 10-11, 137, 152, 163, 207-08, 285, 286, 287, 297

Joint Economic Committee, the, 85

Jones, Luther, 48, 63

Judicial Center, the, 175

Kattenberg, Paul, 288

Katzenbach, Nicholas, 179

Kearns, Doris, 13, 242, 244

Kefauver, Estes, 132

Kellem, Jesse, 48

Kennedy, John Fitzgerald, 9-11, 15, 100, 104, 108-11, 114-17, 121, 125-27, 134, 137, 139, 145, 153, 160-61, 166, 168, 176, 179, 187, 188-90, 195, 205, 224-25, 257, 258-59, 269-72, 277-78, 282, 289, 292, 296, 301

Kennedy, Robert, 13, 115, 121, 132, 138, 156, 158, 187, 189, 190, 193, 203, 209, 211, 221, 222, 224-25, 231, 233-34, 237-38, 243, 245, 262, 271

KGB, 84

Kilgore, Joe, 69

King, Martin Luther, 177, 190, 233

Kintner, Robert, 126

Kissinger, Henry, 242

Kleberg, Richard, 40, 41, 42, 43, 44, 45, 46, 48, 55

Klu Klux Klan, the, 178

Knowland, William, 89

Korea, 153

Chu Lai airbase, 229

Phu Bai airbase, 229

Korean War, the, 83, 151, 264

Kosygin, Alexei, 202, 203, 221

Kosygin, Anatoly, 300

Krim, Arthur, 237

Krock, Arthur, 103, 183

Kruschev, Nikita, 116, 182, 185

Ky, Nguyen Cao, 261, 262, 278, 279, 280

Laos, 151, 153, 255, 271, 272, 292, 294

Latimer, Gene, 46, 47, 48

Lemberger, Ernst, Dr., 14, 213

Levy, Moe, 131

Lewandowski, Januscz, 218

Lewis, William, 143

Life magazine, 192

Lilienthal, David, 222

Lincoln, Abraham, 15, 180, 181, 220

Lippmann, Walter, 154, 171, 199, 297

Lithium, 248

Lodge, Henry Cabot, 218, 260, 284, 296

Long, Russell, 90

Longfellow, 27

Louisiana, 197

New Orleans, 112, 179

Lucas, Wingate, 50, 61

Luce, Henry, 134

MacArthur, Douglas, 68

Magnusen, Warren, 87

Maine, 236

Maiwandwal, Mohammed Hashim, 222

Malechek, Jewell, 241

Mansfield, Mike, 81, 87, 114-15, 152, 179, 198, 205, 219, 255, 259, 271, 273-74, 288-89, 298

Marks, Leonard, 223, 283

Marsh, Charles, 57

Marshal Ford Dam, the, 55

Maryland, 239

Massachusetts

Hyannisport, 110

Masters in Chancery, 77-78
Maverick, Maury, 44
Mayer, Margaret, 113
Mayo Clinic, the, 73
McCarren Walter Immigration Act, the, 89
McCarthy, Eugene, 155, 190, 230, 245, 301
McCarthy, Joseph, 84, 187, 209, 271
McCone, John, 210, 294
McCormack, John, 171
McCrory, Mary, 148
McFarland, Bob, 82
McGovern, George, 245, 274
McKissick, Floyd, 177
McNamara, Robert, 9, 137, 153, 156, 187, 202, 206, 216, 218, 225, 251, 253, 256, 260, 265, 269-75, 278, 280, 282, 284, 287-88, 294-96, 304
McNaughton, John, 288
McPherson, Harry, 12, 135, 142, 186, 284
Means, Marianne, 119
Medal of Freedom awards ceremony, 186
Medicaid, 175, 178
Medicare, 175, 178
Mills, Wilbur, 195
Minh, Ho Chi, 209, 254, 259, 266, 269, 276, 278-80, 287, 290, 293-94, 299, 301, 303
    Trail, 272
Mitchell, John, 239
Mooney, Booth, 26, 93, 99, 118, 144, 166, 191, 192, 217
Model Cities program, the, 174
Moursund ranch, A.W., the, 140
Moyers, Bill, 13, 118, 179, 184, 187-88, 197, 209-12, 226, 245, 284, 288
Murray, James, 87
My Brother Lyndon, 245

Narcotics Treaty, the, 176
N.A.S.A., 115
National Airport, 134
National Crime Commission, the, 175
National Foundation on the Arts and Humanities, the, 174
National Gallery, the, 174
National Guard, the, 203
National Press Club, the, 192
National Security Council, the, 192, 223, 283, 286
National Traffic and Motor Vehicle Safety Act, the, 175
National Youth Administration, the, 31, 44-47, 58, 61, 65, 163
    Director, 46, 49
    Southern Regional Director, 46
NATO, 120
Naval Affairs Committee, the, 56, 60, 64
Nazi(s), 65
Newberger, Richard, 91
New Deal, the, 54, 71, 72, 168, 181, 301
New Frontier, the, 168, 189
New Guinea, 68, 75-76
New Hampshire Democratic Primary, the, 230, 301
New Jersey, 238
    Atlantic City, 159
Newsweek magazine, 153, 192, 221
New Year's Eve, 140
New Yorker, The, 217
New York Times, The, 20, 103, 154, 183, 187, 188, 192, 196, 223, 245, 264, 279, 298
New Zealand, 213, 255, 292
Nixon-Agnew campaign, 136, 238
Nixon, Richard, 58, 84, 121, 132, 135-36, 160, 237-39, 241, 243
North Korea, 256
North Koreans, the, 229
North Vietnamese, the, 237-38, 240, 245, 256, 260, 263, 265, 269, 274, 275-77, 280-81, 289, 293-94, 302

Novak, Robert, 61, 148, 165
Nuclear Non-Proliferation Treaty, the, 176
Nugent, Patrick, 130, 167, 302

O'Brien, Larry, 177, 238
O'Daniel (Governor), 67
O'Donnell, Kenneth, 160, 271
Office of Economic Opportunity, the, 191
O'Neill, Tip, 144, 213
Organization of American States, the, 135, 201
Outer Space Treaty, the, 176

Pago Pago, 165
Pakistan, 226, 255, 293
Panama, 135
Parr, George, 77
Patman, Wright, 43, 44
Pearl Harbor, 68
Pearson, Drew, 168, 171
Pearson, Lester, 199
Pedernales River, the, 132
Pentagon, the, 136, 187, 230
Philippines, 255, 292
    Manila, 218, 255, 297
Pneumonia, 68
Potter, Phil, 149
Precinct 13, 77
Presidential Inauguration, the, 164
President's Club, the, 170, 237
President's Council on Equal Opportunity, the, 197
Princess Margaret, 142
Proxmire, William, 91, 92

Raborn, William, 275
Rather, Dan, 89, 90
Rayburn, Sam, 55-56, 82-83, 86, 91, 102-03, 105, 108-10
Reagan, Ronald, 5, 173

Reedy, George, 52, 95, 97, 99-101, 103-04, 107, 117, 121-22, 129, 130-32, 141, 144, 147, 151, 158, 161, 163, 168, 177-78, 185, 191, 193, 217, 243, 266, 276, 286, 297
Republican Party, the, 88, 103, 161, 178, 179, 213, 218, 224
Reston, James, 20, 154, 196, 298
Reynolds, Don B., 171
Richardson, John, 260
Robb, Charles, 302
Roberts, Chalmers, 145
Roberts, Charles, 153
Roberts, Ray, 61
Rockefeller, Nelson, 234
"Rolling Thunder" program, the, 199, 210, 275, 284, 299
Romney, George, 225
Ronning, Chester, 213
Roosevelt, Franklin Delano, 23, 44, 53, 56, 57-58, 68, 70-71, 118, 168, 181, 185, 204, 300-01
Roosevelt, Theodore, 15
Rostow, Walt, 216, 226, 236, 288
Rovere, Richard, 217
Rowan, Carl, 146
Rowe, James, 55, 58, 76, 95, 107, 238
Rusk, Dean, 127, 131, 136, 187, 203, 216, 221, 224, 231, 236, 273, 279, 282, 284-85, 288, 295, 299, 304
Russell, Richard, 86, 92, 199, 278, 279, 288, 289, 303
Russia, 205
    Moscow, 14, 233, 280, 297
Russians, the, 214, 215, 229, 280, 300
Ryan, Bill, 213

Safety at Sea Treaty, the, 176
Salas, Luis, 77
Salinger, Pierre, 111
Salisbury, Harrison, 220
SALT Treaty, the, 176

Sam Houston High School, 39
Sandburg, Carl, 133
San Marcos Football Team, the, 48
Santayana, 2
Schlesinger, Arthur, 287, 288
Science Advisory Committee, the, 234
Shaffer, Sam, 105
Sharp, Ulysses S., 273
Sheppard, Morris, 66
Sidey, Hugh, 98, 112, 118, 132, 165, 185, 193, 203, 212, 217-18, 228, 284, 302-03
Siegel, Gerald, 86
Sihanouk, Norodom, Prince, 278
Silver Star, the, 68, 69
Singapore, 292
Skuce, John, 63
Smathers, George, 82, 88, 94, 101, 102, 154
Smith, Jean, 121
Smith, Steve, 121
Smith, William R., 77
South America, 186
South Korea, 215
South Vietnamese, the, 119, 252, 259, 261, 263, 264, 265, 271, 272, 273, 280, 286, 294, 296, 300
Soviet Embassy, the, 215
Soviets, the, 14, 176, 203, 229
Soviet spies, 84
Soviet Union, the, 83, 116, 177, 192, 197, 203, 214, 277, 279, 293, 294, 295, 300, 303
Sparkman, John, 85
State of the Union address, the, 150, 161, 181, 185, 195, 198, 220, 226
Steinbeck, John, 166
Steinberg, Alfred, 82
Stevens, Coke, 73, 76, 77, 78
Stevenson, Adlai, 106, 108-09, 132, 198, 288
Stewart, Michael, 192
Strauss, Robert, 170

Symington, James, 215
Symington, Stuart, 85, 104, 108, 109

Taiwan, 117
Taiwanese, the, 119
Taylor, Claudia Alta (*see* Lady Bird Johnson)
Taylor, Maxwell, 157, 163, 260, 270, 273, 274, 279
Taylor, Thomas, 42
Teacher Corps, the, 175
Temple, Larry, 143
Tennyson, 27
Tenth Congressional District, the, 51
Tet Offensive, the, 229, 230, 284, 288
Texas
    Austin, 25, 35, 45, 59, 60, 64, 71, 73, 100, 102, 116, 140, 167
    Cotulla, 37, 39, 45
    Dallas, 64, 122, 125
    Duval County, 77
    Galveston, 56
    Houston, 35, 39, 40, 89
    Johnson City, 25, 74
    Laredo, 91
    Legislature, 22
    Llano River, 167
    Marshall, 32
    Nuevo Laredo, 35
    Pedernales, the, 242
    San Antonio, 35
    San Jacinto, 216
    San Marcos, 32, 34, 35, 39, 40
Texas Democratic Primary, the, 70
Thailand, 119, 226, 255, 256, 280, 293
    Bangkok, 119
Thanh, Au Trong, 262
Thant, U, 159, 222, 266, 279, 281
Thieu, Nguyen Van, 239, 262, 278, 279
Tho, Nguyen Ngoc, 261
Thomas, Albert, 61
Thomas, Helen, 177, 193

Time magazine, 108, 134, 148

Time-Life magazine, 14

Tonkin Gulf
  Incident, 258
  Resolution, 155, 157, 214, 222, 253

Truman, Harry, 72, 78, 131, 168, 178,
  233, 269, 292

Tuesday Lunch Group, the, 208, 283,
  284, 286, 299

United Nations (UN), the, 198, 226, 254

U.S.S.R., the, 206, 293

U.S.S. Maddox, 156

U.S.S. Pueblo, 229

U.S.S. Turner Joy, 156

United States Air Force, the, 200

United States Army, the, 200

United States Bill of Rights, the, 179

United States Civil Rights Commission,
  the, 152

United States Civil War, the, 21, 180,
  220

United States Congress, the, 5, 10, 22,
  31, 43, 53-56, 58-59, 61-62, 80-82, 118,
  139, 150, 155, 157, 161, 167-69, 173,
  179, 181, 196, 199-202, 213-14, 252-53,
  255, 257-58, 265-66, 270, 288, 300-01

United States Constitution, the, 4, 10,
  179

United States Department of Health,
  Education and Welfare, the, 176

United States Department of Housing
  and Urban Development, the, 174

United States Department of Defense,
  the, 187, 202, 265, 300

United States District Court for the
  Northern District of Texas, the, 78

United States House of Representatives,
  the, 60-61, 67, 71, 79, 83, 109, 154, 218
  Speaker, 4

United States Housing Authority
  (U.S.H.A.), the, 64

United States Information Agency, the,
  223

United States Justice Department, the,
  121, 143

United States Marines, the, 200, 286

United States Navy, the, 56, 64, 68, 151,
  162, 200, 285
  Guantanamo Bay, 151

U.S. News and World Report, 226

United States Secret Service, the, 26

United States Senate, the, 14-15, 66, 69,
  70-73, 75, 78-88, 91-95, 101, 106-07,
  109-10, 114-15, 118, 137, 171, 179,
  200, 207, 214, 218, 226, 255-56, 267,
  285, 287
  Appropriations Committee, 87
  Armed Services Committee, 86
  Democratic Campaign Committee,
    87
  Democratic Caucus, 114, 115
  Foreign Relations Committee, 85, 102
  Interstate Commerce Committee,
    102
  Judiciary Committee, 87
  Office Building, 93, 101
  Rules Committee, 171
  Southern Caucus, 86

United States State Department, the,
  146, 187, 188, 213, 279, 280, 285, 300
  Auditorium, 139

United States Supreme Court, the, 180

United States Transportation
  Department, the, 175

United States Treasury, the, 131

U.S. Steel, 169

University of Texas, the, 180

Valenti, Jack, 135, 144-45, 155, 171, 208-
  09, 213

Valenti, Joseph, 155

Vance, Cyrus, 235, 284

Vatican City, 219, 226

Venezuela, 121, 201
Vice President of the United States, the, 4
Vietcong, 163-64, 198, 199, 202, 210, 223, 255, 261, 263-65, 271-75, 278, 281, 283, 286, 294, 302
Vietnam, 9-12, 40, 83, 137, 148, 150-54, 164, 181, 184, 188-190, 195-96, 199-200, 203, 205, 207-08, 215-16, 220, 222-27, 230, 232, 234, 236-37, 251-65, 268-74, 277-304
   Loi, Luu Van, 278
   North, 11-12, 151, 157, 196, 198-200, 202, 205-06, 214, 220-21, 229, 232-34, 236, 254-56, 262, 264-66, 269, 272, 275, 277, 279-81, 286-87, 290, 294-95, 299-300
      Dien Bien Phu (battle of), 269
      Haipong Harbor, 205, 206, 279
      Hanoi, 213, 218, 221-22, 233, 265, 266, 275, 279, 280, 281, 294, 295, 300
      Hon Me, 156
      Hon Nieu, 156
      Le Chang, 280
      Radio Hanoi, 233
   Plank, 236
   Policies, 136
   Saigon, 118, 147, 154, 164, 208, 229, 259-60, 262, 269, 271, 273, 278, 296, 303
   South, 9, 118-19, 137, 151, 154, 157, 159, 164, 191, 196, 198-202, 205, 208, 223, 225-26, 229, 233-34, 239, 251, 252-263, 268-70, 272-73, 275-81, 292, 294-96, 300-02
     My Lai, 265
     Pleiku, 198, 283
   Bien Hoa airfield, 163
   Da Nang airbase, 229

Tan San Nhut airbase, 229
Veterans, 265
Vinson, Carl, 56
Virginia, 247

Wallace, Henry, 58
Wall Street Journal, the, 166
Warnke, Paul, 234-235
War on Poverty, the, 177, 299, 303
War Powers Resolution, the, 3
Washington, George, 118
Washington Post, the, 80, 145, 147, 153, 159, 187, 192, 194, 246, 247, 277
Washington Red, 84
Weedin, Harfield, 64
Welhausen Ward Elementary School, 37
Westmoreland, William, 188, 202, 222, 225, 227, 230, 261, 265, 273-75, 285-87
West Virginia, 109
Wheeler, Earle G., 273, 274, 286
White, June, 53
White, Theodore, 104, 128, 133, 145, 157, 161, 184
White, William S., 49
Wicker, Tom, 88, 264
Williams, John, 90, 171
Wilson, Edith Bolling, 5
Wilson, Harold, 145, 167, 221
Wilson, Woodrow, 5, 230
Wirtz, Alvin, 55, 70, 75
Wisconsin Primary, the, 231
Woodward, Warren, 76
World Bank, the, 287
World War II, 259, 264, 285, 287, 303

Yarborough, Ralph, 76
Young, Harold, 57
Yugoslavia, 294
   Belgrade, 200